JULIE HESMONDHALGH

A Working Diary

OTHER TITLES IN THE THEATRE MAKERS SERIES:

JULIE HESMONDHALGH

A Working Diary

JULIE HESMONDHALGH

methuen | drama

LONDON · NEW YORK · OXFORD · NEW DELHI · SYDNEY

METHUEN DRAMA
Bloomsbury Publishing Plc
50 Bedford Square, London, WC1B 3DP, UK
1385 Broadway, New York, NY 10018, USA

BLOOMSBURY, METHUEN DRAMA and the Methuen Drama logo are
trademarks of Bloomsbury Publishing Plc

First published in Great Britain 2019

For legal purposes the Acknowledgements on pp. 193–4 constitute an
extension of this copyright page.

Cover design: Louise Dugdale
Cover image © Jennifer Robertson, Kyte Photography

A catalogue record for this book is available from the British Library.

A catalog record for this book is available from the Library of Congress.

ISBN: PB: 978-1-350-02569-1
        ePDF: 978-1-350-02570-7
       eBook: 978-1-350-02571-4

Series: Theatre Makers

Typeset by RefineCatch Limited, Bungay, Suffolk
Printed and bound in India

To find out more about our authors and books, visit www.bloomsbury.com
and sign up for our newsletters.

For **Kersh**, with all my love, always.

If the enemy of art is the pram in

the hallway, then its best mate

is the husband in the cellar.

Thanks for it all.

The world is always likely to give us many reasons to think that things are bad and getting worse. Stupidity, ignorance, corruption, cruelty and self-interest success all around us, much of the time, and the cultural industries reflect that fact, and often make the situation worse. But the world also shows abundant evidence of intelligence, knowledge, integrity, kindness and altruism, and if we abandon hope, then in my view we also abandon the possibility of making the world better. Wonderful things get done, made, written and played by people every day . . . There are spaces and people in the cultural industries that actively make good things happen-including products that enhance our understanding, imagination and pleasure, by making us laugh or think hard, and sometimes by shocking or disturbing us. That is why culture matters and that is why the cultural industries matter.

DAVID HESMONDHALGH, *THE CULTURAL INDUSTRIES*[1]

---

[1]Extract from introduction to *The Cultural Industries*, 4th edition, by David Hesmondhalgh, 2019. Reproduced with kind permission of Sage Publishing.

INTRODUCTION

I am so grateful to Anna Brewer at Bloomsbury for approaching me to write a working diary covering the end of 2016 to November 2017. It turned out to be a rich and varied year, not without its upheavals, challenges and frustrations, but full of interesting encounters, huge world events, big conversations and fantastic people doing brilliant work. I think that knowing I had to record the events of my working life made me live a bit more fully too, to be honest, so I have Anna to thank for the extra grey hairs and wrinkles twelve months on.

I've been privileged this year to work alongside some incredible individuals and organizations who are tireless in their efforts to swing open the door of opportunity for people from diverse and working-class backgrounds and to enable them to access the Arts. All of them are doing their bit to fight for proper representation, equality and diversity across the cultural industries: ALT, Les Enfant Terribles, Equal Representation for Actresses, Talent 1st, Act4Change and Actor Awareness to name but a few. Royalties from the no doubt record-breaking sales of this book will go to the wonderful organisation Arts Emergency, and it's the young people who access their services and become mentees that have been at the forefront of my mind as I've written. I hope it'll be a bit of a useful resource for anyone starting out, especially anyone who believes that culture plays an important part in shaping the landscape of a society, anyone who believes that art can help change the world. But I also hope it might be of some interest to anyone just curious about what it's like to be a working actor. I've tried to be honest, and to write in a voice that's authentically my own, so there's a bit of 'adult language'. Sorry if you find that off-putting. Don't stop reading, just skip past the more colourful bits.

I've always wanted to have something published, purely for the joy of the acknowledgements page, but when I got to that bit, I found myself terrified of missing people out. It was longer than the actual book in the end, so I cut it right down. Everyone who is mentioned in these pages, please accept my deep gratitude and feel acknowledged. And there are plenty who aren't mentioned, mainly because they're not part of my working life per se, but are certainly key in keeping me sane and in enabling me to do what I do, i.e., *exist*. Every cup of tea, every lift home, every after-show beer, supportive text, kind tweet, night out, heart-to-heart, recommended book, offer of childcare help, listening ear, shoulder to cry on and warm hug has been appreciated more than I can ever properly express. In the more challenging moments of 2017, my wonderful family, friends and neighbours have lifted and held me in ways that I'll never forget. They know who they are. I daren't list them. But I owe them big time.

I'm hoping that in doling out advice at points throughout the book I haven't come over all lofty or teacherly. I'm still very much learning myself, as you'll see. The very act of writing a diary for publication seems like a bit like an admission of self-importance, and if that tone creeps in on occasion, I apologize. Rest assured, I know I am just a knobhead trying to make sense of it all.

Language is constantly evolving and I have been hyper-aware of this when searching for ways to describe marginalized or underrepresented groups within our industry, a subject that has preoccupied many of us in 2017 and that I talk about several times throughout the year. I looked to Reni Eddo-Lodge's astonishing book, *Why I'm No Longer Talking to White People about Race* (which I can't recommend highly enough) and have taken her lead in cautiously using the terms Black and Minority Ethnic (BME), and, occasionally, People of Colour, when describing people who are not white.

I'm very grateful too for the opportunities I've had that have enabled me to live the life I do now, doing what I love, and I never take for granted the help and support I got along the way, not least from Lancashire County Council who gave me a full grant, aged 18, that enabled me to go to drama school in London.

I hope that by the time this diary is on the shelves, so many of the challenges facing young people starting out now, and documented here, will be of historical interest only; and that a better, fairer, more equal world is around the corner. Don't give up hope, don't stop fighting. Be proud of who you are, and where you've come from. Change is coming, it's within our grasp. I really believe that.

Julie Hesmondhalgh, 26 December 2017

JULIE HESMONDHALGH: A WORKING DIARY

3 November 2016

I'm in MediaCity, Salford, to do a radio play, and – as usual – I'm lost, wandering around from building to building trying to find the MPAS studio. I have no sense of direction and the white maze-like corridors bamboozle me every time. I make it by the skin of my teeth. It's just a read-through today, and a friendly chat over a cup of tea with the producer and her team, the writer and the cast. I'm in and out within the hour and off to Ashton College where I have a longstanding arrangement (and it has been months in the planning) to talk to a group of young people about Arts Emergency, since they are piloting the northern wing of their scheme in the Further Education College.

I grew up in Accrington, a small industrial town in north-west England, not unlike Ashton-under-Lyne, except even further from the bright lights of Manchester. Through a lucky accident of birth, I grew up in a time when young people from backgrounds like mine were supported in every possible way in our journey to becoming artists of one kind or another. I was taken on subsidized school trips to the Royal Exchange theatre in Manchester all through my teens, and had a brilliant teacher, Martin Cosgrif, who taught us A level Theatre Studies and who instilled in us a belief that we could be actors, directors, writers. That we had as much right as the next person to pursue a life in the arts. We all loved performing, but I don't think any of us signed up to that course thinking for a minute we could actually be professionals one day. It just wasn't something that kids like us did. But, after two years with Martin, a disproportionate number of us got into top drama schools. In 1988 when I went to LAMDA on a full grant (covering fees *and* maintenance – can you even imagine?), there were five of us there from Accrington *at the same time*. Three of us in my year of twenty-five or so. Four out of the five of us are still acting.

Young people today are really up against it. The crippling debts that face anyone leaving higher education now, not to mention the devaluing of the arts by policy-makers who regard them as 'soft' subjects, make the choice to pursue a creative degree or arts-led course feel like a daft risk, and one that fewer and fewer kids from low income families are prepared to take. Arts Emergency is a charity dedicated to encouraging these young people to follow their dreams, and to creating an 'Alternative Old Boys' Network' with a mentoring programme that already has 4,000 industry professionals involved. This kind of work is crucial if we're going to have an arts community in this country that truly reflects the diversity of its population. If we're not careful, in a matter of years our arts institutions will be entirely run by the children of the wealthy, and the stories we tell each other will be representative of that tiny stratum of society.

The talk goes well, I think. Ian Kershaw (Kersh), my husband, who mentors a fantastic young English student from the college, comes with me and I manage the PowerPoint more easily than I thought I would. Martha, our fifteen-year-old daughter, is here with a group from her school (hilariously, I had to sign a permission slip to allow her to come and see me talk). I've worked hard to keep the content uplifting, whilst acknowledging the very real and quite bleak backdrop of how hard it is for young artists these days, certainly in comparison to when I was starting out. I spend some time apologizing to the audience on behalf of my own complacent generation for not fighting hard enough to keep in place the things that made our lives so much easier back then. There are positive things I can say, though, about the many opportunities available in the burgeoning creative industries, and that there are people who want to help.

I talk about *Bread and Roses*, the old protest song, with its beautiful line 'Hearts starve as well as bodies'. In my opinion, it offers the template for a good life: you need to balance the bread – having enough to sustain yourself and your loved ones physically with food and shelter and essentials – with the roses – the need to experience beauty, art, music, literature, culture. I feel the government at present would like us to believe that to be an artist is some airy-fairy choice that will leave you starving if you're mad enough to pursue that life. I believe it's possible to have the bread *and* the roses.

There's a good Q&A afterwards with intelligent and thoughtful questions from the young people, including:

How do you cope with being recognized?

Answer: It's not as fun as you think it's going to be, but most people are lovely and just excited to meet someone off the telly, and it takes as much energy to be grumpy about it as it does to just smile and graciously pose for the inevitable selfie.

and

How do you cope with rejection?

Answer: You just have to! It's part of life and part of the job; you have to find ways to lift yourself and be kind to yourself when the disappointments come.

Someone asks me if there's anything I wouldn't do and I talk about the things I've surprised myself by doing over the last few years including sex scenes (*Cucumber*), nudity (*Wit*) and shaving off my hair (*Wit* again). Afterwards, Kersh says he's surprised that I didn't talk about commercials. It didn't occur to me in the moment. I'd be very careful of what I put my face and name to in the name of promoting a product, but of course I'm painfully aware how that kind of choice comes with the privilege of having enough money to say 'no' to stuff. One advert can support a lot of unpaid and interesting work.

I dole out advice like I know something about anything, but try to be honest about how much I'm still learning and how I have to work very hard to remember these things too. 'Course I do. So, for what it's worth, these are some of the things I hope I'm starting to learn . . .

Look after yourself. The Five-a-Day for Good Mental Health are also the Five-a-Day for a Rich Creative Life. So:

1 Move your body . . .

. . . however you can, according to your ability. Get out in the world and breathe the air and get your heart pumping. Being an artist does require some stamina, so stay well, especially if your art is fairly sedentary, such as writing or drawing. You'll have more energy. Tiredness is so boring. Stop going on about how tired you are. Everyone's tired. My friend Brian Astbury set up the then illegally multiracial theatre The Space in South Africa in the 1970s at the height of that most brutal of apartheid regimes. The black actors would work twelve hours a day labouring or cleaning for their rich white employers, then come on the bus to rehearse into the early hours, with the constant threat of arrest hanging over them. When the police raided the theatre, as they did on a regular basis, the black actors would grab brooms that had been strategically placed around the theatre and pretend to be cleaners. They were probably

quite tired. They probably didn't go on about it as much as half the
actors I know. Go for a walk. If you can. Or a swim. Whatever. Move.

2 Connect

Be around other people who feed your creativity, encourage you and
who you support in turn. Champion each other, help each other
develop. Ask for help. You'll be amazed at how much people really
want to talk to you and help you. You've no idea how inspiring it is to
meet young people with vision and passion and ideas, who are trying
to make stuff against the odds. Seek out the artists who inspire you,
write to them, ask for advice.

3 Learn something/do something new

Feed yourself. If you go to an audition or an interview and you haven't
worked for months, you can say that. You can sit and tell them what a
shit year it's been. *Or* you could tell them that you've taught yourself to
play the ukelele by watching YouTube; that you've read some William
Blake, which inspired you to write some poetry for the first time since
you were thirteen; that you've hired a room above a pub and put on a
scratch night of a play idea with some mates. Say how you've listened
to David Bowie's back catalogue, watched Spike Lee's epic film on the
New Orleans flood, genned up on feminism or watched the seminal
box set you always meant to. If you've joined a class, gone walking in
the Peaks or volunteered at a food bank, tell them. You might not be
any better an actor than the person who went in before you, but your
good energy and lust for life will get you the job, I'll bet you.

Take any opportunities that come your way. If someone offers you
a free ticket to see something, snatch it (thanking them profusely,
obviously). If someone recommends a book, read it. If a great theatre
company comes to your nearest town, do what you can to see them

and then hang around at the bar to talk to them about it afterwards. Or tweet them. Read the great plays. You can still order them from the library (at the time of writing). BE ARSED. The world is full of people who Can't Be Arsed. Buck the trend.

4 Be in the moment

I love Facebook. I can happily lose two hours scrolling through the minutiae of my acquaintances' lives. I run a political theatre collective almost entirely on Messenger (8,000 messages between the three of us at the last count). But real life is better. Now and again, leave your phone at home. Be hard to get hold of. Go a different way to work, look up, take out your earphones, listen to conversations on the bus. It'll reboot your brain and make you a better artist. Look at stuff again. OBSERVE. Break a habit. DO NOT BE ON YOUR PHONE IN A REHEARSAL ROOM EVER. It's properly rude.

5 Put something back

Try not to disappear up your own arse. Art is about connecting and creating and making the world better. But try and see the bigger picture. Be pragmatic. A couple of jobs I've done have been quite emotionally full-on in terms of content, especially *Black Roses*. It was a tiny but intense and beautiful play by Simon Armitage about the life and death of Sophie Lancaster, a young woman from Lancashire who died from her injuries after a group of lads attacked her and her boyfriend in a park in 2007 because they were goths. I played Sylvia, Sophie's mum, and the words I spoke were hers, verbatim, from interviews she gave for the piece, interspersed with poetry by Simon Armitage, spoken as if by Sophie. Most nights people sat in silence at the end, and a few people would always wait in the bar afterwards needing to talk to me and Rachel Austin, the brilliant actor playing

Sophie, about how the play had affected them. It's a heartbreaking story and the audience were taken on a little journey through Sophie's life from birth every night, and so they felt the loss of her in some way at the end. It was an upsetting play to be in, and people would always ask how we coped with 'putting ourselves through that' every night, especially with me being a mum of daughters myself. Most nights Sylvia, the *real* Sylvia, would be in the foyer during and after the play selling wristbands and handing out literature about the foundation she'd set up in Sophie's memory, campaigning for better legislation on hate crime and raising awareness about the need for promoting tolerance and diversity in schools. I would have been a proper wanker to come offstage and allow myself one iota of indulgence about how draining it was for me to pretend to be Sylvia every night, when the real Sylvia was there working her arse off to change the world in the face of such horrendous and unimaginable loss.

The same goes for *Wit*, the play about cancer by Margaret Edson I was in at the Royal Exchange earlier this year. After every performance, there would be people in the foyer who had survived cancer or were living with it, had lost someone they loved to it and – in a couple of startling cases – knew they were soon to die of it. It was a complete privilege (an overused word, I know, but very apt here) to spend time with these people and hear their stories. For me, it was a massive part of that job. And because of *Black Roses*, I anticipated it. I talked to the rest of the cast early on about that extra responsibility: how we had a duty to never go offstage and into the bar with any of the usual bollocks about it not being a great show that night for us or how it was a weird audience or how fucking *exhausted* we all were from doing all the acting. That there would be people who might need to talk to us about what they'd just experienced and what they were going through/had been through and that we had to be open and ready for that. And not be wankers.

Yeah, so, as much as possible, TRY not to be a wanker. And if your job gives you a platform to talk about things that matter, climb on that platform and do your best to represent whoever it is you're representing, onstage and off. Put your head over the parapet from time to time.

4 November

Back to the BBC at MediaCity to record my scenes for the radio drama *The Fix*. People sometimes ask me which is my favourite: telly or theatre acting? And it's hard to say. I really do love them both in different ways. Theatre is exciting and a rush, but I like the structure of telly and the piecing together of something that happens when you're filming, the concentration required to block out all the distractions and be in the right moment. But I LOVE radio. Days recording a radio drama are always happy days with lovely people in a chilled environment and it's SORCERY. Sound engineers, studio managers and radio producers are sorcerers. I love the daftness of making the sound effects work and scrambling around pretending to have a fight. Me and the other actor Sophia Di Martino have to do this today in our final, supposedly physical, scene of *The Fix*, huffing and puffing and 'ah'ing and 'OW'ing as we stand by the mic with our scripts, trying not to rustle them as we flail around without actually laying a hand on one another. Bonkers. It's a completely different discipline to the others and I always enjoy it massively.

5 November

Guardian theatre critic Michael Billington reviews Glenda Jackson as King Lear in the production at the Old Vic. I'm interested in his thesis that her life in politics and her experience of 'the world's injustice' may have enhanced her understanding of the role, and his referencing of Michael Pennington's assertion that Lear ultimately becomes a socialist. Out of curiosity I look up the *Daily Mail* review and nearly throw my phone in frustration (oh, what did I expect?). The reviewer is, of course, musing endlessly and in the most disparaging terms about the physical appearance of this powerhouse octogenarian acting goddess. Billington admires her ability to 'think each moment of the play afresh'; the *Mail* thinks she's 'strangely over-rehearsed'.

We saw a preview of the production last week, both Kersh and I nursing massive hangovers, and were completely mesmerized by Glenda Jackson's performance. I am loving this new wave of genderless casting (a phenomenon dismissed as 'daft' by the *Mail*) that allows our most brilliant female actors to inhabit the Shakespeare male greats. And there's no one I would have wanted to see as Lear as much as Glenda. She filled that vast stage mentally, physically and vocally.

Also in today's *Guardian*, a great profile of the playwright Jez Butterworth.

I've been thinking a lot about the opportunities I enjoyed growing up in the 1970s and 80s, and, in particular, being able to draw benefits during the early 90s when I left LAMDA. Jez Butterworth wrote *Mojo* whilst signing on and living in a farmhouse in Wiltshire after university. I helped set up and run Arts Threshold, a little company with its own theatre that we raised the money to build in a Paddington basement. We performed in plays there for more than three years and cleaned the toilets, ran the café and worked the box office too. During this time, I claimed unemployment benefit and housing benefit. The 'dole office' accepted that I was playing the long game, gaining experience in my field in a voluntary capacity, inviting casting directors and agents to performances and eventually getting one of the latter (I'm still with her, twenty-three years later).

I cut my teeth as an actor during those years, and lived with a group of mates who have gone on to be camera operators, award-winning lighting designers, working actors and world-famous movement directors. Rufus Norris, the Artistic Director of the National Theatre, directed his first play at Arts Threshold, which I was in. The state was our benefactor back then, and was Jez Butterworth's too by the sound of it. I remember reading Jarvis Cocker saying that Pulp, the band he fronted for many years, would never have formed without those early doley days of experimentation. Perhaps this has been our greatest failure in terms of what we've failed to preserve for future generations of artists, right up there with free university places and maintenance grants and well-funded further education colleges. That safety net of welfare for the young is no longer there. And we've allowed the culture of benefits to become vilified rather than championed. We pay into a system that is there to support us when we can't support ourselves: that's what welfare is. But sometimes we need that support at the start of our journey, like a down payment returnable in tax later on. That was certainly how it worked for me. I can't imagine what my story would have looked like if I'd not had that support in my early twenties. I certainly wouldn't have been able to live in London amongst my peers, even back then, without housing benefit. We've really messed things up for this generation in the most spectacular way. I think a basic income might be the way forward: a universal £9k a year for everyone. I'd campaign for that.

7 November

Early drive over to Bolton to meet Rebekah Harrison (Becx) and Grant Archer who run Take Back, the Manchester political theatre collective, with me. We're meeting Elizabeth Newman, the Artistic Director of the Octagon Theatre, and Deborah Dickinson, her Associate Producer. Our most recent project was an audio-installation about stateless babies born in refugee camps as part of the Royal Exchange's B!RTH Festival in October. It was a fantastic four-day event examining birth in a global health context. It included seven international plays as the centrepiece, written by women from a range of troubled locations, from Northern Ireland to Syria, each looking at their home country's relationship to birth policy. Surrounding these were various other creative responses to the themes highlighted in the plays, including debates and panel discussions about population, abortion and control. Our piece, *Under Canvas*, was staged in a tent in the Great Hall, the beautiful foyer at the Royal Exchange. The tent was tucked under a staircase and covered in baby clothes that were embroidered with the two main articles of the UN Declaration of Rights, which state a child's entitlement to a state and a nationality. We commissioned twelve writers to respond to news articles and personal accounts from inside the camps and recorded actors reading the pieces. As always with our work, it was hurriedly put together (par for the course when your remit is immediate response; it generally precludes any possibility of funding too). But, thanks to some very talented sound producers and designers and a wonderful textile art graduate, it looked and sounded great and we were very proud of the end product.

We assumed that people passing through the foyer area would just pop in and out, catching snatches of audio as they went, but people often lay down and listened to the entire cycle of work, sitting amongst the blankets and baby clothes strewn around the floor. A group of girls from a school for young mothers in the area came to see it one morning and asked loads of questions and offered to donate some stuff to babies in the camps in France and Greece. They were shocked at the piece about a mother bathing her newborn in a puddle at Calais and wanted to help.

We're now interested in taking *Under Canvas* to Bolton as part of the site-specific festival, REVEAL, that the theatre runs around the town. Deborah suggests that we erect the tent at the Destitution Project, a weekly project in the town centre, providing advice and food and essentials to asylum-seekers. Elizabeth thinks we should play the pieces then record the guests' reactions and responses, then add their voices to the audio recording to tailor the piece specifically for Bolton. It's a brilliant idea. If we can pull it together, we will hopefully exhibit the new version in the foyer of the library, and start some conversations, not only about birth in refugee camps, but about attitudes toward the crisis in a working-class northern town with a large migrant population.

We leave very excited. It's exactly the kind of work we want to be making.

Take Back formed a year ago during the Conservative Party Conference in Manchester when the policies of austerity and the crippling cuts to services were really starting to bite. Under the umbrella of the People's Assembly (the wonderfully broad, left-wing, anti-austerity movement) a few of us wanted to pull together an artistic community and respond creatively to this temporary Tory takeover of our city. We put together an evening of short plays about the current state of affairs with a mash-up of new writing and some Theatre Uncut pieces, which we performed script-in-hand. This was followed by a discussion on the role of theatre in politics and social change.

It was a great evening and what came out of it was the sense of a group of artists wanting to work together in the city to start conversations about the political landscape of our times. Manchester has a great tradition of protest and resistance, and a wealth of writers, actors, directors and producers who are politically engaged, and we all know each other, so it was pretty easy to set something up and roll with it. In the last fourteen months we've produced script-in-hand events on *Hope*, *Capital* (after the March budget), *Protest* and *Togetherness*. *Togetherness* was an immense afternoon of poetry, song and theatre at the Royal Exchange, two weeks after the UK voted to leave the

European Union. It included pieces by Russell T. Davies, Jackie Kay, Anders Lustgarten, Tanika Gupta, Alice Nutter and Brad Birch. We've performed at Festival No 6 in Portmeirion, the Paines Plough Roundabout Tent at the Edinburgh Festival (one bonkers early slot) and, most recently, have created an immersive piece about immigration, control and bureaucracy in a soon-to-be demolished bank in the city centre, as well as *Under Canvas* for B!RTH.

The three of us sort of fell into it. Becx is a talented writer, a politics geek and a force of nature. We met properly, outside of social media, at a People's Assembly demo in London in the summer of 2015. Grant, a visual artist and photographer, came recommended (for his sins) by a friend to film our first gig at the Conference. The three of us met up a few days later to talk about future projects and that was that. We're not even a proper company or a charity on paper yet; we don't have a bank account. We just started in a free space above a pub with some mates, sold it out, and have built on that momentum ever since. We work incredibly well together and these months of theatre-making with them have been some of the happiest and most fulfilling of my career. I'm incredibly proud of the work we've produced, not all of which has worked completely, of course, but I feel we've been successful in pulling together a community of like-minded creatives in this fantastic city and started some interesting and challenging conversations.

Straight after the meeting, we dash over to the BBC. We've been invited as a company to an afternoon of experiencing the newest 360-degree/virtual reality technology with a view to pitching stories to make better use of this developing trend in storytelling. I feel very challenged by, and resistant, to it: the idea of sitting with goggles and headphones on, experiencing a piece of art completely cut off from everyone else, seems *anti-theatre* to me. The whole premise seems to be the antithesis of that communal, shared experience.

One of the films we're shown is an Aardman animation called *We Wait*, about refugees trying to cross the water from Turkey into Kos. It is, admittedly, very affecting. You can turn your head and see people sitting beside you or look out to sea behind you and the sensation of motion in the boat is very effective. But I couldn't help but feel that an ordinary stop-motion Aardman film with its trademark plasticine animated figures would be just as moving. 360-degree requires, at this early stage, weirdly origami-type angular computer-generated images.

I'm not convinced. Grant and Becx, who are younger, and – in Grant's case – nerdier/less Luddite than I am, feel we could contribute something narratively for the BBC to perhaps develop. We discuss a couple of ideas: perhaps a stretcher in an Aleppo hospital, moving through the ruined building, intercut with images of an NHS hospital here or something with multiple narratives on a plane. Might be interesting. I have to leave early, so I leave Becx and Grant to it. They will fill me in when I see them later in the week. I think the key question is *why*? *Why* use this technology? It has to be a story that can be told best by specifically using it, rather than building a story to fit the gear.

Next, to Alra North, the northern wing of the Academy of Live and Recorded Arts.

One of the first-year students, Vic Burrows, tweeted me and asked me to go in to do a Q&A and I said yes, so here I am. An hour and a half with eighty first and second years and post-grad students. It's interesting to talk to young people who are further along in the journey than those I met at the Arts Emergency talk last week. I try (again) to be positive and give them a sense of the wonderful possibilities ahead of them. I also drive home the need to keep 'filling the well', to quote self-help guru Julia Cameron's book *The Artist's Way*, so they can draw on it in dry times: to read, learn and experience as much as possible; see art, watch great films, draw, write poetry, create work. They know how bloody hard it is, they don't need me to reinforce that. I do think it's a dangerous and unnecessary thing to fill young people with fear and dread as they stand on the cusp of entering the professional world, or at the start of their training. One girl asks me if it's possible to be an actor without giving up all hope of ever having a mortgage, owning a car, raising a family. There are lots of questions about auditions. I talk about a lovely clip I saw of American actor Bryan Cranston saying how his luck changed when he started treating auditions as an opportunity to act rather than some hideous test to get through as a means to an end. I love this. I also like to recommend Andy Nyman's glorious little book *Golden Rules for Actors*, with its recurring mantra of 'Be happy, you'll work more', and in which there's a wonderful section on auditions. He says, rightly, that the auditioners WANT to give you the job, they're actually rooting for you, they want you to solve their casting problem. This is so true, I think. The few times I've been on an audition panel, I've been leaning in, positively *willing* the person in front of me to be brilliant.

Lots of questions, too, about the difference between screen and stage acting, always a favourite for students. For example, they want to know whether there's a difference in technique between the two or whether you should just play the intention, regardless of the medium. A bit of both, I think. It's not so much a stage/screen differentiation, as knowing the style of the piece you're in, in the theatre, on the telly, whatever. *Coronation Street*, for example, the soap opera I was in for sixteen years, has a very distinctive style, a slightly heightened reality, and is a bit bolder and more colourful than most telly. I saw many actors over the years disregard this style, perhaps thinking it too broad, and turn in a hyper-naturalistic performance that just disappeared into a bland nothingness on screen. By the same token, there were others who occasionally took the style to an extreme, without it being rooted in character or any kind of truth. The audience know the style and instinctively feel when there's a mismatch. I've also seen many famous and very experienced actors come into the programme over the years and gain a new respect for the actors in the show. No fancy lighting or editing, no mood music or clever shots: what you see is what is broadcast and not many people can pull it off, especially with no rehearsal and forty-odd pages a day to shoot. Same with the writing. All the *Corrie* writers, without exception, could write you a fantastic three-part drama tomorrow, but not everyone can write for *Corrie*. Just think of the sheer volume, the clever and necessary exposition without repetition, and writing for characters over whom the audience feels they have ownership. These writers know they can't get it wrong. It's a hotbed of talent there and I have no time for people who are snobbish about it.

9 November

I get up early and check my phone to learn that Donald Trump has become President of the United States. Shocking and deeply alarming news. You'd think I'd have learned from the Brexit referendum not to go to bed feeling optimistic.

I go into town to meet Becx and Grant and am late because I keep bumping into people who want to talk about the US election result. It's a bit lovely, actually, people need to connect. I'm glad to be out in the world. Over a brew, Becx, Grant and I discuss what we can do as a company and immediately decide to park our next script-in-hand, *Ten Takes on Bodies*, and to use the slot we have booked at the Comedy Store in January, straight after the presidential inauguration, to create an artistic response to what's happened. We think we'll call it *Take Back America*, which is pretty grandiose, but it'll be fairly clear what we're exploring and I don't care. I want to take back America.

I post something online and immediately feel the need to pre-emptively defend myself against accusations of echo chambers and the cries of 'what's the point?' from the Facebook handwringers. The point is to do something, to share a space and start a conversation; to try, using different voices, to make some sort of sense of it and to find a positive way to move forward. Despair just isn't an option. I'm not suggesting for a moment that an evening of theatre in a city in the north of England will bring down the government – the American government! But we have to start with ACTION and community.

Spend most of the day bugged by people talking about building bunkers on social media. DO SOMETHING.

11 November

To Salford's Lowry Studio to see Forward Theatre's *Genesis: The Play* by Frazer Flintham, a production close to my heart, as it was inspired in part by my lovely friend, the actor Morag Siller, who died earlier this year from breast cancer. She was patron of the charity Prevent Breast Cancer (previously Genesis) that funds research into genetic predispositions to the disease and pre-emptive treatment (mastectomies and, in some cases, hysterectomies). She championed this play to highlight the many little-spoken-of emotional and psychological repercussions of the process.

The play was entirely successful in making human a little-understood element of cancer prevention and research. It's some skill to turn science into art in such a seamless way, and movingly but without a hint of sentimentality. The lead character – Rachel, a geneticist who discovers she carries the gene herself – was sensationally played by Helen Bradbury. I love a tough and unsympathetic protagonist: somehow it gives you room to experience what you feel without manipulation. I've seen a few overwrought performances recently, where the actors look like they're mining their souls for the pain of the character and it completely turns me off as an audience member. It seems to me in life that most people will do anything to stop themselves from crying in front of others, rather than wringing every bit of feeling out of themselves, however tragic the situation. A person's attempts to hold it all in are always more moving to me.

Rachel goes into a sort of manic-pragmatic-coping overdrive when she finds out she has the cancer gene and that her daughter might have it too. It seemed a lot more painfully close to life than if she'd dissolved into sobs. Sally Dynevor, my old *Corrie* mate, was there too. Everyone loves Sally. She developed breast cancer while she was playing out a storyline in *Coronation Street* where her character (also called Sally) was diagnosed with the disease. She has been a big supporter of this production and of the charity.

16 November

Take Back meeting at my kitchen table with a curry.

We're doing a talk at the University of Salford tomorrow for the Theatre/Media/Media Production/Performing Arts third years. We plan the general structure, which will involve me introducing us and talking about the *Ten Takes* model (basically ten short script-in-hand pieces on a theme), Grant moving on to the more recent immersive/installation based stuff, and then Becx setting up some exercises on starting theatrical conversations with Trump as a provocation for any issues they might want to explore.

We sign off a proposal for a symposium in Austria called 'Terror on Tour', who have put a call out for supporting events around the topics of borders and terrorism. We've never been involved in anything like this before, but have cooked up an interesting idea (we think) about walls (Trump's proposed wall to keep Mexicans out, the controversial proposals for the wall at the Calais Refugee Camp, and of course the West Bank barrier on the Gaza Strip) and their use in dividing peoples and creating fear. We've proposed an installation type piece using a wall, some projection mapping and perhaps one performer. We'll see.

There has been a huge response to *Take Back America*. We were a bit naïve in thinking that we could possibly do a simple *Ten Takes*, and commission ten writers to do five minutes each. As soon as we put it out on social media we were inundated by people wanting to submit pieces. There's a clear need to channel all these feelings in the aftermath of this shocking election victory that is already emboldening the xenophobes, homophobes and misogynists. If we can achieve one thing with this event, it's to embolden the resistance, to give voice to people who feel incredibly afraid of what the future holds now. Suzanne Bell, the Literary Manager at the Royal Exchange, who was so helpful in connecting us with some of the incredibly talented writers that took part in *Togetherness*, post-Brexit, has forwarded our email to some great American writers and they have all come back to us immediately, offering to write for the piece. And James Graham, who is pretty much the go-to political playwright in Britain (author of *This House* at the National, *The Vote* at the Donmar, *Monster Raving Loony* at Plymouth) emailed us offering a submission. Really exciting and rewarding. It feels as though we're providing something that people need artistically. We're going to have way too many pieces. We'll have to be pretty brutal in our curating and create an online space for the pieces we can't make fit.

17 November

We do our talk at Salford and it goes well. We've never done anything like this before as a company and all three of us enjoy talking about the work and feel proud to show the photos of our past pieces. I take pains to reassure the students that, because of Grant, we look a lot slicker than we actually are, in our Take Back hoodies and with our pretty PowerPoint presentation. Actually, we're as kick-bollock-scramble as they come. We want them to take heart from this and know that if we can pull this work off, so can they.

Becx's exercise goes down a treat and the little groups of five come up with some great ideas, our favourite being a sort of social experiment-cum-immersive piece involving a wall between two groups of people with information being fed to each group about the other and a choice of whether to build the wall higher or knock it down. Brilliant. We might nick it! There are discussions about the fear in the LGBT community, too, and about the bubbles we live in that mean that we're constantly being shocked by these results (for example, the UK General Election of 2015 and EU referendum of 2016). They're a really engaged and engaging bunch, and I think we manage to persuade a couple of them to go for it and set up a company when they graduate. But there are only seventeen of them. Out of a possible 100. Hard at the start not to feel a bit dispirited by the lack of interest. Niki Woods, the course leader, has put in a lot of time and effort organizing this event as part of their enrichment and to give them some guidance as they enter the professional world, and eighty-three of them didn't show.

We talk afterwards about the monetizing of higher education, the extortionate fees and whether a level of entitlement comes with that: the choice of the consumer, the service user, rather than the hunger of the student. Anyway. The seventeen who come are great, so no matter. The overriding feeling we leave with is that the spark that fires everything we do as a company is social justice and politics. It's what gives us the energy to keep doing this, for no money, taking up all our free time really: this belief that we are starting important conversations and helping to shift things. Emboldening each other and feeling less isolated in the face of such a shitstorm of terrible world news. Or something.

19 November

Exciting message from Raz Shaw, who directed me in *Wit* at the beginning of the year for the Royal Exchange. We've been fannying about for months trying to find a London venue for a possible transfer, but the Exchange is such a specific space – a beautiful three-tier in-the-round auditorium that seats about 750, but somehow makes you feel like you're part of a tiny intimate audience. It's a bit of a hard act to follow and we'd all but given up thinking it could ever happen anywhere else, really, especially in a proscenium arch space. The theatre itself was the star of the show in many ways, lending itself to a revolve that became central to the action and also to the feeling of an American operating theatre or a lecture hall. It was one of my favourite jobs ever, partly because of Raz, who I loved working with, and who is a proper mate now; partly because of the ace company and the theatre; but also because it was the most challenging role I've ever had. But I'd come to accept that it was never happening again and was enjoying my growing hair, after having to shave my head for the role, and putting back on the stone-and-a-half I lost (bugger, I'm going to have to shift it again).

There's a sexy new space in King's Cross on loan for a short time from Google apparently, where the musical *In the Heights* is currently playing alongside the all-female Donmar Shakespeare trilogy and *Lazarus*, the David Bowie play. The smaller space is in the round and seats about 400 so that would be ideal, but they need something soon. This might work out perfectly.

I'm rehearsing with film director Mike Leigh all through December for his project about the Peterloo Massacre, then have January to March off before filming, so if we can do it then it would be fantastic. It would mean I'll have the summer filming in a wig for my hair to grow back again. Raz is going to email the cast and creative team and talk to some producers. I start learning my lines again straight away, just in case. There are a lot of lines: I spent nine months learning them last year.

20 November

My old friend Helena Lymbery is up north visiting us from London, on a weekend off from *Harry Potter and the Cursed Child* plays in which she plays a variety of characters. Helena and I were both part of Arts Threshold back in the day and have remained great mates. We have a weekend of eating and drinking and walking the dog and putting the world to rights and arguing about plays we've seen and books we've read, and it's food for the soul. These old friendships. With Kersh, we drink too much red wine and watch the entire second series of *Catastrophe*, the brilliant Rob Delaney and Sharon Horgan comedy, and literally roll around on the floor in hysterics. One of those great weekends in your life where you feel completely whole and content.

22 November

I am in a fug of nineteenth-century research ready for next week and the start of rehearsals for the legendary British director Mike Leigh's film about the Peterloo Massacre, a huge part of Manchester's working-class history. Eighty thousand cotton workers, men and women, with their children, assembled in St Peter's Field in the centre of the city on 16 August 1819. They had marched from as far as Blackburn, Oldham and Stockport to demand equal representation in Parliament. At that time you could vote only if you owned property, and MPs were basically put in place to protect the interests of the ruling classes. The meeting itself was hugely significant in that there were thousands of women there too, organized in newly formed Female Reform Societies. It went down in history because the military waded in on the peaceful gathering and wreaked havoc, injuring hundreds, and killing over fifteen, including women and children. A disproportionate number of women seem to have been deliberately targeted by the sabre-wielding yeomanry.

To say I'm nervous about starting on the film is a bit of an understatement, but I'm excited to be part of it and to work in a different way than for any project I've done before. I've been sent file upon file by the researcher, Jacqueline. And Mike has asked me to think of ten women I know, of a similar age to me, and working class and intelligent, so we can talk through them and do some improvisations and decide on one on which to eventually form the basis of my character. I'm playing a woman called Elizabeth Gaunt who was badly beaten and arrested on the day. I did my initial audition back in the summer: half an hour in an office in Soho, inhabiting the physicality of a friend of mine whilst being observed by Mike. I was absolutely shit. I'd had a cup of coffee too many and I felt quite self-conscious and uncertain. Doing too much, even though Mike had expressly said not to. And then in my caffeinated nerviness I *kissed him* as I left. I kissed Mike Leigh. What. A. Knob. I couldn't believe it when I got the call months and months later saying I'd got the job. Just goes to show. Blimey. *NB: It probably isn't a good idea to plant a smacker on the next director you audition for. I think I got the job in spite of this lapse of judgement, not because of it.*

24 November

Another Arts Emergency talk, this time at Bradford College – a further and higher education institution – to a mix of performing arts students and media make-up students (so I had to adjust my speech slightly for that one). Nice bunch, a couple of bright sparks, a few slouchers and yawners. It went okay. I think the people who really get it are the ones who just know all this stuff anyway; it's just in them to be creative and curious and ambitious. Hopefully I can reinforce that a bit and bolster their self-belief. It's not like any young person is going to listen to me going on and have the scales fall from their eyes and suddenly become motivated, I'm pretty sure of that. I think a few of them today will take up a menteeship. I hope so. As always, I'm moved by the commitment and passion of the teachers and course-leaders, constantly striving for the best opportunities for their students.

Kersh is getting so much from being a mentor. Millie-Jo, his seventeen-year-old mentee, and a budding writer, is a force of nature. She grabs any opportunity he offers to her with enthusiasm and together they've seen loads of new writing, watched the great Sally Wainwright talk about her work and gone to numerous workshops. He even landed her a commission to write a children's play for a little Oldham Coliseum tour of local libraries. She delivered it and it's fantastic.

29 November

Completely bonkers Take Back day trying to fit everything in before I disappear into the mysterious world of the Mike Leigh rehearsal room tomorrow.

I did a benefit for the Working Class Movement Library in Salford on Sunday with my friend Maxine Peake, who's also in the film and has been rehearsing for a couple of weeks already. I could see she was torn between wanting to tell me *everything* and trying to be discreet, letting me experience it for myself when the time comes.

We have three meetings today. The first is with Chris Lawson, a great director who has worked with us many times and who is Associate Director at Oldham Coliseum. A RADA graduate, he has the opportunity to submit something for the RADA Festival next summer and has asked us to be part of it. To propose taking a mash-up of some of our best short pieces of the last year and put on a *Ten Takes* using our actors and some RADA students. He wants to inspire them to be socially engaged as artists, but also to think about creating their own work as a different pathway into the business. He was shocked at a recent London audition for a production up north, when he met a graduate who obviously couldn't be arsed even thinking about working in a regional rep and hadn't even read the play. A graduate! Bloody hell.

Next is the People's History Museum, which is host to a six-month exhibition on LGBT+ history called Never Going Underground. Hayley (my character in *Coronation Street*) was the first trans character in a soap opera back in the day and there was quite a commotion about it at the time, then a little bit of sea change when the audience grew fond of her and wanted good things for her, like equal marriage rights and so on. We were mentioned in Parliament and I became patron of various trans pressure groups as a result. And now Hayley's iconic red anorak (her only coat for sixteen years!) is to be exhibited in the Visibility section of the archive. Proud. But I saw an opportunity for Take Back there, too, so we went in to discuss the possibility of making a piece of supporting work. All a bit tricky as it's been curated to within an inch of its life already, and space is at a premium. We'll see.

And next to HOME Manchester, the fantastic arts centre that opened in 2015, where we're being offered a 'Made at HOME' research and development pot of £1,500 to stage a bit of a play in one of their spaces for a week, trying out some stuff we want to experiment with and maybe doing a little 'sharing' at the end. Result! We love paying people. It's such a rare treat.

At home, Kersh has written the beginnings of a beautiful piece to run in sections through Take Back America: a conversation between a father and daughter about what to do to restore hope after Trump's election, so they collate a list of random (and considered) acts of kindness. He's put a shout out on Facebook and has got some lovely stuff already. He has been sure to reference Duncan Macmillan's one-man play *Every Brilliant Thing*, to which the idea owes something of a debt. He wants to put an envelope under every chair in the theatre with a random act in it for people to take away at the end. I love it. We'll have some angry pieces, I think, and rightly so, but I like Kersh's idea that we can begin to combat all the hatred and fear with a bit of kindness.

30 November

London for the first day of *Peterloo* rehearsals with Mike Leigh. I meet my mate Katie West, a fantastic actor who was in Simon Stephens's

Blindsided with me at the Royal Exchange in 2014, for a (decaf) coffee before we go in and meet the other women in our little 'gang'. Because the cast is so huge, Mike is rehearsing groups in sections, doing individual character work, then putting us together to improvise. Our group consists of Dorothy Duffy, who'll be playing Mary Fildes, Katie playing Sarah Hargreaves, Victoria Moseley playing Susannah Saxton, and Kate Rutter, Christine Bottomley and Samantha Edwards (all of whom I already know, which is lovely) playing made-up characters from the Manchester Female Reform Society. We're ushered into a small, hot room to talk to Jacqueline Riding, the totally cool and sexy historian who we all immediately fall a bit in love with. We talk broadly about the period, the women, the Reform Societies, class and feminism, all of us careful to show we've done our research, but not wanting to show off. These women are great. I feel immediately that we'll all be looking out for each other on this. Mike is funny. Mock-stern and very smart. Everyone will meet at the British Library tomorrow to register and become a member, but I haven't got the requisite ID with me so it'll have to wait.

And that's it for the week. Mike and Dorothy are to work for the next few days and the rest of us are sent off, with profuse apologies from the director, who has fallen a bit behind with rehearsals. All that anticipation, the emotional farewell back home, good luck cards from my family secreted in my rucksack . . . and I'm back home tomorrow!

In the evening I travel up to the Pleasance in Islington to watch my niece, Rosa, in her third-year LAMDA production of *The Revenger's Tragedy*. Rodney Cottier, who was teaching when I was there and who has not changed one iota, has directed and it is fabulously camp with side lighting, full Jacobean costume and many gruesome, brilliantly executed deaths. It's a ridiculous play, but beautifully designed and performed. I really feel that these young people are ready to work, especially Rosa, who shone. I'm so proud of her.

Rosa and I had a big chat about the future, post-LAMDA, in the pub afterwards. Drama schools seem to be very proactive in career development these days, and there seems to be a lot of emphasis on being seen by agents and casting directors, which is great, of course. My friend Laura Dickens works specifically in this area at LAMDA, and is fantastic at creating opportunities for the graduating students as they move into the profession. As someone who had to take a different route into 'the business' (I hate that expression) through fringe theatre and making my own work, I hope that there's an emphasis too on the various other paths that can lead you to paid work. I suspect there is, as this is the college that spawned *The Play That Goes Wrong*, the devised piece that started in a pub for an audience of four and which, following a smash-hit West End run, is now being taken to Broadway by Star Wars producer J J Abrams! I went to a gala performance of it a couple of years back and loved it, but during dinner with the cast afterwards I discovered some of them *still* didn't have agents, for God's sake. Rosa is fretting about how she needs to be in London and how she can possibly afford to do that. I absolutely refute the fact that you have to base yourself in the capital in order to work as an artist. It's two hours on the train from Manchester, where there is a vibrant arts scene, MediaCity, Red Productions, BBC Radio drama, the Manchester International Festival, and countless brilliant theatres and fringe venues. It's affordable, friendly and there are regular trains to London. But for someone like Rosa, whose networks and community of friends are ensconced in the city she trained in, it's a daunting prospect to up-sticks and start afresh in the North. I get that.

5 December

Still no *Peterloo* rehearsals, so am beetling away, reading a book on workers' lives during the Industrial Revolution, the central thesis of which seems to be 'Ah, it wasn't all that bad!'. Hmm. I also managed to cleverly combine a bit of parenting with research by taking my twelve-year-old, Lyss, to nearby Quarry Bank Mill, a National Trust site with working nineteenth-century looms and an apprentice house that was the setting for the brilliant TV series *The Mill*, which I've been enjoying watching again. It's set slightly later in the century than *Peterloo*, but has been so helpful in helping me to imagine the world the cotton workers inhabited.

I'm in London today doing an ADR session for *Broadchurch*, the ITV drama I filmed all summer down in Bristol and Dorset. ADR is Automated Dialogue Replacement (I admit I had to look that up) and involves you watching scenes in which the sound needs finessing for whatever reason, and re-recording dialogue or adding sounds and ad libs for off-camera. I filmed a scene walking along West Bay beach in Dorset with actor Sarah Parish for Episode 3, with the wind howling and sea crashing and the pebbles crunching under our feet, as well as those of the assorted boom operators and cameramen. As the director called 'CUT' we literally said to each other, 'See you in Soho for ADR, then'.

And here we are. Well, here I am. Sarah will be down later to record separately. There is a massive screen in the studio. I really do work hard at not being one of those actors who picks fault with themselves and their appearance all the time. What's the point? My face is my face and my body is my body, and frankly I think it's good to see someone on telly who is a bit wrinkled and scarred and big-nosed and middle-aged and *normal,* whatever that means. But bloody hell, I don't look my best in this show – badly beaten after a sexual assault, and with shit, too-short, post-*Wit* hair. It's fair to say that seeing my face expressing itself all over a ten-foot square screen isn't the best thing that's happened to my self-esteem this year.

I get over myself and get on with it. A digital line moves left to right across the screen and when it hits a static line on the right, you have to say your line, synching it exactly to your lip movements, trying to pitch it emotionally in the right place and even moving your body a bit on the spot, if there's movement in the scene. I really enjoy it actually. It's properly challenging, and I like the technical specificity of it. I do have to do one really difficult scene though, where my character reenacts her rape for the police and gets very distressed. Unfortunately it took place next to a very loud waterfall. It was a pretty full-on scene to film and having to dub it without losing the intensity is a bit tricky. But these ADR lads are brilliant. They do some sort of mixing magic and it works a treat eventually.

I use the time in London to have a couple of meetings, too, including with the playwright Anna Jordan who's writing a new version of Brecht's *Mother Courage* as a co-production for the Royal Exchange and the theatre company Headlong, which produced *People, Places and Things*, the sell-out Duncan Macmillan play starring Denise Gough. The weirdest bit of synchronicity brought me to this job, which will hopefully be happening in 2018. After *Wit*, Sarah Frankcom, the Artistic Director of the Exchange, asked me what I'd like to do next (I'm aware of how fancy that sounds and I don't take it for granted for a MINUTE; it certainly wasn't always like this). I said I didn't have a burning desire to play any pre-existing role really: my passion is for new writing. But someone in the *Wit* cast had mentioned *Mother Courage*, and I remember having seen it as a student at the Contact Theatre when I was seventeen, with the incredible Ellie Haddington in the title role. I felt that a new version of it, in the context of modern warfare and the huge subsequent migration of people, might be really exciting. Sarah said that the Royal Exchange had never produced a Brecht play as the previous Artistic Directors were never fans, and that made us even more alive to the possibility of it. A couple of days later, the director Amy Hodge rang Sarah out of the blue with the idea of a reworked *Mother Courage* written by Anna Jordan and set in the context of the refugee crisis, with a diverse cast and newly composed songs. So I met up with Amy and we got on really well, and Anna was commissioned soon after to start a first draft, which of course will then need the go-ahead from the Brecht estate.

Anna and I have met in passing before, but we're Facebook friends, which has strangely propelled us into a kind of a concentrated intimacy, where we know a little of the minutiae (and of the big events) of each other's lives through that strange filter of the status update and comment button. This was a lovely, short but BIG meeting about the play, her ideas for it and also life, love and loss. I'm really looking forward to working with her and with Amy.

I go to North London to meet Raz Shaw, the director of *Wit,* and we have a boozy evening, where we vacillate wildly between really, really wanting a London transfer to happen and not believing it will, so telling ourselves that it would be better if it was just a wonderful thing, a one-off, that happened, up North, and if people didn't get to see it, then fuck 'em and why should everything have to transfer to London anyway, the bastards. Of course, if we get the go ahead (and it's still 50:50) we'll create a whole new narrative of how we need to reach as many people as we can with this important story. Ha!

6 December

Kersh and I take our daughter Martha and her mate to see Kate Tempest at the Ritz in Manchester. Kate Tempest is a thirty-year-old poet, novelist, rapper and hip-hop artist, who writes and performs searing political epic stories about ordinary urban people. In some ancient cultures, there would be a person called the shaman, who could conjure some sort of magic through wild dance and creativity for the good of the community. There have been a couple of times in my life when I've seen an artist in a performance that has been so off-the-scale of what I thought was possible, channelling something so intense and other-worldly that it felt almost somehow supernatural, like they were summoning something not quite human. It's how I feel tonight watching this tiny, humble, baggy T-shirted poet create an electricity in the room that she says at the curtain call has 'rattled' her, too. People around us are crying. When I went to see Mark Rylance in Jez Butterworth's *Jerusalem* a few years ago, I felt the same. I had turned to Kersh at the end and said 'I don't understand what happened then. That's not acting. That's some sort of shaman shit happening there.' Same tonight. I feel incredibly lucky to be witnessing something so rare and authentic, that makes me want to live better. She also asks us all to properly experience it together in the room and not through a screen, respectfully asking us to put our phones away. I can't tell you what a difference it makes to the energy in the place. I am so glad Martha is there to experience it, too.

Kersh and I talk into the night about how seeing something like tonight's gig leaves you. Does it makes you want to give up on any notion of yourself as a creative or interpretative artist when you've seen the form at its absolute best? Or does it inspire you to work harder, delve deeper, say stuff that matters to you? At the start of the night Kate had talked about the state of the world (it's pretty much what everyone is talking about now, at the dog-end of 2016, with all its losses and with the mess the world is in) and what an important thing it is for us all to be together with strangers in a room sharing an experience. It made me think of what we're *attempting* to do with Take Back.

9 December

Back to London for my first one-to-one session with Mike Leigh. Rehearsals, such as they are at the moment, are taking place on the tenth floor in a strange, seemingly deserted, BT office block on Edgware Road. Mike has been meeting the actors individually and in groups for weeks now and he must be knackered. We've all been told to come in with a list of people we know, who share our gender and who are around our age, and working class. He must have a head full of the friends, relatives and acquaintances of the hundreds of us involved in this epic project. We go to the 'talking room' and I spend two hours talking him through my list of women, one of whom will hopefully be the real-life source for my characterization of Elizabeth Gaunt. I have a list of about twelve fantastic women in my life, some of whom are close friends and some of whom are acquaintances. When we've talked in depth about them all, Mike goes through the list and asks me which of them could translate to the early nineteenth century. It feels quite hard, but actually it's quite clear in some cases. Some of my friends, in all their strength, vulnerability, fierce intelligence and singularity, simply have a very modern sensibility, and some are strangely timeless. My favourite moment is when we sadly decide that my wonderful friend H, one of the best people I've ever known, with her tireless entrepreneurial spirit, and whose latest venture is painting Christmas crockery, is too rooted in the twenty-first century to be the character source for Mrs Gaunt. 'So there'll be no painted plates in *Peterloo*, I'm afraid,' says Mike, shaking his head as he places a cross next to her name on his pad.

13 December

Late for rehearsals for the Mike Leigh film because of massive train delays. It's incredibly frustrating and I immediately regret not coming down to stay the night before, but what can I do? The *Peterloo* team are extremely understanding, thank God, and shuffle things around. But when I arrive an hour and a half after my call, I'm straight into it, and up on my feet for the first time, in a large, hot room with fantastic views of London on two sides. We talk through my remaining list of seven women on whom we could possibly base my character, and starting with the first, Mike asks me to walk around the space, 'getting her moving' while he leaves the room.

The first friend on the list is someone with quite a hard personal and home life, and whom I can't imagine ever sitting and relaxing, unless she's having a quiet moment with a fag. I busy myself in the room, tidying up a bit, examining the blinds, taking note of missing slats, of what needs fixing. This person is not someone comfortable sitting with her own thoughts; she's on the go constantly – almost, it seems, as a distraction from the harsh reality of her circumstances. At some point, Mike comes back into the room and observes me, then after a while tells me to come out of character. Too much messing around with the furniture, in his view. I'm doing too much again. There doesn't have to be any extraneous business. I can interact briefly with other imaginary people, but am not to vocalize or get caught up in scenarios. Mike leaves and returns, and seems a bit happier with what I'm doing. We repeat this exercise with each of the women from my real life who have made the shortlist, until he lands on three he likes the most, or feels are right for the basis of the character of Elizabeth. Available information about Gaunt is sketchy to say the least, other than that she was put into Henry 'Orator' Hunt's carriage at the meeting, after feeling unwell. And that she was subsequently arrested, beaten and thrown into solitary confinement. By the time she was acquitted twelve days later she was in a terrible state, barely able to stand or speak.

Mike leaves me alone for a good twenty minutes as I walk around the room, taking on various physical characteristics that we've discussed and I really enjoy it. It's a completely new way of working, starting from the outside of a character first and finding a physical language for her. The endless walking gives me a sense of how this person might have felt on the long march to the meeting at St Peter's Field. Occasionally I'm able to lose myself in it and a few times I'm just a bit annoyed that I don't have my pedometer on me, because I reckon I'm covering a fair few miles without the satisfaction of clocking them up. When Mike returns, he asks me how it was, we chat for a bit and I'm told to keep hold of what I've found and am released into the afternoon. In the green room I bump into three more actors. There are hundreds of us in this film, and so many of us know each other. Lots of good northern stock.

16 December

Back to *Peterloo* after a meandering few days of really 'filling the well'. These gaps between rehearsals have afforded me the unexpected luxury of some lovely moodling time. I've been reading Patti Smith's beautiful memoir, *M Train*, which I've had for a year but only just picked up. I'm not sure I've ever loved a book as much. I feel very alive to the world because of it, and have sought out soul-enhancing things to do.

Kersh and I saw a fantastic exhibition at Manchester Art Gallery, Strange and Familiar: Studies of British life by Non-British Photographers, which was full of wonderful faces and settings. It made me appreciate afresh the beauty of the ordinary, and reminded me of a conversation with Mike Leigh last week about teeth and how hard it is for him to cast actors for period films because of all the perfect white teeth. Same with eyebrows, I think. The sculpted and tattooed eyebrows that are so fashionable now place women so squarely in the early twenty-first century, as do the smooth, botoxed foreheads and plumped cheeks that are sneaking in, although not to the extent that you see in American actors now. It's such a shame. Not only does it set a standard of appearance that makes ordinary women feel as though their looks are an anomaly, but it also makes the world a blander place. I love nothing more than a craggy, lined and thoroughly lived-in face, with all its experience and character. Even whilst wishing that the face looking back at me from the mirror was a bit less craggy, lined and lived-in at times.

I arrive at rehearsals, full of Patti-esque curiosity and readiness, and thinking I'll be working with the other women in my little team that makes up the core element of the Manchester Female Reform Society. But it's just me again. *Me and Mike Leigh*. I can still hardly believe it, bloody hell. I was obsessed with his films in my teens and twenties, particularly *High Hopes* and *Naked*.

I walk around the big room in character, then get taken off to put on a grey dress from the period and some clogs, then walk around some more. Then I get back into my own gear and we sit and have a chat about my character's family tree. I feel incredibly befuddled by the birth and death dates and the names of all Elizabeth's (entirely made-up) aunties, uncles, parents and siblings. Mike has very strong ideas about how things should be done and you kind of have to sign up for that. For example, he doesn't like his actors referring to their character in the first person, which is easy to slip into. Sometimes I have to fight some feelings of being a little girl again, reminding myself that I'm a reasonably smart 46-year-old, not a school girl trying to impress teacher. It's funny how these old feelings come and get you. Especially, I think, when you're from a working-class background.

I think I hold my own in a slight disagreement about Elizabeth Gaunt's politicization, the fictional journey to be decided between us of how she ended up battered in Henry Hunt's carriage on that fateful August day in 1819. I would like her to be a basically non-political person with a deep-rooted and almost old-fashioned respect for authority and the status quo (the basis of this being almost entirely to do with a real-life testimony describing her as rather incongruously curtseying to the magistrates at her court hearing). My idea is that she has been quietly radicalized by her sparky daughter and her reformer son-in-law. Mike thinks this is quite reductive and that it takes away from her own political agency. But I think that having her as an almost accidental activist – someone who's been persuaded to come to the mass meeting, not entirely comfortable with the crowds and the banners – fits in well with the women on whom I've based her, and also makes starker and sadder the terrible treatment she suffers on the day. That she's the one who ends up beaten and put in solitary confinement is, I think, almost more tragic for the fact that this is her first foray into activity of this kind. Not everyone there that day can have been a political firebrand. Mike agrees in the end.

In the evening I see *Love* by Alexander Zeldin at the Dorfman Theatre at the National Theatre, the renamed and redesigned space which used to be the Cottesloe. It is an incredible and stark play set in a hostel for people waiting to be housed at Christmas, full of incredible characterful naturalistic performances, and stories of kindness and humanity in the grimmest of circumstances. There is a moment in a scene involving an incontinent old lady (played brilliantly by Anna Calder-Marshall) that breaks my heart. My experience is only marred by a couple of obviously very wealthy men in their forties sitting behind me and to the side, for whom the story is clearly just too uncomfortably grim, a fact they feel compelled to signal to everyone by huffing and puffing, looking to each other with smirks and raised eyebrows and glancing deliberately at their expensive watches over and over again. They are seated by the aisle by which the actors exit down the side of the audience, so they catch my eye every time a character leaves the stage, and it pisses me right off. Why do people feel the need to display their discontent in such an overt way? Why can't they just sit neutrally and keep their thoughts to themselves until they leave? It's so rude. I wonder if Anna Calder-Marshall notices too, because in a breathtaking moment at the end of the play when she breaks the fourth wall and staggers into the audience lurching at us without her stick, silently imploring us to engage with her with big frightened eyes, she makes a beeline for them. Two young men in front of me catch her and hold her steady as she passes and I notice one of them angrily wiping away real tears as she moves on. One of the posh blokes behind sits impassively as she leans on him, making no attempt to take her weight. But it definitely challenges him. He's not smirking anymore.

It occurs to me afterwards that the Dorfman is the perfect potential venue for a *Wit* transfer. The theatre at King's Cross now doesn't look like it's going to happen. The figures just don't work, because of the prohibitive rent. Raz Shaw, the director, has tried to contact Rufus Norris (currently Artistic Director of the National Theatre) several times, but to no avail. I think maybe I should give it a go and drop him a line. One last push. I feel as though I'll possibly never play a part so wonderful and challenging and so outside of my comfort zone on stage again, so I might as well try to make it happen again if I can. I won't hold my breath, but, you know, nothing ventured, etc. Can't seem to let it go yet.

17 December

Kersh's birthday weekend, so he comes to London and we eat out and go to see the David Bowie musical, *Lazarus*, at King's Cross Theatre. It's okay. I'm a bit disappointed. It looks beautiful and, of course, the songs are fantastic, but I'm not entirely convinced by the musical theatre-style delivery of some of them and the plot I find to be a bit daft. I leave glad to have seen it, but not really feeling it; just feeling bad about not liking it more when everyone worked so hard.

In the Patti Smith book I'm reading, she visits Brecht's grave in Germany and sings a lullaby from *Mother Courage* to him. I email Anna Jordan, who is working on her adaptation of this play.

We talked in our last meeting about the songs and how they would be styled in our version, bearing in mind that I'm no singer and have a ridiculously low range. We discussed a folk/spoken-word fusion, and it occurs to me, reading this passage, that a Patti Smith style score (but a Lancashire version?) might work really well – that half-spoken, half-sung thing she does on some of her softer songs. Patti is everywhere at the moment. Zoe, the third Assistant Director (AD) on *Peterloo*, was wearing a T-shirt with a cartoon of her on it the other day and we talked about her for ages and she sent me the documentary *Dreaming of a Life*. Then that night Facebook was full of coverage of Patti's faltering version of *It's a Hard Rain* at Bob Dylan's Nobel Prize ceremony. She lost the words twice, but her vulnerability and honest admission of how nervous she felt only added to her beautiful interpretation. She subsequently wrote a wonderful piece for *Rolling Stone* about how the meaning of the song, which is about stumbling and struggling, took her over and overwhelmed her. Pretty much every actor's greatest fear is losing the lines on stage, I think, but it never matters as much as we fear. It's a live art and mistakes sometimes make the live experience more raw, more electric and beautifully human. What a lesson.

19 December

Last day of rehearsals for *Peterloo* until we reconvene next spring. Finally, the women of the Manchester Female Reform Society reunite and there are long discussions with Mike about the origins of the group, the general set-up of the first and second meetings, and our own characters' thoughts, feelings and participation in the activity. It's great to hear about the other actors' characters finally and it's just brilliant to be with such smart and engaged women. No acting, though. No time to improvise, just to lay out the framework. I have no idea how things will work out when we come to film, whether we'll be improvising on set or whether we'll have any kind of script to work with. We'll just have to see how it unfolds. All in good time.

I use the train journey home to catch up on Take Back business. I read the *Take Back America* submissions that have come in already and make a provisional list of ones to be included in the evening in January. There is a lot of poetry and a few monologues, many in a similar (understandably) despairing vein. Once we have all the pieces we can curate something that hopefully has some variety in tone and style, as well as content. Great stuff, though, and nearly all the writers have thanked us for the opportunity to channel some of the big feelings about Trump's impending presidency.

Josh Coates, a Manchester writer we know, is organizing a performance fundraiser for the charity Médicins Sans Frontières on

Thursday, at very short notice, after the completely devastating news from Aleppo this week. There have been mass executions of civilians by rebel forces and the formerly glorious city, the second city of Syria (like Manchester here), has been reduced to complete rubble. There is nothing left and the various agencies and NGOs are trying to organize evacuations of the few remaining survivors, in the most terrible of circumstances and at great personal risk. Take Back will perform two new pieces, one by Kersh, called *Aleppo BB5*, placing the situation here, with me as a Lancashire woman who is trying to survive after the destruction of the north of England. The other, by Becx, is called *I Had to Do Something*, juxtaposing the stories of a young lad in Manchester helping a homeless Syrian refugee he sees on his way to a night out, and a young woman volunteering with the White Helmets to pull survivors out of the rubble in Aleppo.

The BBC Writersroom have got back to us about the virtual reality project. We made the shortlist with our idea, but they went with someone else in the end. I'm a bit relieved. It didn't feel entirely *us* somehow.

Becx and Grant have been to the University of Salford to discuss Take Back being part of a huge festival there in the autumn where we have the opportunity to possibly do a 'best of' performance and be paid! Slowly, these paid opportunities are trickling our way.

And we have invitations from Manchester College to go in and talk to students and from a couple of interesting-sounding events around International Women's Day. The festival in Innsbruck is definitely happening in March, too, as well as the R&D week at the theatre space at HOME and *Take Back America* in the short term. It's going to be a very busy 2017. But Christmas first, and some overdue family time.

2016 has been a hard year for the world: so many losses, so much upheaval. Lots of work to do to make sure 2017 is the start of a new, more hopeful time.

9 January 2017

Back to work after the Christmas break. As soon as my daughters are on the school bus my Take Back comrades are round, the coffee's on and the kitchen table is strewn with bits of paper with the titles and names of the writers of all 40+ submissions for *Take Back America* written on them. They are colour-coded for monologues, scenes or musical pieces and have casting breakdowns scribbled in pencil underneath. Over the next eight hours we read, re-read, eliminate, reinstate, cast and recast until we have two halves of an evening's programme that we hope manages to be diverse in authorship, varied in style and content and that doesn't go on until midnight. We end up with twenty-three responses from a culturally mixed bunch of men and women, including five American writers. We have short plays by experienced playwrights like Kirsten Greenidge, Aditi Apil and James Graham, and new work by young and passionate artists who have approached us with their work. Some of the submissions are bleak and angry; some are hopeful and inspiring. We try to mix them up whilst maintaining some sort of cogency. All the pieces are too long. However, Becx will write to request/suggest cuts. I will write to those whose pieces we can't use with regret and gratitude and ask permission to publish them on our website, and happily inform those who made the final show. We create a mini-ensemble of actors for each half and allocate a director to each section so that each piece runs seamlessly (we hope!) from one to the next, without gaps and hiatuses. We check actor availability, rejoicing when our favourites are free and despairing when they're not, and scrabble around for rehearsal space, which is at a premium in Manchester.

We also decide not to go to Innsbruck to take part in the 'Terror on Tour' event. When we're honest with ourselves, we liked the idea of becoming a bit international (and having a few days in Austria) but the reality is we have so much work to do here and we can't justify the time and cost of taking a piece to a symposium, however interesting the subject matter.

We eat too much bread; drink too much coffee; go off on tangents about projects, plans and ideas way into the future, post daft pictures of us hard at 'work' for our Facebook page. These are, as Becx posts later, the best days.

Later, the internet goes into overdrive about Meryl Streep's Golden Globe Lifetime Award acceptance speech in which she celebrates the diversity of Hollywood and almost cries when she talks about President-Elect Trump and, specifically, his cruel and ugly impersonation of a reporter with cerebral palsy at a rally in the election primaries. She talks about the responsibility of the artist to create and engender empathy.

Later, Trump takes to Twitter to lambast her and her supposedly liberal-elite buddies, and calls her, hilariously, *overrated*. What times these are.

12 January

This is turning out to be a week of strange contrasts. I am in London promoting the upcoming third series of *Broadchurch,* in which I'm playing the guest lead. *Broadchurch* is a hugely successful ITV crime drama starring Olivia Colman and David Tennant, and I spent most of last summer travelling up and down to Dorset, where the series is set, in the shadow of the iconic Jurassic cliffs.

I arrive at Euston and am whisked away to Fortnum & Mason for lunch with a journalist from a Sunday supplement magazine, then to some weird and extremely posh showroom (showing what, I can't quite work out) where I have my hair and make-up done, and where a stylist shows me a line of dresses to try on for the accompanying photo shoot.

Yesterday I was with Take Back at the Destitution Project, a fantastic voluntary run organization in a huge church hall in Bolton town centre. We put up our *Under Canvas* tent, the installation piece we created for the B!RTH Festival at the Royal Exchange and, over the day, we invited users of the project and the wonderful Boltonian volunteers to come and sit and listen to the pieces. We recorded scores of interviews about the personal experiences of the asylum seekers waiting for leave to remain. We listened as they talked through their thoughts and feelings about being in Lancashire, thousands of miles away from home. We talked to the volunteers about what inspires them to help and about the services the project offers. These include English lessons; hot meals; cooking practice using unfamiliar British ingredients; a food bank and a clothing store; as well, of course, as an opportunity to meet people and make friends in this new and unfamiliar environment. We'd put a call out on Facebook over Christmas and thanks to the generosity of our friends were able to bring two carloads of donations to distribute.

Asylum seekers waiting for their court hearing are required to live on a percentage of what the government has deemed the minimum on which an individual or family can survive. Those who lose their case, but who cannot return to their country of origin because of war, political/religious persecution etc., receive nothing from the state. Neither refugees waiting for residency or failed asylum seekers, of course, are allowed to work. These people rely completely on the kindness of others and organizations like the Destitution Project.

The kindness is quite overwhelming – that people are willing to give up a day a week to make life a little easier for others. Interestingly, the demographic of the project-users is ever changing and a constant reminder of what's going on in the world. A few years ago, most of the visitors to the centre were Iraqi Kurds; yesterday most of the people we spoke to were from Sudan, having fled the terrible war there, aided across continents by Refugee Action.

We ran a little art workshop on the subject of 'home' alongside the tent and will exhibit the hand-painted pictures of Sudanese thatched houses and national flowers with the revamped installation at Bolton as part of the Octagon's REVEAL Festival. It was a really humbling experience being there and it felt good to be properly connecting with people in a community that are living with the challenges of this increasingly turbulent and divided world.

And now, in stark contrast, I'm spending the afternoon squeezing my middle-aged feet into Jimmy Choo stilettos and my middle-aged body into Victoria Beckham dresses. I'm having my photo taken (for four hours) under a giant chandelier by an eccentric wild-haired photographer who shouts 'That's my girl!' and 'LOVE!' after every single one of the 1,000 pictures she takes. It's fun. There's room in my heart for this shit. It's part of the job in telly to promote the show you're appearing in and I made a conscious decision when I re-entered the world after *Coronation Street* to just go with that and enjoy it; to remember myself as the dumpy eleven-year-old in her terraced house in Accrington and think how much that girl would have LOVED to imagine her grown-up self spending the afternoon like this.

There's a whole team of people working on this shoot who make their living from it. Martha, my fifteen-year-old, can barely contain herself at the thought that it's someone's job to pick outfits for people. But the reality is that a stylist's job is bloody hard and involves a lot of running around picking up and dropping off clothes; ironing, pinning and steaming; trying to second-guess the peccadilloes of the actors she's dressing; trying to make someone like me, hardly a clothes horse, look half-presentable (Christ). The lovely make-up artist today is on the floor at one point painting over the clusters of varicose veins on my blotchy legs. Two photography assistants heave massive lights and reflectors around for hours. There are nine people in the room making all this happen, and my job is to be cheerful, accommodating and not to be a pain in the arse. To be happy and grateful to be here.

13 January

Press junket for *Broadchurch*. I'm put up in a hotel and then taken to ITV where I spend the day talking to journalists one after the other about all things telly, and about rape and serious sexual assault.

The series starts with my character turning up, desperately traumatized, at the police station in the town, after being raped at a party. The previous series of the show were about a murder investigation and the subsequent trial, and this, the final part of the trilogy, is a departure in that it examines police procedure around rape.

There has been a lot of debate recently around the televizing of sexual assault and the endless crime drama imagery of young girls being pursued in woods, etc., and naked and mutilated female bodies on our screens. It has been incredibly important to the show's creator, Chris Chibnall, and the makers of this series to avoid those controversial cliches, starting, I suppose, with the casting of myself: an ordinary-looking, slightly gone-to-seed middle-aged woman as the victim of the crime (and, crucially, the *survivor* of that crime).

Rape is an act of violence not of sex, and the Manchester Sexual Assault Referral Centre report that the youngest person they ever looked after was a nine-month-old baby girl and the oldest a ninety-year-old woman. There are 85,000 rapes of adult women in England and Wales every year, 12,000 adult male rapes and nearly half a million reported sexual assaults. These figures don't include children. Something like 6 per cent result in a conviction. The first scenes of this series take us, step-by-step, through the procedure when a person who has been attacked comes forward, and we all worked extremely closely with Rape Crisis in Dorset and with Independent Sexual Violence Advisors (ISVAs) to keep this as accurate as possible. It was important to us all to show how things have changed for women coming forward to report these crimes. Thanks to tireless campaigning work from people in the field, gone are the days when a couple of male officers, scarcely disguising their ambivalence towards the veracity of a woman's story, would examine the complainant roughly in the back room of the local cop shop. There is a dignity afforded to the victim now and a starting point of *belief* that women going through this could only dream of ten years ago. There will be helpline numbers at the end of the programme and a lot of the interviews today focus on this element of the work, which is a positive thing.

There will be a press screening late in the month and a cast and crew showing too, so I'm going to wait until then to watch the episode. Everyone seems pleased. Transmission date is the end of February, so hopefully only a few more weeks of 'Are you still doing acting?' and 'How's retirement?' to endure from my fellow shoppers at the local Tesco. My favourite Tweet this week: 'What have you been up to since Corrie, Julie?' These are pathetically ego-denting moments for me, and it takes everything in me not to reel off my entire post-*Coronation Street* CV. Instead I grit my teeth and try to remain graceful and reply, 'Oh, you know, this and that'.

By the end of the day, I'm so sick of the sound of my own voice, I never want to speak again. I can only imagine how bored the publicists must be listening to me drone on telling the same stories over and over, poor buggers.

16 January

A fun couple of days ahead doing one of my favourite and recurring jobs: the latest in an occasional BBC Radio 4 *Woman's Hour* comedy series, written by the legendary crime writer Val McDermid. I play a tough-talking lesbian DCI, solving murders that are characterized by punning on the word 'dead'. Series 1 was *Deadheading,* involving a murder in an allotment, then *Dead Clever* in a university, and now *Dead Pan,* where a food critic cops for it in the toilet of a fancy restaurant. Justine Potter, the producer and director, runs an independent radio production company and working for her is completely different to any other radio experience. Eloise Whitmore, an incredibly talented sound recordist and editor, records everything on the move in Justine's house and car and in the surrounding streets. This has led to many hysterical moments including rolling around on one of Justine's children's beds with Miriam Margolyes (a highlight of my career) and recording a scene outside in the dark in an actual blizzard whilst pretending to be wilting in the heat of an August afternoon in a vegetable patch. The vibe is extremely relaxed with Justine's kitchen serving as an eat-and-drink-all-you-can green room, where gossiping and laughter regularly ruin takes being recorded in the next room. The cast, including Jane Hazlegrove and John Hollingworth, are ace. John is a master of the off-mic 'I'm-still-in-the-scene-even-though-I'm-not-speaking' nasal breath and soft-shoe shuffle. Val comes to watch us, perches with Justine on various settees, beds and floors around the house, plays the occasional cameo, and is a delight. I feel guilty even calling it work.

20 January

I've been approached by Comic Relief to visit one of the projects they've supported through the biennial fundraising extravaganza that is Red Nose Day. I'm to visit Wythenshawe, on the outskirts of Manchester, five miles up the road from where I live. I've been asked to present a regional news piece on an arts and media group called the Community Media Crew, who have been funded by Comic Relief to buy equipment for their weekly radio show, and to take a theatre piece about difference to local schools. The group is made up of adults with learning challenges, or 'mixed ability' as they prefer to be called, and their play is a mainly improvised piece about their own skills, talents and abilities, and about breaking free of the limitations that other people set for us. It's lovely and the children from the local school who've come to the club to watch are completely engaged with the performance. There is a particularly wonderful moment when one of the actresses sings a pitch-perfect a capella version of *Somewhere Over the Rainbow*, and Dennis, a fifty-something man dressed head to toe in army camouflage, stands, salutes smartly, marches over to her and takes her hand for a dance.

John, their group leader and the director of the piece, tells me later how much they've all gained from the experience of acting together, and how theatre has brought several of the members out of their shells and changed them. He is movingly and rightly proud of them, and clearly loves his job.

The information I've been sent suggests that I 'pass on some acting tips' to the actors here, for the cameras, but of course the opposite happens. The little community hall is packed and I talk to them about stage fright. They just laugh at my suggestion that they might feel nervous performing not only for the school audience, but for the viewers at home, too, and tell me that there is nothing to be nervous about. They know their show is great and that they're all knockout in it, so they will just relax and enjoy the experience. They suggest I remember that when I'm next on stage. I'll carry that philosophy with me.

I leave feeling enriched by it all, seeing again, in a completely different way, how art and creativity can fill, enable and empower people of all abilities and stages of life.

21 January

It is the first day of Donald Trump's presidency and millions of people all over the world are taking part in massive Women's Marches in defiance of what many of us view as his misogynistic and racist opinions, and worse, policies. My great friend from drama school Daniel Getzoff is arriving at Manchester Airport from his home in LA at 2.20pm and I'm picking him up, so there is no way I can get to the London demo. Luckily a young student has organized a meeting at short notice outside the town hall in Manchester's Albert Square at 1pm, so Lyss, my youngest, and I set to work making a handmade 'LOVE TRUMPS HATE' sign at the same time as we handcraft a 'WELCOME, DANIEL' sign for the front door.

I hotfoot it into town where about a thousand women, men and children have congregated with their own homemade signs, my favourite being 'My mum hates Donald Trump and my mum likes EVERYONE'. The atmosphere is warm and defiant, and grateful – grateful to this young activist, Jen, who has set up the whole thing on her own and given us Mancunians a place to come and stand in solidarity with the millions marching all over the world. Everywhere I turn I see friends, friends' parents, colleagues, Take Backers, activists and artists of all genders, ages, backgrounds, sexualities and abilities, and I have that familiar feeling of being in love with this city and its people.

I make it to the airport just in time to collect Daniel, one of my oldest and closest friends, but whom I haven't seen since his last visit in 2011. Too long. I've asked him to write and perform something for *Take Back*

America and he's put together a brilliant piece called *Seeking Post-Election Connection (or a Writer's Desperate Attempt to Incorporate a Shattered-Glass Metaphor into Fucking Everything)*. He will pop up all over the space throughout the first half of the evening, creating a structure around which the other pieces will fit.

It is absolutely fantastic to see him and we pick up pretty much exactly where we left off last time we saw each other, as we always do. Some friendships transcend geography and circumstance and ours is one of them. In the evening we drive over to the beautiful Buxton Opera House with Kersh to see Billy Bragg perform. Billy is the English folk punk singer and activist who we have loved forever and whose album *Talking to the Taxman about Poetry* we listened to *constantly* on a legendary road trip across the States in 1990 (the cassette had got jammed). After the show we meet him and excitedly tell him this and just how much it means for us to be seeing him tonight, together, and especially now. This evening he is performing a set with an American singer/songwriter, Jon Henry, singing old American railroad songs, interspersed with some of his political greatest hits, including *Between the Wars*, which makes us cry, with its plaintive lyrics about fighting for a better world; about a helping hand as opposed to an iron fist; about building faith in humanity as opposed to building walls.

At one point, Billy talks about his New Year's resolution to stop posting diatribes on Facebook, but to channel his anger and passion into art again; to write songs rather than shout into the abyss. This strikes a chord with me as the voices of dissent about *our* dissent start to pipe up on social media, decrying today's marches as 'virtue-signalling' and hand-wringing. Solidarity is a powerful thing and today's global act of resistance has certainly rattled those who would like the world to sit back and watch as Trump rolls back the civil rights of women, Muslims, LGBTQI and immigrants. In the days that follow his election, we will all watch in awe and horror at the speed and magnitude with which he brandishes his new power to exactly these ends.

22 January

An early start for jet-lagged Daniel as we drive into Manchester to rehearse the first half of *Take Back America* in the Royal Exchange

Studio. Matt Hassall, who has directed for us many times before, also runs the Young Company at the Exchange and has found us a much-needed rehearsal space. The actors are called throughout the day and, between running pieces with Matt, there is much talk about how needed this artistic response is and how timely. It's very gratifying.

We do a top-and-tail of the scenes right at the end of rehearsals – just the transitions from the end of one scene to the beginning of the next – to make sure it's slick and fast moving, but even seeing these tiny snatches is exciting. Everyone is a bit in love with Daniel and his funny, honest and personal piece about his experience of being American in America on the night of the election and in its aftermath.

23 January

Rehearsals in the Central Fire Station community room all day with our second-half director, Chris Lawson, another Take Back veteran and associate director at Oldham Coliseum Theatre. This second half of the show is more sprawling and complicated. Kersh and Martha's piece about random and brilliant acts of kindness is the thread that weaves through the other pieces, but there are some difficult pieces of writing, which are hard to integrate. James Graham's marvellous piece, *Fascist Beasts and Where to Find Them,* is a lecture by an American academic, set in the future, who lists the ingredients of a full-blown authoritarian fascist state. We, as the audience, tick them off, as in a game of bingo, to see whether the Trump presidency can be retrospectively described as truly fascist or not. In the end, in the game, his regime falls just short. Why? Because of the people who fought him every step of the way. Because of the resistance, the demonstrations, the refusal of ordinary people to allow his policies to become normalized.

I watch Vicky Brazier rehearse with Chris and cry proper springy tears of hope (and fear, I think, and no small amount of overwhelm). I worry that the piece is buried too deeply in the second half. I feel as though this section is not as carefully curated and has too many disparate elements, including a big group performance of a poem written by Millie-Jo, Kersh's Arts Emergency mentee, which is rehearsed too hurriedly at the end of the day.

At teatime, we all move over to the Comedy Store to top-and-tail both halves and to tech the show. The venue is brilliant and the staff beyond welcoming and helpful. Everyone is in good spirits, running scenes, supporting each other and, as usual, I'm blown away by the generosity of all these artists who are willing to give of their time and talent for nothing.

The show goes up late because of latecomers and the whole bottom half of the auditorium is packed with about 300 audience members. Elspeth Moore, a fantastic friend to us and a famous photographer, takes beautiful pictures throughout. When we finally get front-of-house clearance, Becx, Grant and I, who are seated in the front row, climb on to the stage to Green Day's 'American Idiot' and everyone laughs because it feels preposterously rock 'n' roll. We welcome everyone and deliver a pre-emptive strike about preaching to the choir. I steal Kate Tempest's line about us being together in a room being a powerful thing in itself, and say that although we might not be changing any hearts and minds by putting on a show like this, that we hope to open and inspire minds and embolden, gladden and galvanize hearts.

We sit and the lights go down and the show begins with a cabaret drag artist, Jacob, wrapped in an American flag, in a spotlight, centre stage, singing 'The Star-Spangled Banner'. This is immediately followed by an audio of Trump's worst bits (so far): his calls for a wall between the US and Mexico; his assertion that Obama, his predecessor, was the founder of Islamic State, the radical terrorist Islamist group; his chat-show banter about how he'd date Ivanka if she wasn't his daughter.

Then in the silence that follows, a ukulele strikes up and one of our performers, Guy, sings a lovely and gentle song, the entire lyrics of which consist of 'what the fuck?'. It brings the house down. Daniel follows with the first part of his piece and everything rolls together beautifully and smoothly. The mix of spoken word and scenes works a treat, linked by Daniel's ongoing narrative, and every section stands alone, but works as part of the whole with subtle thematic and linguistic links. The first half ends with two beautiful and very different monologues by Rabiah Hussain and Adeel Amini respectively, both talking about the experience of being the children of immigrants. Daniel ends with making us all chant, as he failed to do on a demo in Los Angeles after the election, and we break for interval shouting, 'We believe that we will win!' over and over.

I was right. The second half is more problematic and sprawling. It's fifteen minutes too long. I should have given Millie's piece to one young performer rather than the whole group. The transitions between scenes are a bit under-rehearsed and I regret putting Tim Dynevor's devastating piece about fake news towards the close of the show because, although it ends hopefully, the quotes from Trump's closest allies and advisors ('Would you rather your daughter had cancer or feminism?') are just deeply upsetting and belong at the beginning of the night. Same with James Graham's, perhaps. BUT Amy Drake smashes Aileen Quinn's magazine questionnaire piece that starts Part Two, *What Kind of Angry Woman Are You?*, and the ever-brilliant Chris Thorpe's dry performance of his poem, 'Haircut in Wyoming', are hits. All the actors are just brilliant, as are all the pieces without exception (there is nothing we could have cut) and the Liverpool Everyman's Youth Choir, Generation Now, who stole the show at our Brexit show, end the evening perfectly with a beautiful and angry song called 'It's Not the End'. And everybody afterwards is full of Martha's easy and confident performance with her dad, which makes my heart swell with pride. The problem with having only one performance (and no full run-through beforehand) is that there's no opportunity to finesse or restructure or tighten or improve. But it's also the beauty of what Take Back does, I think. It's a moment in time: not always perfect, sometimes rough around the edges, usually too long, but always heartfelt, passionate, relevant and ultimately full of hope. I feel incredibly proud of what we've pulled off tonight and so grateful to all the brilliant people involved.

And our board in the bar of the Comedy Store is full of Post-it notes with ideas about how to move forward from this moment in time: how to work together to create a kinder society, how to volunteer, how to be active in local politics, how to embolden and galvanize each other in these turbulent times.

24 January

The anti-austerity group People's Assembly has organized a free screening of Ken Loach's latest masterpiece, *I, Daniel Blake*, at the Friend's Meeting House in Manchester, and Daniel and I go along to the packed venue. I've seen the film before, but to watch it here amongst people who are suffering in the same way as the film's eponymous hero is a very different experience. It is a film about how the British government's policy of sanctioning people on benefits, leaving them without money, often for the most minor of 'wrongdoings', is leading to unacceptable levels of poverty, suffering and death among the poorest members of society. There is a scene in the film set in a food bank, which will stay with me forever.

My *Peterloo* friend and comrade, Kate Rutter, who was so brilliant in Tim Foley's piece in *Take Back America* yesterday, is wonderful in the film as a sympathetic benefits advisor. I think she may be the only actor to have worked with both those giants of British film-making: Loach and Leigh.

Ken Loach has dedicated his life to creating art that reflects and comments on the world we live in and the ways in which working-class men and women struggle against brutality and hardship. He has waived any royalties for screenings of the film that raise funds for local food banks. Use of food banks and homelessness has soared in the UK over the last few years of Conservative rule.

There is a lively discussion after the film and a panel made up of benefits activists, members of Disabled People Against the Cuts and a canon from Manchester Cathedral. We talk about what action we can take to help keep up the pressure on the government and to campaign against the draconian sanctions and the epidemic of misrepresentation of benefit claimants in our culture. An inspiring night.

30 January

Donald Trump is not wasting any time. In his first week in office as president, he has repealed Obama's Affordable Care Act, which provided health insurance for the poorest of America's citizens; rolled back reproductive rights for women by requiring federally funded non-governmental organizations to agree to neither perform nor actively promote abortion as a method of family planning in other countries; and reinstated the oil pipe running through the sacred Native American land at Standing Rock. But most shockingly, perhaps, he announced on Friday that he would allow *no* Syrian refugees to settle in the US and that anyone attempting to enter the States from seven predominantly

Muslim countries, including Iraq and Iran, would be prevented from doing so whether they had a visa or not. Chaos broke out at airports across the country as Muslim travellers were handcuffed and held in custody on arrival and protesters mobilized to demonstrate at JFK and LAX among others. The British prime minister, Theresa May, who had been to visit Trump earlier in the week, said nothing. Instead, news broke that he had been invited on a state visit here, with all the pomp and royalty-shoulder-rubbing that involves. An online government petition calling for the withdrawal of the invitation went viral and reached over a million signatures by the end of the weekend. #NoMuslimBan marches were hastily organized in all the major cities in the UK for 6pm this evening.

I'm in London. There is a press screening of episode one of *Broadchurch* and a Q&A afterwards in the afternoon, being held at a hotel on the river, then a cast and crew showing at another hotel later in the evening with drinks afterwards. I have just enough time to scoot down to Downing Street between the two, where tens of thousands of people have assembled, to the seeming surprise of the police, who haven't shut off the roads around Whitehall, but soon realize they have to. The atmosphere is electric and warm and inclusive. Every age, gender and religion is represented here. Young people are wearing 'Proud Child of Immigrants' T-shirts and there are chants of 'Theresa the Appeaser' outside Number 10, and, movingly, 'Say it loud, say it clear, refugees are welcome here'.

In Manchester, my fantastic Martha goes into town by herself and finds the Take Back gang, who have assembled amidst the thousands to do a spontaneous march down Deansgate after a rally in Albert Square. Anger is an energy.

The cast screening is fun. It's good to see everyone again. A few of us have dinner afterwards and I'm not drunk but am all pumped up from the day and knock over my drink gesticulating wildly, splattering red wine over pretty much everyone. What a tit.

1 February

A Take Back road trip to Stratford-upon-Avon to see Anders Lustgarten's play *Seven Acts of Mercy* at the Swan. Anders wrote a fantastic piece called *I Voted Leave* for our Brexit show. It was the only piece that really tried to address why huge swathes of the white working class were disenfranchised enough to vote against remaining in the EU in the referendum, and challenged some of the elitist rhetoric that was thrown at them after the event, branding them all racists. He is a writer who refuses to settle for easy answers and lazy generalizations.

Seven Acts is a magnificent, bold play, bursting with big ideas. It's set partly in the artist Caravaggio's studio in early seventeenth-century Naples and partly in modern-day Bootle in Liverpool, where government cuts are clearing the area of its long-term working-class inhabitants to make way for regeneration/gentrification by way of benefit sanctions and the bedroom tax.

The 'Bedroom Tax', or (more formally) the Spare Room Subsidy, is one of the most dreadful pieces of legislation to have passed in years: cutting a person's housing benefit if they have a spare room in their council or housing association accommodation. Even if they have lived there with their family for decades and their children have now moved away, or even if a room is used for a disabled partner or spouse. It has caused untold suffering and stress with hundreds of people suddenly being unable to meet the rent and getting evicted. Anders expertly juxtaposes the story of Caravaggio painting *The Seven Acts of Mercy* amongst the criminals and prostitutes of Naples with the tale of a young boy attempting to record contemporary versions of the merciful acts on his phone for the benefit of his art-obsessed dying grandad. The Seven Acts are the Bible's dictums for living a good Christian life: burying the dead; visiting the imprisoned; feeding the hungry; refreshing the thirsty; sheltering the homeless; clothing the naked; and visiting the sick.

Afterwards we meet up with Anders and talk about politics and theatre. He is passionate about the importance of giving agency to a play's protagonists so that we're not let off the hook as an audience by being separate from the characters and their struggle, and fearing or pitying them. We should, he says, instead be inspired to take up the struggle with them. He talks about the importance of resisting hiding behind ambiguity and metaphor as theatre makers and writers, and not being afraid *to tell the fucking story.* That we need to empower our audiences to be urgently and actively compassionate. Talking to him is like a shot of adrenaline to your spirit.

On the way home we talk non-stop about plans for our small part of the struggle, about how best to move forward as a collective; the kinds of work we want to make that can inspire people to fight back.

3 February

I have been given some comps for a new play at Manchester's Contact Theatre called *I Told My Mum I Was Going on an RE Trip,* produced by a Liverpool-based young company called 20 Stories High, so I go down with Kersh and Becx. The auditorium is packed to the rafters (and it's a refreshingly youthful and diverse crowd) and four young women are on stage as we settle into our seats, chatting and dancing together. It is a verbatim play about pregnancy and abortion and is about as perfect a piece of theatre as I've seen in many years. I've never seen a verbatim show performed in this way, although I've heard a lot about it and even had a little go at it myself in a workshop once. My part as Sylvia in *Black Roses* was verbatim, but I memorized the transcribed lines with every 'um' and 'er' and 'you know' intact. Here, the four women wear earphones through which the lines they are to speak are played. The lines are real testimonies recorded over months of extensive interviews. The actors speak the words to us as they hear them and with the same dialect, intonation and hesitation. A lot of the testimonies are monologues, but there are conversations between 'characters' (real people), too, and the women synch each section of the play with each other on their MP3 players. They give a 'Standing by . . .?', an acknowledgement from each of them, then a 'And PLAY'. A couple of times, one of them doesn't press Play in time and they have another go. We are in safe hands. There is no pretence that this isn't a piece of theatre.

The effect of this is that we all really listen, undistracted by the tricks of the trade of a more traditional performance. There is no 'how did they do that?', or 'I wonder why they made that choice', because we can see exactly how it works, and they are saying the words as they hear them, with no interpretation added.

The story in the main follows the real stories of four young women: one from Northern Ireland (where abortion is still illegal), one from a Muslim family in Manchester, one from Liverpool who already has a child and one from an unspecified country in Africa where backstreet abortion is the only option when you have an unwanted pregnancy. They also variously play gynaecologists specializing in terminations, doctors who refuse to perform them and young lads discussing the morality of choice. In every role, all four are completely believable, in a way I've never really experienced before. Without any change in costume or physicality they completely transform as they speak the words of whoever is 'in their ear' at that moment. It is hilariously funny in parts, heartbreaking and thought-provoking. It is also incredibly empowering.

There is a section at the end where they talk us through the process of making the piece and give us an inkling of the breadth of research that went into making the show. Then, one by one, they tell us whose testimonies they decided as a company *not* to include. It's a long list: the male anti-abortion campaigner who stands outside family planning clinics showing graphic images of aborted foetuses to the women going in; the London couple who put up young women who have travelled from Ireland for a termination; the boyfriend who insisted it was as much his choice as hers over whether to keep the baby or not. The decisions made over which stories to tell and which to discard can make or break a show like this, and it is to the credit of writer and director Julia Samuels that she has decided to give the young women who were interviewed – those who have *experienced* abortion – the agency in this piece. The play will tour to community centres around the country to audiences of young people and then to Belfast and Derry. I can't imagine the reaction to it there, but it's exactly where it should be seen. It got a well-deserved standing ovation here.

7 February

I've been invited to speak to a monthly meeting of artists, makers and curators called 'What's Next?' at HOME, the arts centre in Manchester. The group's modus operandi is to try to reach wider and more diverse audiences and to keep conversations open between the various cultural organizations in the North West. It's a lovely group, but there's not a non-white face between us, which highlights the problem somewhat.

I've been asked to speak for fifteen minutes on art and activism, the peculiar overlap in the Venn diagram between the two, whether that place exists and, I suppose, if our work as Take Back inhabits that space. The definition of activism is a policy or action of using vigorous campaigning for social and political change, so I suppose that is exactly what we aim to do with our work. I am very glad to have met Anders Lustgarten last week and to have been inspired by him about not being too genteel in a desperate bid to stay impartial or occupying some sort of palatable middle ground. I talk about our need to be bold in challenging social policy that oppresses people, not just in the States where we have a dangerous cartoon baddy to unite over. I mean, how could anyone possibly present an impartial view of the present Republican administration as daily it passes a new piece of legislation that takes away another group's civil and human rights? But, here in the UK, policies are being pushed through at an alarming pace that also reward the wealthy and punish the vulnerable. This very week our government has quietly and shamefully blocked the Dubs Amendment to the Refugee Act, which is a commitment to allow unaccompanied migrant children, of whom there are about 90,000, to settle in the UK – just as we did for Jewish children during the rise of Nazi Germany (Lord Alfred Dubs, who tabled the amendment, was a Kindertransport child himself).

As arts organizations and artists, we need to be at the vanguard of holding our elected representatives to account. Too often fear of losing funding is a factor in the work we choose to make. I talk about that moment in the production of *Love* at the National, where the actors came out amongst us and made us engage rather than observe, and the discomfort it caused among the largely middle-class audience. I find a quote by US activist and gang violence prevention advocate César Cruz that says 'Art should comfort the disturbed and disturb the comfortable' and offer it as a provocation. I swear a bit and feel maverick. But privately I feel some shame. In life I am actually crippled by gentility. I don't like fighting, I don't like not being liked.

In the discussion after the talk I am asked, as I always am, about how to break out of the bubble, the echo chamber we all inhabit in the arts. I say my usual stuff about emboldening each other, about creating communities, about strength in numbers and starting ripples. And I do believe those things. But I know, in part, I am afraid of the world outside my cosy part of it.

There is a by-election in Stoke next week and UKIP (the populist right-wing UK Independence Party) are looking likely to win the seat from Labour. It is a predominantly white working-class area, where the racist invective against immigrants is rife. It's the old trick of pitting people against one other instead of exposing the inequalities of our wealthy society. I should be down there this weekend, campaigning. I should be knocking on doors saying, 'Don't fall for this bollocks, these people do not care about you!' I have excuses. I need to see my old mum. I haven't spent enough time with my kids this week. But the truth is that I'm scared. Of what? Of being told that I know nothing of these people's lives? Of being accused of being part of the liberal elite, another middle-class person telling working-class people what's good for them? And, to my shame, most of all I think I'm afraid of not being liked.

HOME have offered Take Back a couple of weeks of paid research and development with a space to work for the rest of the week, which is so helpful. Becx has written a fantastic full-length play about a rape trial called *My Version of Events.* We're rehearsing that with four actors and a director when everyone's available and holding a sharing on Friday, so to have a space is just fantastic. We also have lots of embryonic ideas that need a bit of time to develop and this time is a huge luxury for us. First up is a meeting with writer/director Janine Waters who runs The Edge Theatre in Chorlton, a suburb of Manchester. Janine and her composer brother-in-law, Simon, work with many community groups, including those for the homeless and refugees, and are keen to pool resources and put in a joint bid for Arts Council funding and do a project. We spend some time during the rest of the day brainstorming possible projects and settle on a site-specific musical about the NHS set perhaps in the training hospital of the uni. We're nothing if not ambitious.

We make a plan for the rest of the week: projects we want to think through and plot, and business we need to tie up. Tomorrow we will film each other talking about our work for the website. We'll also edit together the useable bits from our interviews at the Destitution Project to put together as an add-on to the audio-pieces about birth in refugee camps, for the REVEAL Festival in Bolton at the end of the month.

9 February

This time and space together to think about ideas, make plans and let them percolate, has been incredibly useful to us as a company. We brainstorm ideas about the housing crisis and think about the project on sex work we've been considering for a while. We meet Joe and Will who run the wonderful, relatively new Hope Mill Theatre in an edgy bit of the city, and which is getting quite a reputation as a great place to work. We've had a thought to combine the two elements of our usual stuff, the *Ten Takes* model and the more installation-based work, in order to make a piece that is set all over the entire space, including the toilets, bar and car park, with the audience moving between the spaces to encounter each piece. We are keen to explore the contentious area of sex work or prostitution, and the arguments for and against the decriminalization of it. There are activists who argue that the state shouldn't be complicit in the making respectable of a patriarchal conceit, of men paying for sex and the oppression of women through this work. But in reality, we live in a society in which women need money, need to work around chaotic and underfunded childcare, need to fund addiction, need to eat. Sex work happens. A criminal record means moving out of prostitution becomes almost impossible. It being a crime means that an element of the police can treat vulnerable women as criminals rather than as human beings. The necessarily covert nature of work that has to be underground means that being on the streets is very unsafe, and means that sex workers – of all genders, actually – are extremely susceptible to exploitation and rape. It's a conversation that needs to be had.

Hope Mill is perfect, with its nooks and crannies and doorways and stairwells. We book a Monday night at the end of October, think about which writers would serve each area we want to look at and feel excited about making something in yet another style. We want to be constantly evolving in the work we do, the spaces we inhabit and the ways we present the stories we want to tell.

In between all this plotting and planning I'm listening to hours and hours of radio, preparing to present *Pick of the Week* on BBC Radio 4. It's a weekly forty-five-minute show that airs every Sunday, and basically a 'best of' compilation, the presenter's choice of the best of BBC radio throughout the week. It's a lovely gig (I've done it once before) but it's a load of work. It's not just the listening, it's the timings, the script, the finding of themes to link all the choices together. It uses a different bit of my brain, which is always a good thing, but my head hurts.

It's been a melancholic week on the airwaves, lots of lovely stuff about love and loss, about memory and memoir. I'll start with an Imtiaz

Dharker poem featured on this week's *Poetry Please* – also on Radio 4 – called 'Hiraeth: Old Bombay', which sets the tone. 'Hiraeth' is a Welsh word with no direct English translation but essentially meaning a longing for a place that doesn't exist; a kind of homesickness. I'm going to end with the poet Jackie Kay's Desert Island Disc, my iPlayer choice. It's a beautiful Chopin piece that I think my late dad would have loved. My own bit of hiraeth.

10 February

Today we're sharing the rehearsed reading of Becx's play, *My Version of Events*. The four fantastic actors haven't had much rehearsal so, of course, it's all a bit kick-bollock-scramble in the lead-up to the showing at 1pm. They completely pull it out of the bag in performance.

We have about fifteen industry professionals from TV, theatre and radio coming. We're hoping for perhaps a funded production in a theatre, maybe a tour, to emerge from the showing. Despite not having had a full run, the reading goes brilliantly, although the three of us and director Trevor MacFarlane are pretty twitchy throughout. It feels preposterously intimate in the small, stark space and with several famous faces like writer Russell T. Davies (always so supportive of us) present.

Becx has written a brilliant play. I keep thinking throughout it, 'Bloody hell, this is great writing', and it is clear from the post-sharing discussion that everyone feels the same. It's a joy to hear this group of writers, directors, producers and theatre-makers talking with such enthusiasm about her work and discussing the subject matter in such forensic detail. Such a fascinating conversation about the way young people talk about and experience sex, the role of alcohol and porn in that, and how complex the issues around consent are.

I have to leave a bit early to catch the tram to MediaCity to record my *Pick of the Week*, which will air on BBC Radio 4 on Sunday. Then on to Contact Theatre for the launch of TransCreative, a new arts organization dedicated to unearthing and showcasing talent in the trans community.

I'm appearing as a cameo in a cabaret piece by trans actor Kate O'Donnell called *Hayley and Me*, talking about her life running alongside that of Hayley Cropper, the character I played in *Coronation Street* from

1998 to 2014, the first trans character in a soap. In the show, she usually, at a certain point, picks out a member of the audience to don a wig and anorak similar to those I wore for sixteen years and to act out a couple of scenes with her. Tonight at the given moment I am to appear backlit and in a haze of dry ice and play Hayley. Or rather, play me playing Hayley. Strange one. It goes down a storm with the crowd, especially as we've kept it as a surprise even to mates in the audience – including my friend Annie Wallace, who was instrumental in helping me research for Hayley back in the day and who subsequently became an actor herself. She is currently nailing it as Sally St Claire in the Channel 4 soap *Hollyoaks* and made TV history by becoming the first trans actress to play a trans character in a soap. She only came out to her wider circle of friends last year on her fiftieth birthday and has never looked back. I am so proud of her. It feels significant that she's here. There is a brilliant, vital energy in the whole building.

13 February

Some press is starting to appear about *Broadchurch* and I read a couple of interviews I did the other week. They're okay, but full of really frustrating inaccuracies that won't mean anything to anyone else, but will come back to get me later, I'm sure. 'So your mum and dad were factory workers and you grew up in a council house?' No. I was brought up working class, but we lived in our own terraced house and my parents worked in *offices* in factories. And did a football pools round on Thursdays. It doesn't matter, but I worry that it looks like I'm exaggerating my class credentials or something. One reporter calls me 'unexpectedly normal' and is absolutely determined that I want to be the new Doctor in *Doctor Who*, even though when she asked me I emphatically said 'no', that I'd just like to be a *guest* in an *episode* of *Doctor Who*. Oh well, it's all bollocks in the end I suppose. Nobody really cares except me. And the pictures from that daft photoshoot in London are really flattering, in that I look like my best self, so it's not all bad.

Pick of the Week airs and I say my words, written by me, and that feels good and it gets a lovely response.

Highs and lows. It sometimes feels a bit difficult to retain any sort of equanimity.

I do a phone interview with an academic from York University for a book about actor well-being, and talk about the importance of unions and pastoral care and guiding young professionals through the minefields of the media, both mainstream and social. I talk about having a publicist and sound like a wanker. But the publicists who've guided me through all the press around the higher profile jobs I've done since leaving *Corrie* have been really instrumental to my well-being actually, by looking after that side of it all. It's much more about managing the publicity than about pushing your profile. But it sounds so Hollywood and I feel some familiar shame about my privilege. I'm getting pretty fed up of the sound of my own voice now too, to be honest, pontificating about everything all the bloody time. Once *Broadchurch* is on air (still no transmission date, but it must be imminent), I think I'll take a little step back from being quite so available for comment.

18 February

I am struggling with myself a bit. This hiatus before *Broadchurch* airs is filling me with some anxiety. Some of the press coverage has left me feeling uneasy. I feel as though there's a narrative being spun of my not having worked much since I left *Coronation Street*, which is poking the bear of my ego and this seems to be backed up in my day-to-day interactions on the street: 'Are you just doing theatre these days?' and again, 'Are you enjoying the break?' Hayley, my character in *Corrie*, is a constant presence. I walk through town and people shout her name at me or whisper it to each other as I pass, and every interviewer I speak to asks me about her.

I played a little comic cameo in a short film earlier in the week, which I'd been asked to do as a bit of a favour. I thought it might be fun and I love working, so I drove over to the set on Thursday to deliver my three lines. After a few hours of waiting around (standard) the cameraman came over to set up his shot where I was sitting among all the lovely supporting artists (or 'extras'), and said to the director 'Which one is she? Where's the interest?'. I made a joke about it but knew I was being passive aggressive. I felt small and cross, and angry at myself for feeling small and cross. I'm resenting my own pathetic need for recognition, but only on my terms to pick and choose as and when is convenient to myself. I am fighting some inner c*ntiness for sure.

I talk it through with Kersh this morning and we both realize that we're not putting in the work at the moment. He's been having some similar feelings about his status as a writer. It's all about the status. We both feel a bit lost, I think. We try to unpick our mutual unease. We arrive at the conclusion that we've been getting sucked into a way of thinking about work that focuses on the *consumption* of it, rather than the making of it. It's when this happens that these difficult and unpleasant feelings emerge: arrogance, jealousy, schadenfreude, outrage that we're not being truly *seen*. We've started over the last few weeks to look at our working lives from the outside, seeing ourselves through the lens of others – of how the *world* views us (in our heads; obviously the world has other concerns thankfully) – rather than as how we view ourselves. Instead of concentrating on being true to our own vision or creativity, however small scale or insignificant, we're constantly checking out our positioning against that of our peers. It's the *making* that matters, not the consumption. Overthinking how the work will be received is never a good place from which to create anything unselfconsciously.

A note on jealousy

Ugh. The scourge of creativity and a sure sign you're not 'filling the well'. The feeling of 'why them? Why not me?', the dirty secret thrill of seeing someone fail, the lack of ability to celebrate the successes of others, even those you love. I have been a terribly jealous person throughout my life. I have a wonderful friend, Connie Hyde, who I first met at an audition for an amateur production of *Oliver* when we were twelve and with whom I ended up studying A level Theatre Studies, successfully auditioning for LAMDA and moving to London when we were eighteen. Connie was, and is, stunningly naturally beautiful and talented (she got the part of Artful Dodger; I didn't even make the chorus), but also funny, self-deprecating and loving. I have wasted so much of my life being bitterly jealous of her, despite her being my best and most loyal friend. I recently apologized to her and she wafted it away with her characteristic generosity.

> In a timely article in today's paper, Imelda Staunton touches on this same subject – the futility of constantly measuring yourself against the successes and failures of others. She talks about respecting the job and working really hard; how she wakes at 4.30 every morning thinking about it all. But that she's come to accept that there is always someone above you on the ladder and always someone below you; that you either accept that and get on with it, or get off the ladder completely. That work is who you are.

I spend the rest of the day feeling incredibly inspired. I go to the art gallery and look at my favourite paintings, including *Work* by Ford Madox Brown. Then I see a profound and moving performance in the studio of the Royal Exchange called *The Space Between Us,* a collaboration between members of their Young Company and the Elders Company for over-sixties. It's a piece that incorporates snippets of their conversations from rehearsals, favourite songs, anecdotes, musings on ageing and death, and some beautiful movement. I realize I've never seen this before: young and old people moving together, touching each other, really looking at each other, and it's extraordinary. I have to go to the toilet afterwards for a little cry. The older people saying that they need more time – that they still have so much to do – makes me want to get on with stuff.

Then in the evening I take my mum to see *Funny Girl* at the Palace Theatre in Manchester, starring Sheridan Smith as Fanny Brice. She is out of this world. I can't take my eyes off her. Everything she does is note-perfect, but completely human and raw. This week she was on telly playing the lead in a two-part drama called *The Moorside,* and a couple of times whilst watching her, I felt like just giving up. She somehow manages to be completely her heart-on-sleeve self in everything she does whilst inhabiting a character and transforming herself totally. I think she might be my favourite. Watching her take her bow at the end, lovely and grateful and humble, I feel like I'm watching one of the greats, right up there with Judi Dench or Julie Walters or Imelda Staunton. And because of this week's steep learning curve, I feel inspired to work harder, do better. Not in the hope of ever being as good as Sheridan, but of being the best *I* can be, I suppose.

20 February

The *Broadchurch* transmission is looming, and the publicity machine steps up a gear. It's everywhere. I cunningly schedule an appearance on *Lorraine*, ITV's morning magazine show, for tomorrow in order to get a nice hotel in London for the night for Kersh and me, as we do a whirlwind tour. First up is a fancy private members' club in St Martin's Lane where my old friend Graham Caveney is reading from his upcoming memoir at a Picador publishing showcase. Graham's beautiful book, *The Boy with the Perpetual Nervousness*, is due for publication in August and tonight he's joining a star-studded line-up of writers, including Alan Hollinghurst and the poet Don Paterson, in a select press preview. There is a palpable buzz about his reading, and his choice of passage – about being a shy working-class boy who took refuge in books – is perfect for the assembled audience of publishers, writers and reviewers. Graham, like me, grew up in Accrington in the 1970s and 80s and his memoir is a searingly honest exploration of adolescence, alcoholism and abuse. He does brilliantly and completely holds his own, despite his perpetual nervousness, among such esteemed company. We leave with a belly-full of canapés and armfuls of proof copies.

21 February

Up early to stride over to ITV, five minutes from the hotel, to get made up for my brief appearance on *Lorraine.* There is much chat about my Dorset dialect, which fills me with some trepidation. I hope it passes muster. I did my best, but this is my first telly role in which I've been required to use an accent different from my own broad Lancashire, so some critical ears will be peeled waiting for me to balls it up, I'm sure.

I meet Kersh afterwards and we travel up to The Agency in Holland Park to meet with his literary agent, Nick, and Megan from my agency. Kersh has written a one-woman play for me called *The Greatest Play in the History of the World,* something I've been nagging him to do for ages. The idea is that we put it on with a tiny set (just some shoeboxes) and minimum technical requirements and then it's something we have to hand for the rest of our lives. I can learn it and store it away and then we can return to it whenever we want to throughout our lives, right into old age. We can be on the road, putting it on at festivals and in pub spaces all over the world.

After disappearing to his office in the cellar for a couple of hours here and there over Christmas, he presented it to me in the new year. A first draft of a beautifully told love story, full of exquisite observation and with a time-travel twist. Director Raz Shaw loved it, and our agents too, so we're meeting today to discuss how to proceed.

I've tentatively approached Sarah Frankcom at the Royal Exchange and it looks as if they have a little slot in the run-up to Christmas this year, so the question is whether to start small and low-key and get a bit of feedback, then tour it to Edinburgh and beyond in a couple of years' time. That seems ridiculously far into the future, but that's realistically when we could make a go of it. We decide that this might be the best plan of action, rather than approaching London spaces before it's properly ready. It's a long game. It's exciting to think that we could possibly make it work. I love Kersh's writing (luckily) and it would be romantic to be on the road with him and our shoe boxes one day.

In the afternoon, we all go to the Polish Centre in west London to see Rosa, my niece, in her latest third-year LAMDA production, the musical *Spring Awakening*. God, it's good. They're all *so* good. Rosa is just so wonderful and full of character and charisma. Your eyes are drawn to her on stage. Joe Alessi and Connie Hyde – two of my oldest friends from Accrington College and fellow LAMDA alumni – come too, and they love it. It's a bit of a moment for me, sitting with these friends watching my niece, a shocking twenty-six years after we graduated. Connie has had a big potentially life-changing audition and screen test to play a regular character in *Coronation Street*. I am crossing everything for her. She would love it there, and they would love her still more.

Still no agent for Rosa. I worry for her a bit. It took me three years after leaving LAMDA before I got one, though, and she has plenty in her armour to make her own work if needs be, talented writer as she is.

I have a great relationship with my agency. I've always been with Lou Coulson Associates, since Lou took me on after seeing me in a play at Arts Threshold, the fringe theatre I helped run in the early nineties. Shortly after signing I got a great supporting part in a Catherine Cookson mini-series for ITV playing Rose, the 'plain and ungainly' miller's daughter. It was my first-ever paid job and I learned loads and loved every minute. I was put up in a hotel in Newcastle and was paid £3,000, which seemed like a fortune.

After the mini-series, I did very little in terms of paid work for quite a few years. In 1997, a director I knew from LAMDA director, Helena Kaut-Howson, got me into the Royal Exchange to play a tiny part in her production of *Much Ado about Nothing*, and on opening night I got a bunch of flowers from Lou and a letter saying they were scaling back their client list and letting me go. I don't (and didn't) blame her at all. I was going to auditions rarely and then not getting parts, and they were kind enough to cut me loose when I was in a production with a large company, all of whom had agents I could write to after they came to see their clients in the show. So we agreed to part and on good terms. It's just business.

But then something strange happened. I couldn't get another agent – no one wanted me (that's not the strange bit!) – but I started to get parts again. (Suddenly and mysteriously my luck changed: this sometimes weirdly happens.) A job came in through Lou and I auditioned for a TV crime show, *Dalziel and Pascoe*, and got a juicy guest part, and then the *Coronation Street* casting directors who had been to see *Much Ado* got me in for the role of Hayley. The rest, as they say, is history.

That audition was, absurdly, the easiest of my life. There were none of the recalls and screen tests that are the norm now when you're up for a part in a soap. I just went in for a chat with the lovely casting director, Judi Hayfield, read a couple of lines for the producer, then left. They even paid my train fare. By the time I got back to the house I shared with my mate Joe in London, Judi called to say I'd got the part. This was before mobile phones. Lou, my supposedly about-to-be-not-agent, negotiated my deal and then we just kind of carried on, together, and never spoke of the letter or the fact I was supposed to have been let go. We continued like this for years and then we nearly 'split up' again just as I decided to leave *Corrie*. Some actors change agents regularly and it felt like it was maybe time to move on to pastures new. To have a fresh start. But, once again, no other agent wanted to take me on.

Then, in an act of grace for which I'll be forever grateful, Lou asked to meet up and took me out for lunch and asked me to stay, said that she understood if I wanted to meet other agents and that I should do so with her blessing. And brilliantly she said that she felt it was a marriage. If I wanted to go and have affairs, then I should. And if they didn't work out, she'd be waiting for me. Well, that did it for me. I didn't feel any need at all to pursue any more unrequited love affairs with other agents. I'm still with Lou and her gang now and I couldn't be happier. They've been fantastic in their support of me and in managing this new bit of my career, post-soap. And it feels like a good working partnership. Which is how I think it should feel. We don't work *for* one another, we work *with* each other. They get me, they know the kind of work I'm interested in and what I like to avoid, they look out for me, they've got my back. And the tough times have strengthened our relationship. Just like in a good marriage.

22 February

I drive Martha, my eldest, over to Z-arts Theatre in the Hulme area of Manchester where she's auditioning for the National Youth Theatre summer school. She emphatically does not want me to go in with her – she's determined that no one should know I'm her mum – so I park up nearby as she goes through her speech from Evan Placey's play *Girls Like That* and I wish her luck and wave her off. Thirty-three years ago, my mum drove me into Hulme for the same audition. Weird how history is repeating itself. I hope she gets in. Her piece is great, and I know she'll do well in the workshop, but there are so many applicants for so few places. She has a brilliant time, which is all that counts really. She'll find out in May. Fingers crossed.

My mum texts me and asks me if I'm going to 'put in' for the role of the Doctor in *Doctor Who*, as there is much talk in the press about the need for a woman and/or a person of colour to be next after Peter Capaldi's departure. I forward the text to Chris Chibnall, the writer of *Broadchurch* and the next producer/writer on *Doctor Who* and joke with him that the campaign has begun in earnest now, so he'd better watch out.

23 February

The unveiling of our Take Back 'Love and Solidarity' banner as a few of us join the student-led 'Reclaim the Night' march through Manchester.

There is such a momentum at the moment, such an appetite for protest; a feeling of 'enough is enough'. It's very inspiring to see all these vibrant young people with their inventive and heartfelt homemade signs taking to the streets again.

1 March

To London again, this time to record an interview with Jane Featherstone, the Executive Producer of *Broadchurch* for *Woman's Hour* on BBC Radio 4. The first episode of *Broadchurch* aired on Monday and to say that the response has been overwhelming would be an understatement. The almost forensically detailed first fifteen minutes following the character of a deeply traumatized middle-aged woman (played by me) in the aftermath of a rape, as she's taken through the procedure of examination at a dedicated Sexual Assault Referral Centre (SARC), has struck a chord. It's a massive relief to everyone involved that the portrayal of this process has been universally lauded as groundbreaking. The casting of a ordinary-looking woman of the appropriate age (me); the emphasis on the devastating *effects* of sexual violence rather than the attack itself; the training of the camera on my face rather than my body; the portrayal of a best-practice scenario – all these things have been praised by critics, audiences and experts in the field. I feel proud of it.

I feel weirdly shy around Jane Garvey, the presenter of the show, and don't do my best interview. I even nearly drop a bollock with an accidental spoiler. But it's okay. Jane Featherstone is articulate and assured in spades and is my safety net.

Yet another LAMDA outing in the afternoon to see the students, including my niece Rosa, perform their short duologues for an industry audience in a West End theatre. The scenes are well chosen and wonderfully performed. I have a really interesting discussion with Rosa and her friends over dinner afterwards about diversity in drama schools and the very real and specific challenges faced by actors of colour in Rosa's year, as a tiny minority in that kind of conservatoire setting. Change is happening but it will take a long time to become part of our culture. Thank God for Act4Change, the brilliant organization campaigning tirelessly to strengthen diversity in the arts and supporting people in the industry as they face these hurdles.

I am reading *The Good Immigrant*, a collection of essays written by people of all different ethnic backgrounds, about their experiences of being a minority in Britain. The authors include many actors talking about their deep frustration and anger at the narrowness of representation in the arts and the way they continue to be marginalized. There is so much more work to be done in this area. We're all part of the problem. We have to start listening and stop feeling defensive about our own prejudices, our own privilege; try to look a bit more deeply at how we can move things forward, to progress. On the way back to the Tube I pass three posters for plays on in London at the moment, with not a single black or Asian face on any of them.

In happier news, *Moonlight*, one of the most beautiful films I've seen in many a year, and with a cast made up entirely of black actors, won Best Picture at the Oscars last week.

3 March

To the lovely Oldham Coliseum – which has been around for well over a century – to see the first preview of *Meat Pie, Sausage Roll* by our writer friends Lindsay Williams and Cathy Crabb. I love this place, one of the only theatres I've ever been to where you really feel the audience's ownership of the building and the work. Watching a play here, among this audience, is a unique experience. Tonight they are in fine fettle, loving every moment of this joyous musical about Oldham Athletic Football Club, joining in with the chants, booing the racist baddy, wolf-whistling at the hot young lead in his wedding outfit. The whole crowd standing at the end shout-singing, 'Stand up if you love Oldham'. Brilliant.

5 March

Ups and downs. Highs and lows.

Big NHS march in London yesterday, at which I was proud to speak in Parliament Square to a crowd of 250,000, all uniting against the UK government's health service cuts and privatization. Then today a piece in the *Bolton News* about Take Back's 'Under Canvas' installation at the library, which provokes a shit-storm of fascist comments online, calling us, at best, virtue-signallers and, at worst, lefty freaks who deserve to have our children taken away from us for spreading such propaganda (basically us trying to tell stories about the experience of giving birth in a refugee camp). Blimey. It's best never to read the bottom of the internet, but it's also important to know the depth of feeling about these issues in some quarters, however uncomfortable it is.

I join a panel at the People's History Museum in Manchester as part of the Women in Media Conference 2017. As usual I feel I end up more *inspired* than inspir*ing*. A young children's presenter, as well as agony aunt, Katie Thistleton, is on the panel too and blows me away with her easy articulacy and good advice to the predominantly young female audience. Afterwards, several of them come forward to chat and, as always, I'm struck by what these young, smart women are up against. Several of them are already regretting taking the wrong course at uni because of being dissuaded to follow an arts path. One of them was told by someone in the industry that she should go into the production side of media as she'd have more longevity than as a presenter (she was twenty-one). Pretty much all of them worried about the future being sustainable as freelancers, who may one day want to have kids. There's not much you can say other than keep at it, do it for yourself: create, vlog, blog, write, make, knock on doors, be visible, see stuff, know your world, fill the well, have faith, carry on.

My friend Connie has got the part she auditioned for in *Corrie* and starts next week. Thrilled for her.

6 March

Still no agent for Rosa, despite many of her fellow students having found representation. The career/industry co-ordinator at LAMDA, Laura Dickens, is a friend of mine and checks in to see how Rosa is doing. She assures me (kindly and unnecessarily) that she's working her arse off to find representation for them all, that 200 industry professionals came to the showcases, that she loves Rosa quite independently of the personal connection and is doing all she can. And that perhaps in Rosa's case, the job may come before the agent. This exchange (which of course I go straight back to Rosa with) boosts her considerably and once again we talk about a different way to be in the creative arts, and about how long it took me to get an agent and paid work. She decides that maybe sometimes not having everything handed to you on a plate makes you a more resilient person and teaches you some valuable lessons that *could* result in you becoming a better artist in the long run. What a fantastic outlook. Kersh texts her and once again implores her to get writing.

Woman's Hour airs and they've been kind in the edit and I sound much more articulate than I actually was, fangirling over the Janes.

In the evening I go to a nearby town to see a local youth theatre group, Marple Drama, perform a short, fierce and urgent piece by Anders Lustgarten called *Extremism.* It's about a group of pupils in a classroom dealing with the aftermath of the removal of a Muslim classmate under the 'Prevent' legislation, which gives teachers in schools jurisdiction to report suspicious behaviour that might indicate terrorist radicalization. God, it's powerful. I'm on the front row and hardly breathe during a harrowing section in which a Muslim girl is attacked on a desk. The cast is impressive and during the time I've been coming to see their work I can see how they've grown in confidence as performers and as people. There is a lot of physical violence in the play and I can see that they are looking after each other and staying safe, which allows me to completely be in it with them.

Home for episode 2 of *Broadchurch.* I've not watched this one before and I drive Kersh mad saying things like, 'Aw, that's the little beach café where I used to have breakfast'. Another amazing response from viewers, and the thriller element is kicking in now so people are getting hooked. The viewing figures are incredible (10.5 million for episode 1!) and I'm starting to realize that it's quite a big deal that I'm in this show playing this part. It's exciting.

There's an ace headline in the *Radio Times* this week above an interview I did with them, which makes me laugh. 'We need to see more real people on our screens. Big bellies, big noses, big arses.' My not-so-subtle pitch for more work.

7 March

Caryl Churchill's play *Escaped Alone* is touring the UK and Kersh has got us tickets to see it at the Lowry in Salford. I don't know much about it other than it is about four older women and has a stellar cast: Linda Bassett, Deborah Findlay, June Watson and Kika Markham. I have never seen anything like it. It takes the form of a stilted conversation of half-finished thoughts between the four women as they sit in a back yard in the sunshine, punctuated by apocalyptic monologues from Linda Bassett's character, which contain possibly some of the most extraordinary writing I've ever heard. As the play progresses, we learn each of the women's stories and each has their momentary opportunity to describe to us their inner lives. The section in which the seemingly cheery simple soul of the group recites the words 'terrible rage' over and over again, with increasing ferocity, will stay with me for a long time. I felt exhilarated after it. Even just seeing these four older female actors owning the stage so completely was remarkable in its rarity. But the play itself had so much to say – in the most abstract, but crystalline, ways – about what it is to be a woman, and specifically a woman over sixty, in this world.

8 March

International Women's Day and Martha, my smart, cool, fiery, engaged, funny, feminist eldest, texts me from school in the morning to say that as she's stepped off the bus a group of lads from her year were standing waiting for her, chanting 'Fuck women!' The little shits. Kersh is taking her to Liverpool tonight to see *I Told My Mum I Was Going on an RE Trip*, the fantastic verbatim piece about abortion we saw the other week. A good antidote. Spending time with her amazing dad, reminding her that there are good men standing with us, and seeing that wonderful piece full of young women's voices. My youngest daughter is starting kickboxing at the community centre. I'm at the Coliseum in Oldham talking to a group of women about the boundaries we face and the importance of supporting each other and celebrating each other's successes.

11 March

I'm so out of the habit of work at the moment that today comes and bites me on the arse.

I've been asked to speak at a day-long conference at Doughty Street Chambers, a progressive set of barristers' chambers with offices in London, Manchester and the States. The theme of my particular panel is 'being heard'. We also offered up a couple of Take Back pieces. The initial plan was to show a reading of a shortened version of Becx's rape trial piece, but the actors weren't available so Becx has, as she puts it, 'scragged off' a new piece about sex work for me to perform, to run alongside a piece that Kersh wrote a while ago in preparation for our sex work project later in the year. In all of our memories – including the writer's – this piece, *A Nice Man,* was a monologue, so Kersh was set to perform it (he was an actor before he became a writer). But at 2am when I crawled into bed, pissed, after a night with mates, he mumbled, 'I think there's more than one person in my piece'. I find it in the morning, and it is indeed a three-hander between a rapist police officer, a raped sex worker and an investigating officer. After some frantic phone calls, a friend, Martha Simon, steps in to save the day, and we have a hurried rehearsal in a spare office at the chambers during the lunch break of the conference.

The pieces go down a storm. We've all been unsure as to how our bit of theatre would be received in the middle of all these top-level talks from highly qualified experts in their field, but someone says afterwards that it was amazing to see a short play get straight to the heart of an issue in five minutes, when a lawyer wouldn't have even got started on their first point. Becx's 'scragged off' piece is a monologue about a sex worker trying to make a better life for her daughter, and who endures a vicious attack by a client and whose greatest fear is being exposed. She can't report the attack to the police because she works from an illegal brothel and she will put the other women at risk of arrest. It's full of detail; her daughter nagging her to buy eggs after work for her food tech lesson the next day and writing EGGS in red pen on her mum's hand, the lettering later obscured by blood. Kersh's play follows straight on, based on a horrible real case, in which the rapist actually got his comeuppance (much to his indignation), as the woman he raped was 'just a prostitute'.

I really enjoy performing today. There's an energy in the room, that deep listening silence you sometimes experience during a piece, and I realize how much I've missed acting in front of an audience. It's been a while.

The panel I'm part of is exceptional. A wonderful, gobby Glaswegian barrister chairs it and there is a city councillor, a human rights lawyer and a TV journalist (my mate Jude Moritz) all speaking about their experiences of being heard or helping others to be heard. Harriet, the lawyer, was subjected to a hate campaign on Twitter after daring to question the appropriateness of a hateful 'bikini-ready' billboard campaign. Sarah, the councillor, talks about the importance of supporting each other as women and championing one other. Jude describes her incredible experiences interviewing women who have turned their tragic life circumstances into campaigns for justice: Sylvia Lancaster, mother of murdered Sophie Lancaster; Girl A from the Rochdale abuse trial, who was brave enough to speak out against her abusers and her subsequent treatment by the police; and the women of the Hillsborough Justice Campaign, among others. I talk about class barriers and the importance of art in making women's stories heard. The panel before ours was about reproductive rights and I referenced *I Told My Mum I Was Going on an RE Trip* as a piece of art that could make huge strides in changing attitudes when the play tours Northern Ireland and the Republic.

It is exhilarating to talk to so many smart and respected women afterwards, at the top of their field, really championing the use of art and culture to spread awareness and affect law making and implementation. One of the leading officers in the Rochdale sexual abuse case was there: she resigned from Greater Manchester Police in order to speak out about the appalling treatment the girls had to endure after coming forward, constantly disbelieved and fobbed off by the agencies employed to protect them. She is excited to tell me that Lesley Sharp is playing her in an upcoming TV series about the case, called *Three Girls*, which we agree will do much to shift public attitudes about the women at the centre of these real stories, often so misrepresented by the media.

We leave full of ideas and issues we'd like to explore in future work. An unexpectedly brilliant and inspiring day.

13 March

Again, I am finding it a bit difficult to practise what I preach in terms of keeping my well filled and staying creative in this in-between jobs period. I seem to be spending a lot of time talking about creativity (and writing about it here) and *consuming* art and culture, but am doing little to actively engage creatively at the moment. My days fill so quickly and easily with emails, Facebook (the enemy of productivity), interviews, family; I feel like a part of me is stagnating a little. These hiatuses, in theory, should be a time for writing, learning new stuff, pushing out of my comfort zone. I can fill a morning wrapping birthday presents and pootling down to the post office. I go for a run, my first long one in a while, up the hill at the back of my house, and the space and sky are good for my soul. I start to think about the next Take Back show, *Take Back our Bodies*, about starting work in earnest on that, how we need a piece on Ireland and reproductive rights. I have an urge to take a dance class. I miss the intensive movement sessions of a rehearsal room. I bought a ukulele last summer and set myself the goal of learning one song and performing it in the bar of the hotel we go to in Wales every summer on our holidays. But I haven't even picked it up yet. I could do with some singing lessons in preparation for *Mother Courage*. I need to start learning lines for the epic one-woman play that Kersh has written. Still nothing from Royal Exchange about a possible slot there. Need to chase that up. And no word from HOME about a space for *Take Back Our Bodies*. And nothing back from Rufus regarding my email about *Wit*. Meh.

14 March

Have revisited *The Artist's Way* by Julia Cameron, an old book on creativity, a sort of Twelve Step programme for blocked artists that we all read in the 1980s and 90s. It's changed my life more than once, I'm almost embarrassed to report, and was a huge factor in my daring to leave *Coronation Street* after sixteen years. If you can get past the slight corny Americanisms and New Age spirituality, I can't recommend it enough. The idea of 'filling the well' comes from there and it's a book I return to over and over when I'm feeling a bit stuck. Today it gives me a little push to do some stuff for myself, to resist duty and have a bit of luxury. I book a massage, practise the piano for the first time in years, read some Mary Oliver poetry, take myself off to a café and drink coffee reading my book, pretending to be a mysterious traveller in a foreign city. I listen to The Specials, do some weeding, sit drinking tea in the spring sunshine, buy some daffodils for a quid. I feel a bit more myself again for it.

16 March

Amy Hodge, who will direct me in *Mother Courage* next year, calls. Anna Jordan, the writer, is snowed under with work and will struggle to deliver a second draft of her new version in the next couple of months, so Headlong, who are co-producing with the Royal Exchange, have decided to push back the production into the summer or autumn season in 2018. I feel fine about it. I'm hoping that *Broadchurch* might open up some possibilities for more telly work once I finish on *Peterloo*, so it gives us a bit more time. *Broadchurch* is being well received, which is a massive relief.

17 March

Manchester Theatre Awards at HOME. We have a great day. It's a good old get-together; a few drinks with mates. I win Best Actress for *Wit*, and Take Back win the Stage Door Foundation special award: a trophy and £500. We are completely shocked as there are no nominations and it's only part-way through our friend Caroline Clegg's introduction of the award, when she mentions political theatre, that we start to realize she might be talking about us. I say over and over to Becx, who is sitting beside me, 'Is it us? Is it US?', until Caroline calls us up and we do a rubbish overwhelmed speech, halfway through which I pull myself together and manage to say something semi-coherent about what we do as a company. *Wit* loses out to another Royal Exchange main house show, Hugh Whitemore's *Breaking the Code*, directed by Rob Hastie, and I feel disappointed for Raz, our director. At the UK Theatre Awards last year, Raz won Best Director and I lost out on Best Performance to the wonderful Paapa Essiedu for his Hamlet, so at least I got a chance to thank Raz and all the company this time, and Kersh of course, and to dedicate it to my late friend Morag Siller's memory. Morag was being treated for cancer while the show was on and died shortly after the run. She was texting constantly throughout and I had a photo of her on my dressing room wall, which I kissed every night before going on stage.

Raz and I talk afterwards about why we feel a bit sad, and think it's because this really feels like the end of the road for *Wit* now. We should have been doing it in London now, riding on the back of the *Broadchurch* publicity (and now both our awards) and before filming starts with Mike Leigh. But it didn't happen, and we have to make our peace with that. We have Kersh's play to look forward to and Raz is considering setting up a production company in order to make the work he wants to. He asks me for ideas, and I start to think about us commissioning a black writer to write something to do with white privilege. I feel it everywhere at the moment. My eyes are being forced open through reading Nikesh Shukla's *The Good Immigrant* and, in particular, through talking to black and Asian actors and creatives. The awards ceremony today was fun and we had a lovely time but it was impossible not to notice the lack of diversity among the nominees and, in particular, the winners.

22 March

Tracy Brabin, the actor-turned-MP who won Jo Cox's seat after Jo was murdered by a right-wing extremist at her surgery last summer, is hosting a Parliamentary debate on working-class access to the arts in the Commons. She has asked me to take part. But it is my friend Tom McAlpine's funeral today so I'm unable to attend. Tom was a Manchester legend, and for many years he ran with great humour and charisma the charity Moodswings Network, which supports people with mental health difficulties.

Later in the day I turn on my phone to text Tracy and ask her how the debate has gone, and see on Twitter that there has been some sort of attack on Westminster. A car has ploughed into crowds on Westminster Bridge and a man has been shot as he attacked a police officer. Tracy is safe, locked into chambers, along with a group of visiting schoolchildren. As the day progresses, sketchy details are released and by bedtime there are four people confirmed dead, including the police officer and the attacker. A terrible day.

28 March

Everything feels very up in the air at the moment. I feel in a strange place. I just want to work. But there is some sort of expectation, because of *Wit* and because of *Broadchurch*, I think, that I have to start making choices that move my career forward. I'm saying 'no' to a few things because the next job has to take me onto another level. Or something. I don't know. Thank God for Take Back. I can hammer away at that without any of the other bullshit affecting my choices. And I can quietly beaver away at Kersh's play, *The Greatest Play in the History of the World*, throughout the next few months, which will be something lovely to work towards. The Exchange have offered us a weekend in December, but they can't produce it. We'd have to fund it ourselves and come in as a visiting production. I think this will suit us as it means we'll have ownership of it going forward. Our big plan for the future: me, Kersh and a suitcase full of shoe boxes (the set) travelling the world in our dotage.

My old friend from LAMDA, Zara Ramm, is at the West Yorkshire Playhouse in Leeds in *Pink Mist*, Owen Sheers's astonishing play about three young men from Bristol joining up and going to Afghanistan. It's a physical and visceral production that leaves me reeling. I have seen some amazing theatre this year so far.

29 March

Nothing, the Young Company production at the Royal Exchange, opens in the studio. There was a production of the play last year, which went on to win a Manchester Theatre Award earlier this month, but I didn't catch it. So I'm seeing it with fresh eyes tonight and no small amount of nerves as my daughter Martha is in it. *Bugsy Malone* it ain't. My God, what a dark and nihilistic piece, beautifully adapted by Amanda Dalton from the novel by Janne Teller, about a teenage boy who decides that life has no meaning and takes refuge up a plum tree. His friends, played by a cast of extraordinary young people from an exciting array of backgrounds and with different abilities, take it upon themselves to prove to him that life matters by creating a 'heap of meaning' made up of things that are important to them. It all turns pretty dark, in a *Lord of the Flies* kind of way, and the audience are left shell-shocked as the play reaches its brutal conclusion.

Martha is just brilliant, completely present and committed. I couldn't be prouder. She doesn't want anyone at the Exchange to know I'm her mum, which I think is admirable, but which means I can't bask in her reflected glory afterwards and have to skulk off to the train alone. She is loving every second. We have completely lost her to the theatre. Brilliant. How wonderful to find something that you love when you're fifteen.

30 March

To the Royal Exchange again for the matinee of *The Suppliant Women* in the main space, a 2,500-year-old play by Aeschylus brought bang up to date by David Greig. It's being performed by a massive cast of 30+ young women drawn from all over Greater Manchester. There are three professional actors and then this wonderful community chorus playing a group of refugee women fleeing forced marriage. Most of the play, an hour and a half of it, is spoken and sung in perfect unison as a chorus. I have been asked to 'offer the libation' at the start, an ancient Greek tradition in which a civic representative (I'm not quite sure how I qualify, but never mind) thanks everyone involved and pours a bottle of wine around the edge of the stage.

It is an incredible production and the chorus is just beautiful and so together and slick. The play is hardly ever produced because of the large numbers of cast involved. Martha is with me and we both find the sheer scale of it, all those young female voices lifting up together, a very moving thing. I meet some of the chorus afterwards, and it's clear they have had a life-changing experience working on the piece, just as Martha has had doing the Young Company production of *Nothing*. There is a light in their eyes as they talk to me about how it's been for them, being part of something like this, with so much to say about the world, that makes me teary and hopeful.

3 April

I receive an intriguing phone call from John McGrath, the Artistic Director of the Manchester International Festival (MIF). Lemn Sissay, the wonderful poet and broadcaster and Chancellor of the University of Manchester, has approached him about a project. John used to run Contact Theatre in Manchester back in the day and turned around so many young people's lives as director there, as did Lawrence Till before him. Lemn's story is well documented, as much of his writing is about his extremely traumatic childhood and adolescence as a young black man in care. His Ethiopian mother asked for him to be fostered at birth in order for her to complete her studies, but her baby was renamed and given to a family against her will. Lemn spent the first twelve years of his life as Norman (named after his social worker), the 'adopted' son of a deeply religious white family in a white Lancashire mill town. His mother never consented to Lemn's name being changed on his birth certificate or to him being legally adopted, so when he reached adolescence, the family he had lived with since he was a baby were able to put him back into care, cutting off all ties. Naturally, Lemn, adrift in the world, lost his way. Poetry and theatre, it's fair to say, saved his life.

Subsequently he's set up a charity that provides Christmas dinners to young care-leavers every year. Recently Lemn has decided to seek compensation from the local authority social services for the deep trauma he has experienced as a result of their negligence and institutionalized racism in their treatment of him as a young boy, and as part of this, he has had to undergo an intensive psychiatric assessment. Now, many of Lemn's friends and acquaintances who have received a similar psychiatric report in the past have found the reading of it a triggering experience, leading to depression and sometimes suicide. So the receiving of the report is an extremely delicate and difficult thing to know how to handle. Because Lemn has always felt most at home on stage, he has decided to have his report *read to him live* for the first time in front of an audience. John would like me to be the reader, at the Royal Court, at the end of the month. What a complete honour. I know Lemn a little bit, love and admire his work, and feel sure that I am up to the job. I feel that I would be solid and warm, and that I would be able to look after Lemn by sharing the stage with him, terrifying as the prospect is.

4 April

John McGrath calls again, and gives it to me straight. A month ago when Lemn first had the idea to have his psychiatric report read to him in front of an audience, Lemn approached another actor, very well known, and with a similar story to his, to be the reader. He/she didn't get back to him, and as time was running out, John said to Lemn that they needed to cast someone else. And, of course, last night, the other actor rang him back and is available after all. Their shared background makes complete sense of it and it is a coup to get them too, I get that. I tell John that I will keep myself available and am happy to step in even at a day's notice, if something happens that means the other person can't do it in the end. It's a horrible call for poor John to have to make, and I feel bad for him, especially as I'd been so up for it when he'd approached me. But I do understand. I've had to write a couple of difficult emails myself today, gently telling people that we're not able to use their pieces in the next Take Back show, so it feels strangely appropriate for me to be the recipient of a 'let down' call. I do feel sad, though. I felt as though I was perfect for this strange and delicate task. I don't often feel that.

5 April

John emails me and tells me that Lemn and the other actor have met and have decided together that he/she isn't the right person to read his report to Lemn after all. John doesn't say why, but I wonder whether it might be a bit triggering for them both, with their difficult, similar histories. So I will be doing the job in the end. I am absolutely thrilled. It is a huge responsibility; I feel incredibly honoured to be trusted with it.

Lemn's great friend Louise Wallwein, another poet and playwright who grew up in care, also found safety and solace and self-expression at Contact back in the day. She has written a version of her fantastic one-woman show called *Glue*, about her life, for BBC Radio 4. Susan Roberts, the director, has contacted me asking me to play her social worker in this new version. So, at the end of the month, within days of each other, I will have the privilege of helping to share these two extraordinary and painful stories by two people I love and whose work I greatly admire. Their survival and art continue to be an inspiration to me. I feel very happy.

17 April

We're back from our family holiday and Kersh and I head straight down to Dorset for a special screening of the last-ever episode of *Broadchurch* at the Electric Palace in Bridport. We have a fantastic couple of days seeing the sights, taking pictures of each other pretending to be Hardy and Miller (the show's detectives, played by Olivia Colman and David Tennant) in the shadow of the iconic Jurassic Coast – ending the whole experience where it began, which feels perfect.

There is such a buzz in West Bay about the last episode; people have loved this series and I feel very proud to have been a small part of it. Proceeds from the screening are to go to Dorset Rape Crisis Support Centre and The Shores, the Sexual Assault Referral Centre that helped us so much with our research for the *Broadchurch* storyline. The incredible staff are special guests, as well as a couple of survivors who have been generous enough to share their stories with me after managing to turn their lives around and becoming counsellors for Rape Crisis. I've learned so much doing this job: shocking facts and figures and stories, that I wish were made up, about the epidemic of sexual violence in this country.

18 April

Prime Minister Theresa May has announced a snap general election on 8 June. Here we go!

20 April

A Take Back outing for Grant's birthday to see the National Theatre's production of *Our Country* at HOME in Manchester. It is the NT's response to Brexit and is part curated from interviews with people who voted Leave or Remain in five distinct regions of the UK, and part poetry by Carol Ann Duffy. Penny Layden plays Brittania, breaking her heart over all the division, and also channels David Cameron, Boris Johnson, Michael Gove and, in one profoundly moving moment, Jo Cox, the MP and Remain campaigner who was murdered at her Yorkshire surgery on the week of the Referendum. Jo's words, 'We are far more united and have far more in common with each other than things that divide us', from her maiden speech in the Commons, have become iconic, and were more apposite than ever in this context.

As usual I will have to sit with it for a few days before I can fully process how I feel about the piece as a whole. I get so carried away by the live experience and my complete love of being in the theatre that often I can be a bit blind to the faults or problems with a play or production. Everyone seems to cautiously like it. We have a few questions: first, about the choice of regions (Scotland, Wales, North East England, South West England and Leicester), and who was left out and why; the representation of the BME population (there was one Asian actor in a cast of seven); and the rather cavalier approach to cultural stereotyping and the verbatim form. But I liked its rough edges, its chaotic structure. And, strangely, unlike some of the people we talked to afterwards, it didn't make me angry or hopeless; rather it made me feel a kind of fondness for our ridiculous little nation with all its clans, identities and vernacular. I feel quite sanguine in a kind of ''Twas always thus' kind of way about how united AND divided we are. It's an ongoing project apparently, as Brexit unfolds. It will be interesting to see how it evolves. And how differently it's received, region to region, as the production tours.

I have been ill since our holiday over Easter with a rotten and debilitating cough and cold that I'm completely sick of. I nearly had to leave the *Broadchurch* screening and *Our Country* because of ill-timed coughing fits.

24 April

I'm starting to feel a bit frustrated by some to-ing and fro-ing with the Royal Exchange about us taking Kersh's play, *The Greatest Play in the History of the World*, to the studio there. After initially offering us a weekend slot before Christmas, they're now bumping us to a Tuesday and Wednesday with no technical support at all. Myself, Kersh and Raz Shaw, the director, are keen to have a soft launch of the production at the Exchange. It makes complete sense for us to be there, with me and Raz involved and with Kersh being a former Bruntwood winner back in the day.[2] I think we perhaps haven't been clear enough about how passionate we are about the piece. Also, it's possible there's been some blurring of lines between what we think of as a soft launch with the

---

[2]The Royal Exchange's high-profile biennial playwriting competition.

production values that an audience might expect from this team, and what the Exchange might have misinterpreted as a scratch or work-in-progress sharing? I email everyone to try and sort it out, as I think we're all on different pages at the moment with it, and it's making Kersh in particular feel a bit crap and unwanted. And it's a beautiful play. It deserves better.

25 April

I think my interpretation of events was correct. There has been some miscommunication – which I have to take responsibility for – about what exactly we'd like from the theatre, so a meeting is called for next week to discuss just that. The Exchange can't offer us any money, so we'll be a visiting production, but we do need proper technical back-up. It is a programmed, ticketed event, and I will be spending the rest of the year learning the lines so I want it to look like a proper thing. Sarah, the Artistic Director, Ric, the Senior Producer, and Amy, who produces the Studio programme, have also put their heads together and offered us a weekend in November. This is a far better option for us. Then we can take it from there in terms of how we want to proceed, and if and where we'd like to tour it. We're all much happier now. Just some crossing of wires I think, and me underplaying my hopes for the piece probably.

An all-day Take Back meeting at our favourite café, The Koffee Pot on Oldham Street. Our next project, *Take Back Our Bodies*, is imminent and we still have lots of organizing to do in terms of the show itself, and selling it. I'm quite relieved that it's a lot shorter than *Take Back America*, but it's still quite sprawling. It's such a wide remit in terms of the subject matter and, at the moment, something seems to be happening every day that we feel needs to be included with some urgency. In the last two weeks there have been accounts of concentration camps for gay people in Russia and horrific stories of the torture and murder of gay people in Chechnya. Our own government is pushing through a policy in which single mothers will lose their benefits for any third child unless they fill in a form stating that they have been raped. On just about every level this is reprehensible.

Meanwhile, the row rages on in America (with plenty of champions here) about the planned policy to stop trans women using female toilets. Kersh has written a powerful piece about the decriminalization of abortion in Northern Ireland; there's a campaign around this at the moment after a mother was arrested for procuring abortion pills for her pregnant teenaged daughter. We learned lots about this topic at the Doughty Street Chambers International Women's Day event in March. We also have pieces on rape as a weapon of war; slut-shaming; fat-shaming; ageing; porn; fifty years of the Wolfenden Report, which recommended the legalization of gay sex for those aged over 21 in the UK; sex for people with disabilities; the availability of PrEp (the drug that reduces the chance of getting HIV) on the NHS; and the pressures on young people to conform to standards of appearance. And, threading throughout, will be Take Back regular Sandra Cole's painfully honest vignettes about what it has been to be a black woman growing up in Britain. Because of the personal nature of the pieces, we're also asking our writers to film a sixty-second piece to play before each section, talking about their inspiration/provocation for writing their piece. I think it will be a powerful night, but we all feel strangely nervous about it.

There is also much discussion about our planned production of *My Version of Events*, Becx's play about consent. We have been given some incredibly helpful free legal advice from Doughty Street and Becx has rewritten it. We now need a director and are struggling to secure a complete and diverse cast for a week's run without funds to pay people properly. Becx has had an idea to make the whole thing much more of a Take Back affair. Keep it script-in-hand, with panel discussions after every sharing and with some sort of supporting installation around some of the key issues. As we're chatting, Grant, in his brilliant and no-fuss way, designs a set that will transform immediately afterwards into an exhibition space. We talk about almost blind-casting each evening's performance, with actors of all ages and ethnicities, and not just the twenty-somethings that a straight reading of the play would require. We end up very excited about the prospect. We ask the actor and director Noreen Kershaw to direct and she is enthusiastic and supportive as ever in her response.

Saw Bill Naughton's *Spring and Port Wine* at Oldham Coliseum with my mother-in-law in the evening. Lovely, traditional production of a much-loved play set in 1961. The Oldham audience is in customary fine voice, ooh-ing and aah-ing their way through. Proper.

25 April

To MediaCity to record my little bit as Social Worker in Louise Wallwein's beautiful radio adaptation of her one-woman stage play, *Glue*. I take her a collection of poems by one of my favourites, Mary Oliver. There's a line at the end of her poem 'Wild Geese' about the world constantly announcing our place in the family of things.

Lou's search for family, and her love of nature, as well as her huge and generous heart, are some of her most defining characteristics, I think. That and her ability to really live the good moments. Which she most definitely is doing today. Another landmark in her life.

29 April

I catch an early train to London and head to the Royal Court where I meet the director John McGrath and producer Sarah Sansom in preparation for tomorrow's sharing of Lemn Sissay's psychiatric report in the theatre.

We are shown into a tiny, blue, soundproofed room, which is a set for an upcoming immersive piece. We drag a table and chair to one side so I can start reading through the massive thirty-something-page document. It's a very harrowing read: a relentless inventory of neglect, emotional and physical abuse, of lies told, of a life of being treated as a threat and outsider, and a subsequent diagnosis of pretty much every possible disorder from post-traumatic stress to alcohol abuse. And a prognosis of a continued lifetime vulnerability to all these things. Everything is in there. The only changes are to protect the identity of people who aren't involved in his abuse: ex-girlfriends and so on are referred to as A, B and C. It takes me an hour and forty minutes to read through it, some of it almost impenetrable psychological test results with much repetition throughout. I get to the penultimate page before I lose it. It's not one particular sentence that gets me, but the cumulative horror of what I'm bearing witness to, I think. Especially the endless fucking racism: personal, institutional and societal. I try, unsuccessfully, to carry on about four times before I get my shit together. Better this has happened today, hopefully. Then Lemn arrives. He's on good form, but is clearly a bit wired. He has no idea what's in the report or what conclusions it reaches. He wants to tell some jokes and funny stories throughout. John has written in four breaks during which I will ask the same three questions:

How are you doing, Lemn?
Do you want to say anything?
Are you okay to carry on?

Lemn is already thinking of what to say. I recognize this impulse. We gently talk to him about how his role in this unique event is just to listen. To resist the impulse to entertain, to perform, but to just hear the words and respond honestly. If he has a plan of what to say, he may (as I think I would) spend the time thinking, 'When's the next break?', 'Will that story work?'. As we speak, the monumental realization of what is at stake for him suddenly hits him like a ton of bricks; it's as if this is the first moment he's fully understood what this is going to be, and he becomes very upset and overwhelmed. It's good, we all agree. It's fucking huge, this.

We all go out in search of a good cup of tea (forget it, this is London) and as Lemn and I walk and chat we find a child's homemade beaded bracelet on the pavement. I pick it up and pocket it: a good luck charm.

Lemn leaves and John and I start working through the text, breaking up paragraph-long sentences with endless added parentheses and commas to help me make sense of it, and trying to work out how to make the transition between the explanatory language and Lemn's quoted testimony, which sometimes appears in the middle of a sentence, unannounced by a handy 'Mr Sissay said . . .'. Without me doing some sort of Lemn impersonation or actually miming the airborne quotation marks, it's sometimes hard to make the differentiation.

I am supposed to be seeing my mate Joe in Albert Camus's *The Plague* on the other side of town, but the trains are slow and I don't make it, so go back to a café near my hotel and have a couple of glasses of wine and do a load of work on the 'script'. It's so important I get this right. I go to bed listening to an old recording of Lemn's *Desert Island Discs* to feel close to him.

30 April

It's hard to put into words what an incredible day in my life this has been. I can't really process it yet. I wake up all kinds of wobbly – the most nervous I've been in years, I think – and have to meditate my arse off for a good hour to get myself in any kind of fit state.

Lemn posts a poem on Facebook:

I am the bull in the china shop
And with all my strength and will
As a storm smashed the teacups
I stood still.

I arrive at the theatre at noon and John and I do some work in the theatre space. I've never performed downstairs at the Royal Court, only upstairs in the small space, and this in itself is quite a moment for me personally. Although today is emphatically NOT about me. Jez Butterworth's *The Ferryman* is previewing at the moment and looks set to be a smash hit, but – this being a Sunday – the stage is free. So some curtains cut off the bulk of the set and a chair and side table have been set in front of it on one side of the (really little) stage, and a desk and chair for me with a big jug of water on the other. I can be heard fine. It feels intimate compared to the Royal Exchange, the theatre I know best, which is in the round and on three tiers. We find a way to mark the moments in the report that are direct quotes of Lemn's words, by reading them in an evidential way, in rather the same way a lawyer does in court. I feel very nervous. It's the enormity of the task and its deep resonance for my friend, but I think it's also the fact that I only have one crack at it. No previews, no notes, no 'hmmm, that bit didn't quite work, Julie. How about trying it this way tonight?' Just one chance. Channel 4 News are coming to film it and the *Guardian* are doing a big piece with Lemn and have come to take a couple of set-up shots of us. My black dress is rejected because of the black curtain backdrop and I look like a floating head. Luckily I have a back-up outfit. Lemn looks dapper as ever.

Kersh has travelled down and meets me at the stage door for a much needed bloody hug. I'm given Lucy Davis's lovely office overlooking Sloane Square as my dressing room, and have to make several trips to the toilet. My, the nerves have got to me. Lemn gives me a book and a beautiful card that I will treasure forever.

At 5.50pm we're called down to the stage and have a big cuddle. I am worried that the cold reading of the official document might leave Lemn feeling as though I am disconnected from his story. I give Lemn the bracelet we found together, with its C, love heart and A beads. It stands for Courage and love and Attentiveness, I tell him. I tell him my heart is with him totally, even as my mouth spouts the hard facts of his life, and the damage done to him. And then we're on. The love and warmth for Lemn from the audience is palpable. We stand together centre stage and Lemn reads a page of his blog from a few weeks ago when he decided to do this. It ends:

> One reader
> One table
> And me.
> It will be called *The Report*.

He sits and I check he's okay and start. I am a bit stumbly and dry-mouthed. The first page is a list of the Consultant Clinical Psychologist's vast qualifications. People tell me afterwards that Lemn is very animated during the first section. He is also drinking loads of water. The jug is on my desk. A few people confess they become extremely concerned that he'll go thirsty, but after about twenty minutes he dashes off and gets another bottle. The audience are Oldham-like in their audible responses and it's lovely. They gasp at the reported recollections of his childhood: his white foster mother tearing at his hair with a nit comb, the schoolyard racism, the renaming of him as Norman after his social worker, his files stating at the age of six that he's expressing a 'wish to be white'. Most heartbreaking is the decision to hand him back to social services, when he was just twelve; his normal and small acts of pre-teen rebellion (like getting a biscuit from the tin without asking) branded 'the Devil's work' by his ultra-Christian foster parents; and then them blurting out to him he was a product of rape. At the age of twelve he was put into institutions, taken away from everything he'd ever known: grandmas, grandpas, siblings, cousins; gone forever. It was years later when he discovered that his Ethiopian birth mum had begged for him to be returned to her, and wanted him to grow up among his own people where he wouldn't face discrimination. During one of our breaks, when I ask Lemn if he's okay and he wants to carry on, he thanks the audience and says he couldn't have done it without them there. Someone shouts, 'We're here for you, Lemn!', and everyone applauds and I don't know how I don't weep. Lemn does.

Some of the most painful passages are about the intense shame he has been made to feel about himself, and his fear of rejection, which cause him to seek superficial connection through his fame and at the expense of personal relationships. This is why we're here tonight. This is his safe place. In front of an audience, in the theatre.

By the end of the two hours, we have heard it all, sometimes multiple times: the same terrible damage presented over and over from source after source with the conclusion that Lemn will never get over what has happened to him, that his childhood was stolen from him and that the effects will be life-long. There is rage in my voice as I read some of these passages. Recommendations are made for his continued treatment and support and for compensation from Wigan Social Services. Lemn looks hollow. Everyone tells me afterwards that for the last half hour he is still and haunted, his hand at his throat.

All funds from tonight will go towards the Foundation Lemn intends to set up to help and support young people in care and care-leavers.

The rest of the night is a blur. We are whisked away for interviews with Channel 4 News. I meet the psychologist who wrote the report and the lawyer who commissioned it. I meet foster carers, adults who grew up in care, young people currently in care. There are poets, comedians, journalists, DJs, actors, directors, graffiti artists and social workers in the bar. Everyone wants to hug Lemn, everyone wants to compensate for the love that was stolen from him. This has been a new kind of theatre. I've never experienced anything like it. I hope it's a healing thing for that beautiful man.

1 May

A day of normality at home. Hanging washing out in the sunshine, getting the kids' bags ready for school tomorrow, cooking tea. Family seems a precious thing. I am lucky that this is my normality.

Beautiful piece by Simon Hattenstone in the *Guardian* that really honours Lemn and what he did yesterday.

2 May

This Take Back has been a tough one. I think I understand why now. The topic, *Bodies*, is naturally bringing up difficult things for the artists involved. We're asking people to talk about painful and personal things, to write and perform pieces that have deep resonance for them, and there are some raw emotions flying about that are manifesting themselves in occasional defensiveness, a little bit of preciousness about the pieces and no small amount of fear, I think. I realize that we really have to look after everyone in this piece, more than ever before; to make people feel like they have a safe space to discuss some of the really challenging subject matter and to feel listened to and heard. Sometimes in making a show you can become fixed on the finished product and forget to be mindful of the process, and to be gentle with everyone's tender hearts. It's a very exposing thing to talk about the body as a battleground, from inside the war. The process should always be kind.

I am fielding Take Back calls all day whilst running around between *Peterloo* fittings in London. *Peterloo!* I'd almost forgotten about it. I go to Cosprop in Archway and three ace women led by Jackie, the designer, layer me up with chemises, corsets, dresses, woolly socks, clogs, shawls and bonnets. It was a boiling hot August day on the day of the massacre and my character has a fainting fit that means she gets carried up into the main speaker's carriage. Bloody hell, I'm not surprised she passed out with all that clobber on. There'll be no acting required if we get a warm spell during filming.

Then up to Camden for make-up fitting with Chris. Basically there will be none. She tells me this nervously because many actors' idea of no make-up is actually 'no make-up make-up', ie. subtle corrective cosmetics that make you look like you just have naturally lovely blemish-free features and no bags! None of that here. But I do need a wig. We try on a couple and settle on a blondy grey. I'm going to look about 100.

I have a bit of time before my off-peak train is due, so I wander aimlessly around Bloomsbury ironing out Take Back issues on my phone, when who should I bump into but Lemn Sissay. We are so astonished to see each other, so soon after Sunday and completely randomly. I abruptly end my call to Becx and we just hug for ages on the pavement and get a bit teary and take selfies for Facebook. He's doing okay. Channel 4 News are running a piece tonight. He's feeling good and taking care of himself. It is so good to see him.

I get home to a few emails from my agent, which my stupid phone hasn't allowed me to see all day. I have an audition for a voiceover for a supermarket (quick Google of ethics brings quite positive results, especially re: waste reduction), a Christmas special of a gameshow and an offer to play a 'comedic fairy' in pantomime. Funny old world.

3 May

I meet Becx and Grant and we go to see Noreen Kershaw at her gorgeous higgledy-piggledy house in north Manchester that feels like it's in the middle of the countryside. Noreen is completely ace: a champion of young artists, a fabulous actor (she was the first Shirley Valentine), an accomplished director and a friend to everyone. She is piss-funny too, and has made us a pie! What's not to love? We sit round her big kitchen table, with sleeping one-eyed dogs at our feet, and talk about our ideas for *My Version of Events*. She gets it, she gets it all, and has fantastic suggestions too. She is passionate about new writing and loved the scratch reading of the play we did at HOME, so we're really thrilled she's on board.

In the afternoon I meet Raz and Kersh at the Royal Exchange and we meet Ric, the producer. Sarah and Amy aren't around, but Ric is incredibly reassuring and generous and honest about what kind of support they can offer us for *The Greatest Play in the History of the World*. He's obviously read and liked it, too, which Kersh really needed to hear. It looks like we'll put it on as associates and cover costs the Exchange can't offer with an Arts Council grant, if we can get one. We pin down the November dates in the studio as well, and decide to aim for five or six shows. It's only an hour long. A hell of a lot of lines for me, though. When Ric leaves us, we have a read-through just for ourselves and get very excited about how to bring it to life. It's such a beautiful story, full of ideas and science and poetry. It has a love story at its centre and a message of cramming it all, of living a life with meaning, of making it count. It's so Kersh. (Note: it probably isn't The Greatest Play in the History of the World obviously, but you have to see the play to understand the title. FYI.)

5 May

I am making my directorial debut in *Take Back Our Bodies*. Tonight I'm working with actor Sandra Cole on her short monologues that will run through the evening as a thread. There is very little directing to be done at all. The pieces are so painfully raw and personal to her, dealing as they do with some of the shocking racism she's encountered in her life, and she reads them with such grace and humour and warmth and fierceness, I can only watch and marvel. We make some tweaks and tiny cuts and highlight some moments, but she is just sensational. She starts by singing a bluesy version of *Maybe It's Because I'm a Londoner* which sends shivers down my spine, and then goes into a brilliant monologue about constantly being asked where she's from, and the frustration of her questioners when she replies, honestly and straightforwardly, 'London'. We rehearse at a new rehearsal venue, Hope Studios, in the Northern Quarter of Manchester, and it is fantastic. Rehearsal space is always a nightmare to get hold of here, and this many-roomed studio space is just superb. When I get home, Rosa, my niece, has arrived on the train, and we sit up drinking too much red wine and talking about theatre until the early hours.

6 May

An early start for us all, as rehearsals for *Take Back Our Bodies* start at Hope Studios at 10am. We have booked two rooms, one for Ian Townsend and one for Kate Colgrave-Pope, both of whom are directing five or six pieces each. Cherylee Houston, who plays Izzy in *Coronation Street*, is directing her pieces at Contact all day, as she is a wheelchair-user and it has better access. I've stepped in to be in Kersh's short play, *The Eighth,* about the proposed decriminalization of abortion in the Republic of Ireland and Northern Ireland, because Sue McCormick, who was supposed to do it, is already in two pieces with two directors. The piece is a music hall number in the vein of Joan Littlewood's Theatre Workshop, with an Englishman, an Irishwoman and a Scotswoman all walking into an abortion clinic. Kate is just fantastic. She gets the form, the style, and whips us into shape easily within the hour. The rest of the day is spent darting between Hope and Contact, making sure everyone has everything they need and that everyone's comfortable with what they're doing. We all meet for a top-and-tail tech, just working through the cues with the ace Contact team. We've asked all the writers to make a sixty-second film to play on a screen before each piece, explaining their inspiration and provocation for writing about what they have. It's a device we've used before when we had our *Ten Takes on Capital* and it worked well. The films are all unique to the writer. Anita Pandolpho is filmed in her allotment shed to introduce her one-woman play about ageing. Kersh gets our daughter Martha to talk about abortion rights on his behalf, because he believes it's a woman's right to choose. Sandra introduces her pieces with a close-up of her skin against her white boyfriend's, with a poem about skin both separating and connecting us. Becx leads into her piece, *One Form*, with a long close-up, shot in silence, of the 'exemption form' women are being forced to complete in order to receive Third Child Tax Credits if that child is a product of rape.

Everyone seems relaxed and in good spirits as the house opens at 6.50pm. We go up late because there is a huge queue at the box office and we have a nearly full house, which is wonderful. It is also, without doubt, our most diverse audience to date. The subject matter has brought in a new crowd. Rupert Hill and Liz Carney open the show with a lovely duet called 'In My Mind I'm Free', based on a Stephen Hawking quote, and telling the story of a couple of teenagers who are only able to speak to each other online. The whole evening runs without a hitch. Every piece is perfectly pitched and I'm very pleased with myself about the running order, which was a complete headache, but which seems to hit the right note in terms of contrast in tone and seriousness. Rosa appears in eighteen-year-old Millie-Jo's play about shit magazines and self-image. Later she performs a beautiful Sarah McDonald-Hughes monologue about slut-shaming and consent and kindness. She is knockout. You can hear a pin drop when she's performing. My old mate Johnny Voe has joined the cast after years away from the stage and is chilling as a Chechnyan father and anti-gay warrior. Peter Keeley, a bit of a Manchester legend, who has been feeling increasingly marginalized as a writer and performer with cerebral palsy, performs in his own duologue with Toby Hadoke about disability and sex and gets the biggest laugh of the night with his line 'I've been blown out more times than a monk's candle'.

Sue McCormick nails Lisa Holdsworth's sketch on being fat, circling cake on stage like a vulture, until – with the killer line quoting Chekhov, about never having a loaded gun on stage without firing it – she shoves a big piece in her mouth, raises her fist and shouts 'BANG!' Melissa Johns, a new actor in our gang, delivers her own heartbreaking and piss-funny scene about dating with one arm. Guy Hargreaves opens the second half in yellow Speedos playing a ukelele and singing about John Lennon, Yoko Ono and the virtues of eating your peas. Zoe Iqbal's fabulous sketch about porn and gender roles is hilarious and there isn't a dry eye in the house after Becx's play on rape as a weapon of war. Josh Val Martin's perfect three-hander between gay men of different generations, perched on the edge of the stage, chatting about their experiences and ending with the shooting in a club in Orlando, breaks my heart. Sandra ends the whole evening with *One Body*, making us all hold hands in the audience and connect with one another.

We get a standing ovation. Amazing. And the bar is buzzing afterwards. So much to talk about, so many people's stories told and properly heard, some people finding their voices for the first time, some people making their long-awaited comeback on stage. Sandra says that Take Back nights are always healing experiences, which is not a bad review, and it feels that way tonight. It feels good to be in a room with good people, talking about stuff that matters, planning what to do next. There is a general consensus that this has been Take Back's best yet. There is a list of signposts on the programme: organizations and volunteering opportunities relating to the pieces, from PrEP to policy, from addiction support to solidarity with gay men in Chechnya. We want people to take this feeling out into the wider world and change things.

8 May

Thirty days until the general election and time to put my head above the parapet and throw some energy into trying to get the Tories out. I hate it. I hate the way it makes me feel: exposed and grandiose. But apparently it helps get the message out. I make a little film for social media in my back garden with Jonathan Reynolds, my local MP. He's a good fella, even though we don't agree on everything. The campaign against Labour leader Jeremy Corbyn blazes on, in the media and within the Labour Party. I believe Corbyn to be a genuine, honest and authentic man whose socialist principles and values are in line with mine. I campaigned for him to be leader. But there is a schism in the party and there are many of my friends now I can't even talk to about him. I don't understand it. I feel like this is a moment in history when we have a real opportunity to build a better society, but there is such animosity towards him. I know that if we lose this election, the Corbyn supporters will be blamed for the failure, but half of the party just hasn't got behind him and there is so much at stake. Now is not the time for fighting among ourselves. I have been asked to introduce him at the Manchester launch tomorrow, in front of about a thousand activists. I've shared a platform with him before and he is always rapturously received. It's quite something to witness.

The party want to see my speech ahead of the event. I tell them I don't normally write anything down: I just turn up and speak from the heart. They really want to see what I'm planning to say. So I write a poem. It's not serious – more Pam Ayres than Carol Ann Duffy – in the tradition of Lancashire gatherings, where someone always whips out a ten-stanza ditty to mark the occasion, with slightly dodgy scanning and some half-rhymes. I often perform one at these kind of dos because I'm not a politician and no one wants to hear the same things over and over, especially from someone from the telly. I apologetically send it, emphasizing that it's meant to be a bit shit and will delivered humorously. Which of course instantly renders it unfunny.

But the policy team would prefer if I made the same points without the poem. They think the press will be mean to me. It doesn't quite match the tone they're going for. Which I assume is dry and po-faced. I'm pissed off. Why get me in? This is what I'm for surely? To connect with the gathered crowd in the way I know how? Get a local councillor in. I feel mistrusted, censored and a bit humiliated. I think it would've gone down a storm. Meh. I watch the news with a sense of despondency, which I resent, because that's not my default setting. Bloody politics is making me a miserable bastard.

I think we're going to have to do a Take Back response to the election. Maybe on the Monday after the result. Give a handful of writers the weekend to respond and put on an evening. I have a feeling we might need to get everyone together, and very probably not to celebrate, unfortunately.

9 May

Lessons learned today. We turn up at EventCity, a huge cavernous conference centre near the Trafford Shopping Centre on the outskirts of Manchester, and the scale of today's launch becomes apparent. The huge hall is packed to the rafters with activists, the world's press is in attendance, including the BBC's formidable political editor Laura Kuennsberg, plus the entire shadow cabinet. A huge banner announces, 'FOR THE MANY, NOT THE FEW'.

Oh my good God, the poem would have been a car crash. They were completely right. This is proper shit going down here. I ask the organizers how many speakers there are, and they casually say, 'Oh, just Ian (Lavery, Elections and Campaign Co-Ordinator), you, then Jeremy'. I am not here as a bit of light relief after twenty Labour activists: I'm Jeremy Corbyn's warm-up. I meet loads of people from across the spectrum of the party, from campaigners in their 'Save Our Chorley A & E' T-shirts to people with disabilities who have been completely shafted by the Tories. I have about a thousand selfies taken before taking my seat next to Andy Burnham, the newly elected Mayor of Greater Manchester. Not for the first time in my life, and especially lately, I think, 'What the hell am I doing here?'. Ian Lavery does a rip-roaring barnstormer of a speech and I get up and speak from the heart, a few words scribbled on a bit of A4, knees knocking, completely pretending to be someone who takes this shit in her stride. I talk about my pride in being part of a movement of people who give a toss about stuff and how we have thirty days to get on the right side of history and get the message into the homes, hearts and minds of people who have been disengaged from party politics for too long. Thirty days to stand up for what we believe; thirty days to save the NHS. I then welcome Jeremy Corbyn on stage as 'a man who has dedicated his life to giving a toss about other people'. He does a great speech. The response to him is as warm and riotous as always. Not that you'd ever know it from reading the papers, largely owned by a handful of right-wing media moguls.

Later when the video goes out on social media and the news sites I get a bit of flack on Twitter. I'm either a B- or a D- or a Z-list soap actress, depending on who is tweeting, and should stay out of politics and stick to my day job. I've never really understood that argument. Is it only politicians who are permitted to engage in politics? For me, this is a once-in-a-lifetime opportunity to have a government in power who want equality and peace, whose policies reflect my own deeply held principles. I have no hidden agenda. I have zero interest in a career in politics (I don't have a thick enough skin, for one) and sometimes my earnings put me in the higher tax bracket, so I would be someone required to pay *more* in tax if Labour got in.

Generally, though, people are lovely and appreciative of me sticking my head above the parapet without apology. I get a lot of messages that fill me with hope. And I hope I've helped embolden a few people. But there is a LOT of cortisol at large in my poor old body. These last couple of weeks have been an adrenaline-fuelled roller coaster and I need to keep my eye on not getting completely stressed out.

I get asked to go on Channel 4 News, but I want to be at home with my kids. I'm jumpy as hell. But very proud to have been asked to be part of today.

15 May

Becx's dad has passed away after a long illness. Bless her heart, she's still determined to carry on, business as normal, and turns up for an interview with an online magazine about our work at Hope Mill. I am grumpy because they want to film us and we weren't told in advance. I am a bit twatty, I think, and feel bad afterwards and buy loads of coffees to prove that I'm actually quite nice. Dick.

All three of us are feeling a bit beleaguered and unphotogenic for different reasons. It's a good interview, though: it's always a pleasure to talk about what we do because we love it and explaining it makes us feel good about what we've achieved. We then move straight into a good but slightly overwhelming meeting with the Artistic Director of Hope Mill, Joe Houston, and Sundae, a brilliant PR agency who have been charged with creating a funded piece of theatre for the Migration Lab.

The Migration Lab is a huge University of Manchester-funded research facility, but involving academics from all over the world. We've been drafted in to pull the facts and figures together and make some sort of immersive/installation experience over a few days in October. It's exciting. We can use our slot that we had reserved at Hope Mill for the sex work project and park that for now. That issue is going nowhere. Our experience at the Doughty Street Chambers taught us the very real impact of performance in terms of getting information across in an imaginative and engaging way. Migration and the refugee crisis are obviously topics we're very interested in anyway, and this will be an opportunity to pull some random ideas and inspiration together into something cohesive. Bringing humanity to the numbers.

As usual, Grant, with his visual art background, has tons of wonderful ideas to make beautiful images and projections about the movement of people all over the space. We'll hopefully integrate these with actual pieces of performance. We have a couple of days slated in June to meet with some of the academics at the forefront of the work.

16 May

More Take Back planning at the café at HOME in Manchester, where we revisit Becx's play and decide to cast only age-appropriate actors for the rehearsed readings over the week. We feel that the language and subject matter is so specific to a particular generation, the piece will lose some of its power if we cast older actors. We have enough great young actors in our community, we think. We set to planning a cast of four for each night's sharing with an eye, as always, on diversity. We also start to think about visual artists we can approach to provide an exhibition space around the subject after the performance and Q&A each evening of the run.

We also discuss the need to create a response to the upcoming election result (whether good or bad!). We decide to use the Monday night at Hope Mill after the election and, before *My Version of Events* starts on the Tuesday, to put on ten short commissioned plays written after the results come in and over the weekend. We choose ten writers who will have a unique take on the outcome and get in touch. Everyone is very keen and feels they'll need an outlet for the joy or (more likely, alas) the despair.

In the evening I go to the 53two space in town to see *JB Shorts*. *JB Shorts* started a few years ago now in the basement of the Joshua Brooks pub, primarily as an exercise for TV writers to flex their creative muscles and write some theatre. The template was six fifteen-minute plays on any subject at all, and years on, JB has become something of a Manchester institution. Kersh has a piece in this run, *JB Shorts 15*, called *Keep Breathing*, a hilarious two-hander starring the excellent Amy Drake as a spin class instructor ('Hacienda Spin! I say Whoop! You say Whoop Whoop!') who, in the course of the fifteen minutes, finds her mojo, dumps her horrible boyfriend *and* the spin class for proper cycling in the real world and a life of self-fulfillment. It's brilliant, a perfect JB, and goes down an absolute storm. As usual in Manchester, most of the audience and cast know each other, and the writers and directors are running the box office too, so there is a lovely party atmosphere in the bar afterwards.

18 May

To Liverpool with Mum for lunch at the Tate, a rainy run along the docks in the wheelchair and a matinee of *Billy Elliot*, possibly my favourite musical ever. What's not to love? It features cross-dressing little boys, the miners' strike, a whole number lampooning Thatcher and some of the finest set pieces ever known to theatre (Billy ballet-dancing amongst the riot shields, young Billy dancing and flying with his older self). I started crying from his first pirouette and have not a scrap of make-up on by the standing ovation. What a tonic. Political theatre on a grand scale.

21 May

Lemn Sissay's fiftieth birthday party in Manchester's beautiful King Street Townhouse, with drinks on a terrace overlooking the Town Hall as the sun sets, and speeches from some of his oldest and closest friends. A moment in our lives. How lucky I feel to be there celebrating that beautiful human being, to whom I now feel forever connected because of the experience we shared the other week at the Royal Court.

22 May

A day that Manchester and the world will never forget.

Kersh and Martha left in the car at teatime to go and eat in Manchester before going to see Ariana Grande perform at the Arena. Martha has loved Ariana since she was a young teenager and although she's now a bit of an indie kid, a piece of her heart will always belong to her first music love. So this was her Christmas present from us last year: fantastic tickets right at the front, within arm's reach of her heroine.

At 10.35pm Kersh rings me. Lyss is in bed; I'm catching up on *Corrie*. There's been a loud bang and a lot of panic at the gig. No one knows what's happening, but someone has been on stage and announced that there is no need for alarm: a huge balloon has popped next to a microphone apparently. Martha is upset because there is widespread panic, but nothing to worry about, they're on their way home. They've left the Arena and are walking to the car as they call. I idly check Twitter, which tells a very different story. There are rumours of people being injured from shrapnel from an exploding speaker, people have been hurt in the crush, there has been a bomb, there are widespread injuries. I tweet what Kersh has told me from inside the arena: nothing to worry about, it's a balloon. Kersh also tweets in an attempt to reassure people who are speculating. Loads of people retweet it.

By the time Kersh and Martha get home, it's clear that it is no balloon. The emergency services are out in force and, as we sit, shell-shocked, watching the rolling news, the true horror starts to unfold. A suicide bomber has walked into the foyer area where people were starting to leave and where parents were waiting for their children to come out, and has blown himself up. All three of us, and Kersh and Martha in particular, are struggling massively to come to terms with the narrative they thought was the truth as they left the concert, in spite of the mayhem around them, and the reality of the situation. It is immensely confusing and frightening.

A researcher from *Good Morning Britain* phones before my family even arrive home, having seen my tweets, asking me to go on and talk about it. I give him short shrift then feel bad.

We delete our earlier tweets and apologize, and are trolled by people who, for some unfathomable reason, think we've been making a sick joke, rather than reporting what had been told to the assembled audience. Martha is beside herself. She had questioned the veracity of it all the way home because of the sheer numbers of emergency vehicles and helicopters that appeared almost instantly, but Kersh had just believed what he'd been told, very possibly because he needed to in that moment. He has got them home safely and calmly because of it. But we go to bed knowing there have been fatalities. The true horror will fully emerge over the coming days.

22 May

There are twenty-two dead and many, many more injured. Martha sleeps until late, I ring school and tell them. The mothers of two of our neighbours' school friends are missing. The local GP and his wife and daughter are in hospital. The world is in shock. There is a vigil in Albert Square and Kersh and Martha bravely go in. I stay home with Lyss. It is packed in town, apparently. Tony Walsh, the fantastic Manchester poet, performs his piece 'This Is the Place' about our city, its people, music, history, invention and unbowed spirit. The video of his beautiful reading goes viral almost immediately. On the way to the vigil Kersh and Martha stop off to see the waitress at the restaurant they ate in last night, at HOME, who'd chatted to them about their plans for the rest of the evening. Kersh woke up thinking about her, guessing she'd have been worrying about them, knowing that they were there. She sees them as soon as they enter and runs across the restaurant to throw her arms around them in relief and gratitude. Not everyone was so lucky.

23 May

Martha goes back to school, but struggles. No one has the language to talk to her about what has happened. She feels bad for feeling so wretched when she knows she was incredibly lucky, not only to have got out alive and uninjured, but to have not witnessed the horror close up as so many did. She is throwing her energy into fundraising.

The tattoo artists of Manchester are donating funds from Manchester bee tattoos to the Emergency Fund for the victims, so Martha is buying henna to make temporary bee tattoos for children and young people.

I'm so proud of her. I go into town to record a monologue for *Music Week* on BBC Radio 3 about a deaf woman who begins to imagine she can hear music. It's a lovely piece and a welcome distraction.

Afterwards I go and see the flowers and tributes that are starting to fill St Ann's Square. It is a strangely disconnected and disconcerting experience as there are scores of TV crews and reporters there. Later I write this and post it on Facebook.

Things I saw in Manchester today

3 friends sharing lunch and stories on a bench in the sunshine.

A young suited man with eyes full of tears walking away from the huge tower of flowers in St Ann's Square.

A procession of town hall workers transporting armfuls of memorial bouquets from Albert Square to St Ann's.

A tiny little girl laying a bunch of Sweet Williams for me, then solemnly shaking my hand as I thanked her.

An elderly lady standing next to me, gently placing her hand on my back as I had a little cry.

Three no-nonsense lanyarded women handing out cakes to homeless people on Cross Street.

A young man in Waterstones with 'FREE HUGS' scrawled on a bit of cardboard around his neck getting a lesson in proper hugging ('come on, get in there!') from an older, more experienced hugger (me).

A gang of men in matching 'Fuck the Terror' T-shirts striding down Market Street.

Children chasing pigeons in the sunshine in Piccadilly Gardens, picnics, bubbles, ice-creams.

Everywhere, on every front page, the faces of the missing and the lost.

People smiling at each other in a sad, knowing, looking-out-for-each-other way.

Manchester, I've never loved you more.

28 May

Kersh, Martha, Lyss and I spend the day at Crosby Beach picnicking and watching the beautiful Antony Gormley statues emerge from the sea as the tide rolls back. It feels good to be at the coast. The two mums from our neighbours' school have been identified. They died in the blast waiting for their daughters in the foyer. All the names have been released now.

In the evening I go to Stockport where a vigil is taking place for Martyn Hett, one of the twenty-two victims of the attack: a huge *Corrie* fan, known to all of us in the cast because of his hilarious YouTube videos about his favourite characters. The park is packed and his friends and family line up to speak about their beloved life-loving, camp-as-Christmas, 'pain in the backside' Martyn, with breathtaking strength, dignity and love. #BeMoreMartyn is the theme of the event. Love life like he did, we're told by his mum, his dad, his stepdad, his partner; live it to the full, be yourself, don't apologize for who you are.

I went tonight because he loved *Corrie* so much. Someone had placed a Hayley mask, with a bee drawn on the cheek, at the foot of the life-size photo of him that formed the centerpiece of his 'shrine'. I thought he might have liked that I was there. A few of us from the cast and production had made it down, with the same thought. His boyfriend told me he would have loved it. But I got so, so much from being there. I'll never forget it as long as I live.

30 May

I feel completely out of the loop with everything else in my life apart from my family and the tragedy of last week. My *Peterloo* schedule has come in. I don't start until July. Two weeks' rehearsal, two weeks' shooting and two weeks on hold. I have to sign a confidentiality clause, saying I won't discuss anything about the project to anyone. Adam Penford, who is taking over Nottingham Playhouse, wants to meet me about a potentially exciting project next year. I finally have a date to meet 'the client' at the supermarket for the possible voiceover job this Friday. I've been asked to record a piece about my cultural highlights for *Front Row*, BBC Radio 4's arts programme, next week.

I meet with Becx, Grant and the director Matt Hassall to discuss our interview today for a supported scratch festival of work-in-progress at the Royal Exchange called Co:LAB. We'd put in a proposal a fortnight ago that was based around reactions and narratives surrounding an inciting incident. This no longer feels entirely appropriate because of last week. We cobble something together instead and meet producer Amy Clewes and associate artistic director Matthew Xia to discuss it. We discover, to our amazement, that we've come up with something rather exciting: a movement-based piece where the performance itself is the focus of false reporting, social media rumours and subjective cultural interpretation, that we can possibly develop further for the Migration Project piece, too. We have so much on at the moment, it won't be the end of the world if it doesn't work out, but it seemed to go well.

1 June

Steven Greenhalgh, the new UK rights director at Samuel French publishers, is up in Manchester to see *Persuasion* at the Exchange and has asked to meet Take Back to talk about our work and the possibility of publishing some of it. Becx and I meet him at HOME (Grant is working, doing his proper job, whatever that is) and he is very excited about what we do and would like to read *everything*. It still amazes us to be taken half seriously, so it's quite a thrill for us to have been even heard of further afield, let alone pursued in this way.

We all go to the press night of *Persuasion* in the evening, which is a completely bonkers imagining of it by Jeff James, complete with Spandex bikinis, actors sliding face-first through foam and a rave music soundtrack. It's bloody glorious and exhilarating, but will, I'm sure, be HATED by many. They've been having twenty to thirty walk-outs a night in previews, from Jane Austen purists and theatrical traditionalists no doubt. Wonderful.

2 June

A very early start and to London for my 'test' for the advert. I've never done a commercial casting before and it's a treat to be *paid* to attend and have my train ticket paid for, too. It's in a super-trendy advertising agency in a Soho mews and I'm shocked to see the number of people in attendance. There are six people squeezed into a tiny studio while I am in a glass booth, being instructed. *More familiar! More likeable! Cheekier! More over-the-garden-fence! More smiley!* They are actually very lovely, and the man in charge astonishes me on introduction by immediately announcing himself as virulently anti-Tory, and saying that he's got me in because of my Jeremy Corbyn speech. And there was I thinking that it might LOSE me work. Go figure. It works to be true to yourself, kids!

I love being in London. I'm re-reading Patti Smith so wander around kind of pretending to be her for a few hours, like a wanker, sitting outside the patisserie Maison Bertaux in the muggy sunshine drinking coffee and writing in my notebook. Bliss.

5 June

More horror unfolding this morning. Terrorist attacks in London – a van killing pedestrians on London Bridge and multiple stabbings.

It's the One Love concert with Ariana Grande at Old Trafford Cricket Ground this afternoon, and Kersh and Martha have been given free tickets because they were at the Arena last Monday. Inevitably the events in London will cast a long shadow over the day. Our children are growing up with this terror as the new norm. I can't process it at all.

6 June

Another whirlwind day trip to London. I've been asked by *Front Row* to record a piece for their new slot 'Hooked', where people talk about their cultural favourites. I do my entire interview about Manchester's artistic response to the Arena attack: the bee murals popping up all over; the spontaneous a capella outbreaks of Oasis's 'Don't Look Back in Anger', which has become the unofficial anthem for our grieving city; Tony Walsh's vigil poem, 'This Is the Place'; and Antoine Leiris' memoir, *You Will Not Have My Hate*, written after his wife was killed in the Paris shootings, which I returned to in the days after the tragedy at home.

In the afternoon, Kersh and I go to LAMDA, get a whirlwind tour of the super-duper new building (so posh and state of the art) by A J Quinn, the TV lecturer there, and see Rosa as the lead in Robert Holman's *Holes in the Skin*. She is just great in it.

8 June

General Election Day. I wake up early, sick with hope and worry, and go down to the train station in our village to leaflet and rally with my local Labour Party. Then later we join our MP and do a bit of heartening canvassing nearby, and on to our neighbouring constituency to leaflet outside another train station and have a cup of tea at the Glossop Labour Club. It feels like the world is out campaigning for Labour and there is a feeling of great positivity tempered by pragmatism.

We've been caught out before, but the exit polls come in at 10pm and the news is amazing. Labour have possibly gained many seats, not enough for a majority government, but enough to stop the Tories from increasing their majority (which was the point of Theresa May calling this election in the first place). Again, we're all wary. Exit polls have been devastatingly wrong before. But as the night unfolds (and I'm up until 4.30am) there are more and more surprises. Canterbury turns red. Amber Rudd, the Home Secretary,[3] demands a recount (she ultimately wins by literally a handful of votes), Labour steal Sheffield from Nick Clegg, the former leader of the Liberal Democrats. The mood among the Labour supporters online is jubilant. This is better than we could have imagined. Jeremy Corbyn wins his Islington seat with 40,000 votes and the turnout is high – higher than in years. By the morning it's clear that the Tories have scored a massive own goal, but more than that, everyone is forced to concede that Corbyn has mobilized and inspired young people to vote in their hundreds of thousands and that his campaign, on a socialist agenda, has been a massive success.

He's going nowhere as leader of Labour. We even win Kensington! For those of us who stuck by him throughout, there is a quiet sense of vindication. And it feels good.

---

[3] She resigns from this post in April 2018.

12 June

Frantic rehearsals begin for *Ten Takes on the Result*, Take Back's response to the election. Our ten writers have worked over the weekend and delivered on Sunday afternoon in time for us to cast, check availability and schedule rehearsals around people's day jobs and multi-casting.

Kersh and I have been at Raz Shaw's fiftieth in Rye at the weekend and I spent the half of the hungover journey home that I wasn't driving doing just that. As rapid responses go, this is as rapid as it comes I reckon.

We are so lucky to have the space at Hope Mill tonight as we set up for *My Version of Events*, which opens tomorrow. Becx, Grant and I run between Hope Studios where half the actors are rehearsing, and back to Hope Mill where we're teching the week's show. As soon as we're done we turn the space around. The set for *My Version of Events* is a simple rectangle with one row of chairs on four sides and four strip lights. *Ten Takes on the Result* is staged in proscenium on a raised platform at one end of the space, so lots of shifting furniture to be done.

We programme two showings, at 7pm and 9pm respectively, because the theatre is smaller than our normal capacity and the appetite for this response is large. Especially as Tony Walsh of the wonderful post-attack Manchester vigil poem, has written a new one for the election, commissioned by the *Guardian*, and has agreed to open for us. It is a brilliant piece about young people becoming engaged and crossing the line into changing the world. He's like a rock star now, is Tony. A neighbour's eleven-year-old comes to the 7pm show with her mum clutching a handwritten book of poems written in class, inspired by 'This Is the Place'. People line up afterwards to be photographed with Tony. It's wonderful. Poet as pop star. We talk a little bit about how his life has been turned upside down and how it's taking some getting used to. He's on the front of the *New Yorker* this week, for God's sake.

The *Ten Takes* that follow Tony's more than hold their own. There is a lovely rough-and-readiness to the makeshift stage and houselights, and Rupert Hill and his singing partner Liz Carney start us off with a beautiful duet, again about the kids making it all okay, called 'Turned Out Nice Again'. Sue McCormick is next with a clever and heartfelt play about how losing sometimes means winning, and how winners are not always right. And how right(-wing) is usually wrong. Sue is a committed activist and her voice being part of this means a lot to me. She is a comrade in the truest sense.

Lindsay Williams, one of our best and regular writers, has written 'Toppled', a super-clever sketch about a Tory bus coming off the road. Becx has written basically a love poem to everyone who stuck with Corbyn called 'A Little Story About Hope'. And Rosa, my niece, has written a fantastic poem called 'The Naughtiest Thing I Ever Did', a reference to the Prime Minister's awful election interview during which she was asked what was the naughtiest thing she ever did, to which she replied something along the lines of, 'Oh gosh, I ran through fields of wheat'. Four young female performers nail it and it brings the house down. Zoe Iqbal ends with a monologue, 'Blind Faith', about the inherent goodness of people that ends, 'Great Britain, I know you love me really. And I love you too, you daft cow'.

It is a wonderful warm night, full of love and laughter, and as usual there is a lively bar afterwards with many people saying how much they needed tonight after the craziness of the last week. It feels like a celebration. And at one point during the second show, I step outside myself for a moment and really acknowledge what we've created here in our city, and how we've almost inadvertently become a bit of an institution. I smile to myself indulgently like a proud nan.

At the end of the night we turn the space around again to get the set ready for tomorrow. Eight grey flats, constructed by Grant and his dad, surround the playing area and they weigh a ton.

13 June

Rehearsals for *My Version of Events* start. Noreen Kershaw meets the actors of the day, some of our favourite Take Backers, and works through the day in the space. Visual artists bob in and out with the pieces of art they've created for us to exhibit on the back of the flats and turn around in the interval. There is some brilliant and exciting stuff. A bed with rape statistics almost imperceptibly embroidered into the duvet cover. A demi-mannequin, legs apart, on a plinth, pasted with magazine images. A whole show of work by an art student from

Birmingham about sexual violence, including daubed slogans and disturbing, beautifully worked paintings.

The play goes down very well. It is beautifully written and very thought provoking. After the interval every night we will have a Q&A and discussion, and tonight we're joined by a worker from Trafford Rape Crisis. Becx facilitates and does really well, but it's very interesting to hear what people have taken from the reading. The definition of consent is very clear and we have it displayed on one of the exhibition boards, and Amy from the charity is also very clear: if a woman is too drunk to consent, it is rape. The mixed audience find this hard to accept. The play is very much designed to provoke debate and to explore the thornier issues around consent, but at times the conversation descends a little frustratingly into pub semantics: 'What if the *man* is too drunk to consent?' 'What if she'd said "yes" right up until the moment she became unconscious?' Lots of talk of *grey areas*. For me, when there is an expert in the field present, when someone works at the coalface of sexual violence every day and knows, *to the letter*, the laws surrounding consent, I like to shut up and listen to what she can teach me, you know?

We'll structure the discussion differently for the rest of the week. Great, though. This is what we do, start the conversations – even if they don't always go the way we'd like, or had maybe envisaged.

14 June

I have my Manchester bee tattoo. Clay, my talented tattoo artist, is an actor, fine artist and care-leaver. As with the other tattoo artists in Manchester, he is donating the proceeds to the fund for the survivors of the Arena attack and the families of the victims. We put the world to rights as he painstakingly reproduces a beautifully detailed worker bee onto the top of my left foot. I love it.

15 June

The Royal Exchange have offered Take Back a space for Co:LAB and maximum funding. We quickly put together a paragraph and a title for the publicity and decide on *Shooting the Messenger*. It will be a durational and immersive piece in the studio, and will give us an opportunity to develop some ideas for the Migration Project, too. I spend some time trying to put together a mash-up of previous Take Back shows to take to the RADA Festival and pull together a small cast to come with us to do two sharings. Actor availability is an issue, as is the relevance (now) of some of the pieces, but I get there in the end, settling on nine pieces to be performed by seven actors, incorporating the NHS, Brexit, Trump, the Election, war rape, immigration, porn and protest. There are, believe it or not, quite a few laughs in there, in spite of the subject matter.

I also finally engage with the 'workshop' we have with academics from the University of Manchester next week about the Migration Project we're to deliver at Hope Mill later in the year. We've been sent so much information that it's a bit daunting, but I find a way through and structure something around the specific areas of interest and expertise they have researched, finding examples of our work to support it, as examples of what we do. The idea is to show the amount of information a short piece of theatre can get across really. Then hopefully we can mine them for information and ideas, so we know specifically what they'd like us to explore as part of the project.

Martha is performing with the Young Company today and tomorrow in a great little project called *Table for Six*. The audience are seated at tables in the café in the Great Hall at the Exchange and actors from the company, dressed as waiters, hand out menus of six monologues written by members of the young company, which can be delivered in whatever order the 'customers' like. Then one of the young actors comes and performs it for your table. Martha has been working hard rehearsing her part as a young woman with Asperger's trying to find a relationship with God. She does really well, so assured and confident, holding our gaze, even as her little sister does bored faces and her grandma – not realizing Martha's in character – tries to chat to her.

Good showing of *My Version of Events* tonight, which I take my mum to see. Audiences have been pretty good, although we have struggled to sell it. I figure people think that the subject matter makes for a very heavy evening, but actually Becx's writing has a light touch and is full of detail and character. It's not graphic in content at all. But we have put a trigger warning on the publicity, so it may have scared people off.

There has been a terrible fire at Grenfell Tower, a high-rise in London's North Kensington. It looks as though many lives have been lost. The footage is just devastating.

16 June

I've been offered the advert voiceover. I'm relieved because I'm eating away at my saved *Broadchurch* tax money. I haven't really earned much since I finished filming in September. But I'm a bit uneasy, to be honest. I still feel a bit uncomfortable about advertising. I console myself by thinking of it as supplementing all the unpaid Take Back work, and promise myself that I'll donate a chunk to a food bank.

Noreen Kershaw isn't available to direct *My Version of Events* today so Esther Dix has stepped in. She doesn't want to use Nor's very specific choice of lighting state (just the four corners spotlit) preferring a general state for the actors to move about in. Cel Spellman is the perpetrator in today's 'version'. Cel is one of the loveliest men on earth. He played my son in the Channel 4 series *Cucumber*, but is also a Radio 1 DJ and TV presenter, and has a huge following (especially among the demographic we'd like to reach with this piece), so we're selling well tonight.

We leave Esther and the cast to it while we go over to The Edge Theatre and Arts Centre in Chorlton to unveil a plaque celebrating a new studio space. We are also there to see 'The Boothies', members of the Booth Centre which cares for homeless people/people with addictions. They are, under Janine Waters' direction, performing a show written specially for them, about an arts centre struggling to stay open during the Spanish Civil War. Ambitious and political stuff. They do absolutely brilliantly and revel in the adulation of the assembled local dignitaries and the Manchester theatre glitterati, taking it all in their collective stride. Several of them tell me afterwards that they never in a million years thought they'd be able to perform in front of an audience and what a life-changing experience being part of the group has been.

Tonight's show is fabulous. I really like Esther's take on the play and the slower pace brings out new things for me as an audience member. The cast are strong too. The Q&A is challenging again. But it's all part of the fun. The play is certainly making people talk and argue and look more closely at an issue around which there is still so much misinformation and confusion. It's clear to me that consent, and sex and relationships in general, should have a clear and essential space in our children's schooling.

Meanwhile, in London, the terrible fire at Grenfell Tower has exposed multiple local and national government failings: in the fire safety of the structure; the consistent failure to engage with the complaints and concerns of its (poor) residents; the closure of fire stations across the capital; and in the way in which the victims and survivors have been treated subsequently. There is talk of cover-ups and social cleansing, and tonight there was a mass demonstration where angry local people stormed the council offices in Kensington then marched to Downing Street, calling for an end to the government. Everything is changing. People have died in their scores, possibly hundreds. People are furious. Theresa May will surely have to go.

17 June

Can't be at Take Back today. As a family, we have a long-standing plan to go to London to see Kneehigh's production of *Tristan and Yseult* at The Globe. None of us has ever seen anything there before and it's a great experience. It's boiling hot, so thank God Kersh has got us seats in the balcony and not standing in the sun as groundlings (yeah, not *that* socialist, eh?). The show is classic Kneehigh: inventive, hilarious, full of music and dance, storytelling at its very best, and at the end Kersh and I are weeping, of course, much to the amusement of the girls. I would *love* to work with Kneehigh. The thought of being in Cornwall, living together as a company, creating a show and travelling the world with it completely appeals to the romantic in me. But, alas, I don't have any of the skills required to be part of it (clowning genius, musical talent, physical theatre experience) or indeed a life that could support that kind of wandering troubadour existence. Maybe Martha will do it and I can live it vicariously.

We even manage to get to the Tate for a bit afterwards. There's a room dedicated to art and politics, where I find brilliant quotations by Picasso and dissident Chinese artist Ai Weiwei about an artist's role as a political being; about participation in society being a human need, not an artistic choice; about artists being alive to events that require a whole-hearted response; that freedom of expression is inextricably linked to the beauty of life.

In New York, the outdoor theatre in Central Park is staging a version of Shakespeare's *Julius Caesar* that unapologetically casts an unmistakably Trump-like figure as Caesar. People are actually storming the stage and trying to stop the production because of the negative view of the President. The Right hate it when politics infiltrates their cosy notions of what art should be and do: the idea that artists should exist only to entertain the wealthy and give them a much-deserved night out amongst their own. In their view, we mustn't challenge their version of the world or question their privilege.

19 June

At the moment, I'm doing so much admin and producing for Take Back, which I enjoy immensely, but I need to make sure that I stay creative, too. With this in mind I've sent my one-woman show, *These I Love*, to Alison Vernon-Smith, who produces radio comedy. I wrote it after my dad died, and it's about my childhood and the unexpectedly beautiful poetry and diaries he left for us, spanning decades. I did a scratch performance of it a couple of years ago, in a little room above a pub in town, and had a bit of radio interest, but everyone at BBC Radio 4 seemed to want me to turn it into a drama, with scenes, when actually I think it needs to be performed as is, in front of an audience and recorded. A few people who saw the scratch night have mentioned it to me recently and it's spurred me on to pursue some sort of life for it again. It may come to nothing, but I'd like to do more with it.

Meanwhile, *Wit* has reared its head *again*. Raz, the director, is waiting to hear from Trafalgar Studios to see if they want to produce it. Whatever. I am so much fatter now and have so much hair, it will be like starting all over again. Which, of course, I will love. But I have to pretend I don't care so I won't be disappointed again. I know Raz feels the same.

20 June

A lovely offer has come in from Bill Buckhurst, a director I met at Raz's fiftieth last week: a small part in a film he's directing based on the

Richard Cameron play *Pond Life*. It's one day's filming but in stellar company: Siobhan Finneran, Sian Brookes and Sally Lindsay. It'll have to work around the other film, so fingers crossed. Mine is a tiny part (a couple of scenes) but it's a fantastic script, very much with the young people it's about at the heart of it. I'm up to play Angus Imrie's mum. Angus is on the two-year course at LAMDA and I saw him at the duologue showcase a few months ago. He is clearly very talented and a name to look out for.

22 June

We have an all-day workshop presentation with the Migration Lab and Sundae, the PR company in charge of the process of turning the research material into a piece of theatre. We all meet at Hope Studios along with Esther Dix, Zoe Iqbal and Hayley Cartwright, who have worked on a couple of pieces with us to give the examples of our work to the assembled academics and researchers from the University of Manchester. There's a bit of a strange and awkward atmosphere which makes me jumpy and inappropriately loud, making jokes that no one laughs at. I don't know whether everyone feels a bit nervous and uncertain in this alien environment but my God, they're a tough crowd.

I've spent some time reading through the various areas of interest to the Lab, and have found from our archive of shows a variety of scenes and recordings to support the research on borders, journeys, agency and home. We also show Grant's promotional film for our refugee immersive piece, *I Forget Your Name*, and play a couple of B!RTH tent recordings about journeying and displacement. Grant has created a mood board to illustrate an idea we've had for a dance piece in a black box space, with chalk line borders and boxes that the performer will break up during the movement. As usual I feel proud of the depth and scope of the work we've produced, and I feel like everyone is given a good taste of the kind of work we're interested in, from scenes and sketches to more installation-based projects. What the academics think of it all, I don't know.

As I introduce each section, with increasingly nervous desperation, Fiona and Tom from Sundae and the Take Back gang nod and grin enthusiastically from around the edges of the tiny airless rehearsal space to compensate for the rather inscrutable faces of our invited audience. Luckily, things warm up a bit in the afternoon when the conversation opens up to ask them all what they would most like us to explore in the piece and what they're most keen to convey to an audience of policy makers and punters. Some interesting ideas are discussed; we're particularly struck by the idea of a Hierarchy of Belonging, based on where one is from, how long you've been here, your social class, the colour of your skin, etc, and also the idea of personal borders: the moment when one consciously becomes a migrant because of poverty, war or perhaps the dream of a better life for one's family. We have plenty to work on and with. The Lab itself is keen for us to explore the macro/micro of migration, pulling out individual stories from the numbers, the data. Becx, Grant and I leave with our heads bursting, and luckily have a long drive to Hull Truck to discuss it all. We're seeing two of our favourite Take Back veterans, Danielle Henry and Olivia Sweeney (my one-time National Youth Theatre mentee), in *Mighty Atoms*, an all-female production about boxing. We make plans all the way there and back.

23 June

To London to do some more recording for the advert, finessing the 'test' I did earlier in the month and adding some pieces for a radio campaign. The boss, who I really like – the one who got me in because of my Corbyn speech (oh, the irony) – keeps taking the piss about how I can afford my 'new conservatory' now, which makes me squirm with embarrassment, but I front it out. The reality is that I can carry on doing a year's worth of Take Back shennanigins for free because of this one hour of 'work'. Crazy.

Looks like *Pond Life* is happening, too, as I get an email requesting my (ever-expanding) measurements.

24 June

A difficult and quite stressful morning. Take Back are taking part in the RADA Festival next week, at the request of Chris Lawson, one of our regular directors and a RADA graduate. As a project it's fallen off our radar a little bit. I programmed nine pieces for it from our back catalogue last week and approached some actors. One of our lovely regulars, Shila Iqbal, emails apologetically saying she has to film in her new sitcom next week and the dates clash, so we are an Asian actor short which impacts on a couple of specific pieces as well as on our diverse mix.

I have a difficult phone conversation with Chris during which it becomes apparent that we're all a bit out of sorts. It's a classic case of miscommunication – something I normally try to avoid at all costs, God damn it – but the pace of the last few weeks and the number of projects we've had on (as well as other work) has meant that we, as a company, have been hard to get hold of. Chris didn't want to push things and step on our toes, so had taken a step back. We interpreted this as him disengaging. Shit. I think everything is okay by the end of the call and he calls me a bit later to say he's found an ace actor to replace our Shila, and who is based in London. I create a playlist for between the scenes; he's organizing extra rehearsals for tomorrow in Manchester with the actors who are available. Horrible and tense though: Chris is a good mate to us as a company, and to me personally, and it's upsetting to have had such a tricky conversation. I think it's sorted though. Lessons learned on my part too. DEAL WITH THINGS AS THEY COME UP.

I go to see the band Elbow play in Dalby Forest with Kersh and our mates Al and Amy, and it is so good to drink pissy lager and dance and sing along and laugh ourselves to sleep in a campsite bunkhouse. I have felt a bit weighed down by duty and responsibility of late.

27 June

Oldham Coliseum with Kersh and mother-in-law, Joan, for a deeply affecting and beautifully designed production of *The Father* by Florian Zeller, translated by Christopher Hampton, about a man (played by Oldham legend Kenneth Alan Taylor) living with Alzheimer's. I've never quite seen anything like it. You experience the world entirely through the protagonist's eyes, so several actors come on as his daughter, her husband, a nurse, then change identities as pieces of furniture move or disappear between scenes. The result is disorientating, but incredibly clever. It feels like a brave and bold piece for this brilliant little theatre, and the audience are with it every step of the way. You can hear a pin drop.

At home we catch up on Jimmy McGovern's fantastic series, *Broken*, starring Sean Bean in a career-definer as a Catholic priest working in a poverty-stricken area of the North West. It's gruelling viewing, but completely of the moment, and as beautifully shot as you could ever hope to see on British telly.

Martha comes home from her last session with the Young Company and is not in a good way. The incident at the Arena has taken its toll on her; delayed shock perhaps. I am not going to go to RADA with Take Back; I'm needed here.

29 June

The last couple of days have been exhausting and hard. The four of us take the train into town for the opening of the Manchester International Festival (MIF). The conceptual artist Jeremy Deller has made an installation called *What Is the City but the People?* – a giant catwalk bookended by huge screens in Piccadilly Gardens, down which Mancunians parade as their photos and stories appear on screen. I don't really want to go; I don't feel like doing anything apart from being at home, but it's good to be with all the family and the event is absolutely wonderful, so thank God I didn't miss it. Lemn Sissay is here in his full university chancellor's robes. Bez from the band Happy Mondays dances around him. There are singers, councillors, bakers, dog-walkers, cyclists, florists, refugees, homeless people, a couple on a blind date (!), a pair who run a food bank from the boot of their car, a Muslim taxi driver who turned off his meter on the night of the Arena bombing and worked all night taking people to safety. It is an absolute spectacle and one of the most life-affirming pieces of art I've ever seen. For the first time in days the rain stops. Manchester is out in force. We opt out of the opening party to be with our children. At the moment being together feels like the most blessed thing in the world.

The show at RADA goes well apparently, although one of our actors has been struck down with food poisoning and has had to be replaced. I feel terribly guilty for not being there. I feel a bit shit about everything at the moment. Wracked with all sorts of things. And quite unmotivated. First bit of filming next week for *Peterloo*. Don't feel ready.

1 July

I take Martha and a couple of her friends to see the first preview of *Fatherland* at the Royal Exchange, part of the MIF. My old mate from Accrington and LAMDA, Joe Alessi, is in it and I'm looking forward to it. It's a collaboration about fatherhood between writer Simon Stephens, Frantic Assembly's Scott Graham and Underworld's Karl Hyde. Simon Stephens wrote about its inception in his working diary three years ago, so it's been a long time in the planning.

Everyone is furious with me for being there on the first preview. But I'm a good audience, and I love the seat-of-pants edginess of early showings. In lots of ways it's a glorious piece of theatre; Karl's music is heart-stopping in places; the actors are ACE (especially Joe); it looks beautiful; there are moments, set pieces, that really work; and it carries you along as a theatrical experience, for sure. But there are troubling things about it for me. The fact that it features a huge cast of men, with no women, and an overwhelmingly male, white creative team, seems almost too obvious to mention. In an era when the battle for 50:50 representation for women actors is at full whack, it feels, well, *weird* to be watching something so man-heavy.

But more problematic (and it pains me to say it because I love everyone involved) is what I felt was the narrow scope of the stories about fathers (and sons) they've chosen to tell. There are two fantastic black actors in the cast in leading roles, but it is really obvious to me that the verbatim testimonies they're performing are from white men. You can't, surely, tell exclusively white stories, then cast a couple of black actors and think that that's diversity sorted? Three actors in the piece play Simon, Scott and Karl and are questioned and challenged by a made-up character throughout: about why they're making the piece, how exploitative or self-indulgent it is. Who is it for? It's a clever device that allows for self-deprecation, but he doesn't ask some of the questions many of the audience will have: why no women? Why such a limited scope of stories? I couldn't help but think of all the stories I would have loved to have heard – sons of fathers who have transitioned, children of armed forces dads, gay sons of Muslim patriarchs, macho dads of disabled kids . . . The show ends up being about men's difficulties in communicating with their kids and dads, and about forgiveness of shit fathering. Which is all great, but I feel it could have been so much more. I acknowledge that that would have been a different play, and not the one that this team wanted to make, so that's a bit unfair on my part. We can all think of what we'd prefer to have seen after the event.

Good, though, to feel alive with the questions and conversations around it. Which means a worthwhile night at the theatre, I reckon.

6 July

The first day of filming for Mike Leigh's *Peterloo* in Lincoln.

I am working with a fantastic bunch of women. We are bonneted and clogged and striding the cobbled hilly streets of Lincoln shouting for 'universal suffrage!' and 'liberty or death!' It causes quite a sensation in the town, and the crowds of bystanders film our every move on their smartphones, even as we all stand wafting our many-layered skirts, legs astride, trying to get some air up there. It is boiling. Which is lucky really, as 16 August 1819 was a famously hot day. We finish much earlier than expected so I manage to get home.

7 July

What if Women Ruled the World? at the MIF. Vicky Featherstone directing, an ensemble of actresses, plus six female experts in their field. The focal point is the Doomsday Clock, an imagined concept involving a team of people in the know citing how close to midnight (the end of the world basically) we are at any given point in history. So, for example, we were five minutes to midnight during the Cold War, the Cuban Missile Crisis and the Arms Race of the 1980s. We're *two and a half* minutes to midnight now, unsurprisingly. It's a great piece: the performers are perfect, the space is immense (the disused Mayfield train depot at Piccadilly Station, now a vast warehouse), the sound design is epic. Tonight's experts include a psychotherapist and campaigner against female genital mutilation (FGM), a UN human rights lawyer and an Afghan education activist. The premise is that after a nuclear attack, women now outnumber men five to one, so we have the power. We have three minutes to turn the clock back and save the world: how can we do things differently? Tonight's panel decide: by promoting equality with men; not exacting revenge; by banning all nuclear weapons; educating all our children creatively; ending neo-liberalism and the celebration of greed; calling out FGM as child sexual abuse, not cultural practice. I love it. Some audiences have struggled with the merging of theatre with discussion, and this conceit was a bit hit-and-miss at times, but this is why I love MIF. It's a bold experiment. I can actually feel my mind broadening as I wallow in the privilege of listening to all these incredible women. I don't think I love anything more than hearing people talking in a passionate and informed way about their area of expertise.

13 July

Another MIF: seeing the legendary Manchester band New Order at the old Granada Studios. It's funny to be back at Stage One, my *Coronation Street* home for so many years, and I have an experience verging on the spiritual in there. The band are being supported by a twelve-part synthesizer ensemble from the Royal Northern College of Music, all in rows of lit 'windows' high behind the stage, and conducted by Joe Duddell. After the stress of the last few weeks, there is a moment when I'm watching the band and I'm dancing and I feel completely at home, in my body, in the space, in the lovely crowd. Just fantastic.

14 July

The last day of MIF and also of the Greater Manchester Fringe, which I've not really been able to support with everything that's been going on. But Rosie Fleeshman, one of our Take Backers, is performing her one-woman play, *Narcissist in the Mirror*, at the little space above the King's Arms pub in Salford. Noreen is there, with musician Noddy Holder. The Fleeshmans are quite a legendary Manchester family, all actors, and

Manchester has turned out to support Rosie and the director, her mum, Sue Jenkins. We have brought Martha with us and it is the most perfect choice of piece for her to see right now. Rosie is only twenty-three and has turned some of the struggles and challenges in her life into a funny, moving and honest epic performance poem covering the need for attention and love, acting, dating, sex, mental health, loneliness and narcissism. It is an incredibly accomplished and gripping piece of work and she gets a well-deserved standing ovation at the end. Martha is beaming throughout; it is completely speaking to her and I hope inspiring her. Afterwards Rosie tells me that it was performing in *Take Back America* in January that gave her the confidence to write and perform the show, and to see herself as a maker rather than an unemployed actor. Marvellous. That we are helping people find their voice, as a by-product of what we do, is just music to my ears.

Afterwards we meet Joe and fellow *Fatherland* actor Nick Holder who dash over after their show to the Mayfield Depot again, this time to see *10,000 Gestures*, an astonishing and experimental piece choreographed by Boris Charmatz, involving twenty-five dancers in the vast warehouse space performing 10,000 human gestures in an hour, with no single movement repeated. At one point they climb into and over the audience. A woman dressed as a ninja sits astride me and breathes into my ear. We're all close to tears at the end: I can't really explain why – it's not a rational thing, it's visceral – and again I'm so glad that Martha has had the opportunity to witness such beauty and talent. This festival has broadened all our minds and hearts.

We have received full Arts Council funding for Kersh's *Greatest Play in the History of the World*, thanks to a perfect application by Raz and Ric Watts at the Exchange. This is great news and means that we can have our dream creative team to design and light it, as well as create a score for it. Exciting.

16 July

Jodie Whittaker, my mate from *Broadchurch*, has broken the internet. She is the new Doctor in *Doctor Who*, the thirteenth, and the first woman to ever play the part. It is the BEST news. She is so ace and hilariously funny. The vast majority of people, it seems, are over the moon, but a handful of online commentators are upset. Apparently a time-travelling Doctor with two hearts who regenerates every couple of years into a different body can't possibly be a woman. Because that would be preposterous.

17 July

We are now in Kent with *Peterloo*, rehearsing and filming the first meeting of the Manchester Female Reform Society. We're all pretty nervous, and when Mike takes Dorothy and Vic off to rehearse their 'addresses', the remaining four of us are palpably relieved to have been given a stay of execution for a couple more hours. Honestly, I don't know what it is, possibly the element of the unknown in this process, but we're all shitting it. We will be filming in a beautiful (and cool) room that is part of the historic ropery at Chatham Docks, and, when the time finally arrives, we are trussed up in our corsets and clogs to rehearse there.

We walk around on our own outside for a little bit, at Mike's instruction, to get into character – 'warming up', as he calls it – then come in and start improvising. When we film, there will be scores of supporting artists amongst us too, so it's a little forced and unnatural at first.

Dorothy and Vic are fantastic as the president and secretary respectively, delivering their speeches with passion and conviction when the moment comes. I feel compelled to say things as my character, but really because I feel I ought to, to look like I'm doing something. Afterwards, Mike basically tells me that I'm shoehorning my character's agenda into the scene rather than just being there in character, and he's right. So when we do it again, I don't say anything. My character, the way I've created her, just wouldn't. Perhaps I should be worrying about the fact that I'm not really going to be in this film much at all, but honestly, I feel so glad to be a part of it and it's fine.

After lunch, the sparks start lighting the room so we reconvene, rather incongruously, in a wedding marquee in the grounds. It is hilariously hot. Mike works and works the speaking actors and finesses and fine-tunes the lines, making sure the dialogue is on point, dialect and era-appropriate. Caroline, the second assistant director (AD), types it up as we work, until we have a fixed scene. It's fascinating to watch the process: from improvised generalizations to a set scene, with all the necessary ideas in there, and no extra flabbiness. We all feel the need for a glass of wine afterwards and go to a nice pub where we get pissed, talk non-stop and kill ourselves laughing about the day and how we were all moments from keeling over in the heat. I am having such a good time. What a joy to be working with these women.

19 July

Mike Leigh's energy is something to behold. It's not a sparky, quicksilvered momentum in any way, but a deep focus and ability to keep going for hours and days and weeks at a time. Often after a day's filming, as well as prepping for the next day, he'll rehearse with the next batch of actors. After a couple of hours, we're all ready to drop. It's intense in every way: the heat, the sheer volume of people in the room, from the huge crew to the seven of us and the 60+ supporting artists (who are brilliant, it has to be said). Mike is seventy-four. It just shows what doing a job you love does for a person's spirit and longevity. It's a long day's filming, but I enjoy myself watching the process, positively revelling in the talent of my new mates who do the meeting scene at least fifteen times and never drop the ball once. Poor Chrissy is really ill, has been sick all night and is an absolute hero. I don't know how she keeps going. In any other job, she'd have been sent home for sure. Vic's ankle is bandaged up after an old injury came and got her at the weekend and she just gets on with it uncomplainingly, jumping to her feet to deliver her incredibly complicated speech over and over. The supporting artists are a sparky and instinctive bunch, and take the piss out of me for not having any lines ('You're one of us!') and for needing so much attention from wigs and make-up before my one shot of the day. My wig has drooped, my bonnet has drooped, my make-up has all but slid off and I have to be almost completely redone.

20 July

Back home and I'm going to see the National Theatre Live screening of *Angels in America: Part One* at the cinema at HOME.

NT Live is such a brilliant thing: it gives audiences all over the country the opportunity to see some of the very best theatre around. *Angels* has completely sold out at the National Theatre – tickets are like gold dust – so how wonderful to be able to watch it in the cinema. Part One, *Millennium Approaches,* runs at three hours forty minutes with two intervals, and next week is Part Two, *Perestroika*, which runs at about four hours twenty. It flies by. It is just a perfect piece of work, a bloody masterpiece. Every line matters. Every actor is outstanding. The staging is beautiful, the sound heartstopping. I feel sick with jealousy. I would give anything to be in a show like this.

21 July

I get an urgent message from my agent saying that the supermarket need me to get to a studio as soon as possible, within the next few hours, to re-record *a word* from the commercial voiceovers. I drive over to the Sharp Project, the huge creative office and production space in Manchester. I meet the engineer who bustles me into a booth, where I spend ten minutes (with the London creatives directing me down the line) changing the phrase 'good value' to 'great value'. Bonkers.

24 July

Kersh texts me as I'm on the way to Doncaster for my one day on the film *Pond Life*. He's read an interview with the actor/director Paddy Considine who has said something that strikes a chord with both of us: that there are three types of job – one for the wallet, one for the CV, one for yourself. The voiceover is definitely for the wallet and today is for me. I have a tiny part in the film as a mum, ghosting around the outskirts of the lives of the young people the script focusses on. And it is a beautiful script. Angus Imrie, a friend of Rosa's from LAMDA, is playing my son, and he is not only brilliant but completely lovely. It's the last week of filming and he has won everyone's hearts. As usual, it's high glamour for me in the costume department in a too-tight denim skirt, short leggings and a sad T-shirt. The film is set in an ex-mining community in 1994. I realize that I have basically had the same hair since 1994 apart from the brief *Wit* bald period, which works out well but is a bit embarrassing. Equity come to visit the actors at lunchtime and, as usual, I'm shocked that some of the cast aren't members of the union.

I don't think that a lot of people realize that all our contracts, our pay, our insurance, our breaks, are Equity-negotiated. We *are* the union. It stops us from being exploited and from working in unsafe conditions, and their unbelievably great pension scheme means they pay out a pound for every 50p we contribute. It's not unusual for young people not to even know what a trade union is, which is a bit depressing.

I can't emphasize enough to all actors the importance of becoming a member and paying your dues. You will get it back a hundred-fold in worker rights, peace of mind, decent pay and protection from exploitation. The more of us who are members, the stronger the union is.

Filming goes well. I find it a bit hard when I have so little to do. I just have to trust that I'm playing the truth of it. I did all the work: gave her a backstory, etc. I don't know what else I can do really. The producer, Rienkje Attoh, drives me back to the station at the end of the day and I ask her about her upcoming projects, and she tells me about a kind of docu-drama she's making with Baby Cow Productions about Lemn Sissay. 'Do you know Lemn?', she asks. Hilariously, it turns out she saw *The Report* at the Royal Court but had no clue that it was me on stage with him (hair brown at the time, glasses on). Ha! Master of disguise. I tell her that I'd love to be involved in this project if there's anything I can do in it. Lemn is becoming the Kevin Bacon of my life: six degrees of separation between everyone in the *world* via him.

My Facebook timeline is full of excitement today about Michelle Terry becoming Artistic Director at Shakespeare's Globe. I don't know Michelle, but she's an actor as well as a director and I know loads of people who have worked with her and love her. Everyone seems to think it's very good news.

There's also a massive stink that rumbles on about gender inequality in BBC pay. The top earners' salaries were published last week and the disparity is completely shocking. The *Strictly* presenter Claudia Winkleman is the highest female earner on £450,000, which is a *quarter* of what the highest male earner, Chris Evans, brings in. Twenty high-profile female BBC employees have written an open letter to Tony Hall, the Director-General of the BBC, to demand equity. Meanwhile, the controversy over a female Doctor Who continues with much hand-wringing about loss of male role models for boys. As someone who has sat through many an action blockbuster with my two daughters I can say with some authority that the lads are doing okay for onscreen representation. Bloody hell. We are 50 per cent of the population. That the casting of a woman is being branded in some quarters as 'political correctness gone mad' is just crazy. It's a shocker that we're still having these conversations in 2017.

27 July

I have been procrastinating wildly about knuckling down to line-learning for *The Greatest Play in the History of the World*. Every day I wake up with a plan to spend an hour on it and every day I do every other feasible job on my list first, until I run out of time. November is a distant elephant, but it will be here in the wink of an eye, I know this! So today I will drag myself away from important Facebook business and get on with it.

The most commonly asked question of any actor seems to be, 'How do you learn all those lines?' When you're in a soap you get pretty good at it, just through necessity. Sometimes you have twenty pages to film the next day, so it's a matter of giving yourself enough time to familiarize yourself with the dialogue in the days preceding so the task is less daunting when the clock is on. There are people on *Corrie* with photographic memories, so they can literally pick up the pages on the day and wing their way through: it's a kind of genius. Certainly, during my years there my short-term memory became super-developed (possibly at the expense of the rest of my poor brain). I could almost see the words on the page as I said them on set, to the point where if we got a rewrite and my lines were in different places on the page it would completely throw me. For theatre, I think you use a completely different part of the brain. The lines need to be absorbed to a level at which they become part of you, so that when you're performing you can be free to be properly in the moment. I am hyper-aware that in even writing about this I'm on the edge of wankiness, but I do think that's true. Sometimes, and it's only really rarely for me, I can feel so free with the dialogue that something happens that allows me to be completely in the scene and things can happen that are unplanned and spontaneous but absolutely of the moment. I wonder if really great actors are in that zone all the time, and the rest of us dip our toes into it occasionally.

A lot of the time, I can be acting away but also noticing the yawning elderly man two rows back or how I didn't quite hit the timing of that little exchange, damn it. I'm fascinated by the number of levels on which the brain seems to operate simultaneously. Desperately attempting to remain engaged and in character the other day, for example, rehearsing the scene with Mike Leigh in the boiling hot marquee, I seemed to be able to listen to every word my fellow actors said (to the point of almost knowing their lines), react (I hope) appropriately, whilst at the same time running a constant internal monologue that took in the bluest-blue of Dorothy's eyes and Vic's poor ankle; noted with admiration Chrissy's fierceness; pondered whether this kind of sweating did you good like sauna sweating and if I was ridding myself of toxins as I sat in my many layers of costume; clocked the tantalizing supply of water on the other side of the space and how thirsty I was, knowing I hadn't really done enough to warrant getting up and getting a bottle. Would anyone have been able to tell that these were my musings in that moment? I'm not sure.

Suffice to say that this fulsome entry on line-learning has been a welcome distraction from, yep, line-learning. The only way to learn lines is to work through them, bit by bit, going back over yourself and doing whole sections at a time, until they're in. Get on with it. You've just got to do it. I don't think there are any shortcuts, however many apps they invent. I find it easiest when I'm out walking the dog.

And speaking of lines, how on earth did the cast of *Angels in America* do it? Seven hours of performance. We see the second half tonight, four hours of it, NT Live at the cinema again, and we leave feeling like this is surely one of the greatest plays ever written. Every member of the cast is brilliant too. When I did *Wit* I had a lot of dialogue and was on stage the whole time. I started learning it in April to begin rehearsals in December. And I got a lot of credit for learning those lines. And a lot of (welcome, but misplaced) sympathy for putting myself through that performance every night: pain, death, and especially getting naked at the end. That play was an hour and a quarter long. Andrew Garfield as Prior in *Angels in America* puts himself through what I can only describe as an emotional wringer throughout the entire seven hours of the two parts. He physically contorts in pain, weeps and screams and loses it and dies and lives again and talks and talks and *feels* every second. The others aren't far behind either in terms of what their characters go through throughout the course of the show. It makes me feel like a total rookie. And watching Denise Gough and Susan Brown almost makes me want to give up, they're so, so damned good. I mean, what's the point? I could die happy, just having seen this production of this play. It's perfect.

Now get on with your line-learning, you dick.

Oh, and while I'm at it:

All the cast of *Angels in America* were beaming at the end as they came on for their bows. I CAN'T STAND IT WHEN ACTORS SIGNAL TO YOU HOW EXHAUSTED THEY ARE, HOW HARD THEY'VE WORKED, IN THE CURTAIN CALL. You know what I'm talking about. Stop it. Smile and be gracious. I always spot the ones who are gracious and graceful and grateful for the applause.

31 July

Tax day.

My advice to any actor is, for God's sake, educate yourself about tax. Get a pension through Equity and, if you can afford it, get a good accountant (rather than a dodgy one). You must always put aside a percentage of your earnings for your income tax payment at the end of January, *plus* extra for the advance payment on the year ahead, and then another advance payment at the end of July. So it's always more than you think because you're paying ahead too. *And pay your taxes proudly and fully*. Remember the MPs' expenses scandal? We were all outraged by all the stuff that had been offset against their tax (famously a duck house and a moat, as I recall). There are all sorts of ways you can reduce the tax you pay and most of them are legal, but what is *legal* and what is *morally correct* are sometimes two different things. Taxes are what build schools and hospitals and roads. Do the right thing. Be part of the culture shift that says, 'I am PROUD to pay my tax fully and on time'. This country loses billions to tax evasion every year, a massive amount in comparison to what we lose in, for example, benefit fraud (FACT: check it out). Be one of the good 'uns.

Having said all this, my fantastic socialist accountant (seriously: how wonderful – and, let's face it, unlikely – is that?) rang me today with my bill for next January and it is pretty eye-watering for a little girl from Accrington. I promise I'm not telling you this to show off. I had a good year last year (April 2016–April 2017) because of *Broadchurch*, but I've earned, ahem, significantly less since then. That's a freelance life for you. I've been dipping into my tax money to buy food and pay bills etc, waiting to be paid for the supermarket voiceover, but I'll definitely have the balance by January, plus the advance. I understand that some people think it's inappropriate or vulgar to talk about money and it's a hugely sensitive subject, I know. But honestly, it's so easy to think you're loaded when you've got a nice job, but sometimes that money has to seriously last you, and you HAVE to proudly pay a big chunk to keep our society on its feet. So, as ever, as a veteran knobhead who took years to get my head around this stuff, PLEASE, don't be a knobhead. There's nothing romantic or artistic about being shite with money and getting bollocked by an HMRC employee, I assure you. It's terrifying when you can't pay. These people are like trained assassins. Don't say I didn't warn you.

In other news, I am practising what I preach and have learnt seven pages of *The Greatest Play*. Well done me for doing my job.

Rosa has graduated from LAMDA and has an agent, an audition for a Channel 4 comedy pilot and a recall for a theatre tour.

Martha has gone to London to do her fortnight with the National Youth Theatre (NYT). Kersh took her down and settled her in to her halls of residence (I'm banned because she doesn't like people recognizing me and connecting her to me, sob). He brilliantly found a gaggle of girls in the next room, invited them all out for some tea and they jumped at the chance and were absolutely lovely. So he has left her with new friends and a fridge in her tiny room, nervous but happy. We are now listening to Joni Mitchell in our kitchen, drinking wine and weeping.

2 August

I'm in London with Lyss having some us-time while Kersh writes *Eastenders*, and Martha is at the NYT. We are seeing our mate Sara Poyzer play Donna in *Mamma Mia!* in the West End, for, I think, the fifth time. I love this show. And Sara is so sensationally good in it. I weep with pride every time I see her sing 'The Winner Takes it All'. There is more than enough room in my heart for this kind of unapologetic theatre joy. It is irresistible. I challenge you to resist. Thrillingly, Sara is also writing a book (provisional title: *Here I Go Again: Mamma Mia and Me* – bloody brilliant). It's about her four plus years travelling the world with the show, offering a real insight into the universe of the touring actor: keeping it fresh; staying well mentally, vocally, physically; keeping your relationships healthy (her husband, Richard Standing, played her onstage lover, Sam, until a couple of months ago); staying alive creatively. And still enjoying it. After FOUR YEARS. Also the wild variations in audience reaction from South Korea to Dublin to Tel Aviv, and the politics of all those places too. As seen from the viewpoint of a visiting performer.

Lyss and I also go to *Shrek's Adventure!* in County Hall on the South Bank: a celebration of the much-loved DreamWorks film and franchise. I spend about £1 million on photographs and light-up Donkey ears. I positively revel in the brilliant actors' performances in the 'live action' bits as we move around the space, just nailing it as a narcoleptic Sleeping Beauty, a dozy torturer, a Sloaney Cinders and Princess Fiona herself. I can only imagine the ultra-competitive casting process to be part of this. It was the same back in my day with the Museum of the Moving Image (MOMI) where newly graduated actors would be dragged over the casting coals to play Eisensteinian Russian revolutionaries and silent movie stars. It would have been easier to get a part in an actual Eisenstein film, I reckon. The quality of the performers is so high, it makes me realize (again) how many brilliant actors there are out there.

I have had friends (and I think this is a rare thing) who have literally lost their homes because of a dogged determination to only work as an artist, to be paid only for what they have trained hard to do. As I have previously discussed I was lucky enough to be involved in Arts Threshold for many years, while the benefits system supported me, but I've also worked as a (bad) cleaner, a (usually drunk) bartender, a (shortlived) street cleaner in Wembley, a children's entertainer and face-painter at the Chicago Pizza Pie Factory (how I got my Equity card, as part of Variety Equity no less!) and in PR, God help us all.

As an actor, you will most likely have to take work other than acting gigs. Just try to find something that gives you a bit of flexibility and time off for auditions. You might be better working in a café than acting in something like *Shrek's Adventure!* if the people who employ you are more willing to let you go for meetings (I don't know if this is true, I'm just using that as a hypothetical example). A lot of people who want to be actors ask me about extra work, and I don't know how to advise really. It's such a different world as a supporting artist, and I think the days are gone when you could be plucked from the background and given a leading role, as happened to the late Bill Tarmey, my wonderful *Coronation Street* colleague, all those years ago when he was chosen to play the legendary character Jack Duckworth.

As I may have mentioned before (as much to remind myself as anything else), the important thing is to stay active, stay creative, fill your well. Surround yourself with people who are making and doing and not whinging about how no one is giving them the chance to make and do. Both types can be found in any job.

3 August

Tricky email exchange with the makers of *The Acting Class*, a soon-to-be released documentary about working-class access to the profession. Maxine Peake, Chris Eccleston and I were all interviewed for it, amongst others, and it is already getting quite a lot of interest and coverage, which is great. The problem is that I don't like the trailer. Which has stopped me from sharing it on social media. I feel the need to explain to them that I'll support them however I can in promoting the film on its release (Q&As, etc), but I just don't feel comfortable sharing the trailer, which begins with what I feel is a quite mean-spirited slow motion montage of the privately-educated Damian Lewis, Benedict Cumberbatch and Eddie Redmayne triumphantly collecting various awards – the purpose being to highlight how these posh actors are taking over the world, I suppose. I feel that to focus on them is to be divisive and leave us open to accusations of sour grapes, which can only be counterproductive. They are no more to blame for their background and life circumstances than I am. I feel it's too personal, too them-and-us and I don't like it.

Dee and Mike from Inside Film get back to me straight away to reassure me (there's even a bit in the film where I talk about my mates from drama school who were Etonians, and how ace they were/are), but I think they think I'm worried about the documentary itself. I'm not. I just need them to know why their constant bids to get me to share the trailer on Twitter have been left unanswered. The way we conduct ourselves as we have these important conversations is crucial, I think.

4 August

Team Take Back reunion at The Koffee Pot. It feels great to be back with Becx and Grant, making plans and organizing upcoming projects. We start by having a debrief about *Shooting the Messenger*, the Co:LAB experiment about fake news that took place at the Royal Exchange a couple of Saturdays ago. I couldn't be involved because I was at a friend's wedding, but Kersh and the kids went along for an hour. I think the project was bold and definitely experimental, and not to everyone's taste. It was a durational piece lasting over three hours so much depended on at which point you dropped in, too. Kersh and Martha had been a bit perplexed as to the politics of it all, and I was slightly concerned that the theme had got lost in some of the theatrical madness: Sandra watching the action on a screen in her pyjamas in the studio foyer, Yandass dancing for the entire period in a chalked box, Becx writing news stories from left and right perspectives, Gemma and Charlotte live-tweeting, Olivia and Will acting as security guards. Judging from the feedback in the days that followed, some people really got it and some people had found it unclear and confusing. Everyone had decided that Yandass was a refugee being 'held', which was interesting as that was never stated. Some people chalked messages and pictures in the space, some just stayed and watched onscreen with Sandra in the foyer and discussed immigration and race and some audience members got a bit over-involved and lairy, taking on the 'security guards' to the point where Olivia had to ask them to leave, have a cup of tea and calm down. People endlessly tried to engage with Yandass, which was heartening. Our conclusion: an exhausting experiment, successful in parts, from which we can take a few things into our next projects.

Our most pressing job is to firm up plans for the big symposium at the University of Salford at the end of August (again, in my absence, as I'm filming). We need *Ten Takes on Protest*, a selection taken from our previous shows, and a cast to perform them. We're also erecting the tent that featured in the B!RTH festival. Then there's the Tory Party conference in the autumn. Rather than the original plan of a durational piece, we opt for a *Ten Takes on Resistance*, to be performed, we hope, at Central Methodist Hall, where we started out nearly two years ago at the last Tory Party conference. It will hopefully serve as a celebration of how far we've come since then, too. I barely knew Becx back then and met Grant that evening when he came to film the show. My job tomorrow is to recruit ten writers in the first instance. We'll hopefully do the show on Monday 2 October, the day after the huge demonstration in town.

We also talk about the structure of the Migration Project, which we're thinking of calling *The Hierarchy of Belonging*. We need to know exactly how much money we're being given from the Lab at the University of Manchester first, before we can properly plan, as it affects how many actors we can use and how many pieces of installation etc. We have a good idea of what we want to do, though, converting the theatre space at Hope Mill into a warehouse with cardboard boxes and pallets and suitcases, and with a mixture of art, film, audio and live performance. The centrepiece will be a film of Yandass dancing in a chalked grid, until she is covered in chalk (as trialed at Co:LAB) as we play audio of social-media comments about refugees that Tom at Sundae PR has collated for us already. We think we'll ask the Young Company at the Royal Exchange to record these for us. We're thinking we might get away with using only two actors, which means we can pay them properly hopefully. I'll be rehearsing *Greatest Play* at the same time so, again, my involvement will be a bit limited. But there's plenty I can do in the run up for sure. We have an idea to have a box of mobile phones in the space, ringing, and when you pick one up, you listen to a recorded audio monologue about crossing borders. I will again get on to recruiting writers and actors for that. I'm excited!

5 August

Two things catch my eye on Facebook. Alan Cox, my old LAMDA mate, shares a brilliant interview with the actor and former Doctor Who Tom Baker, who talks about his disastrous run as Macbeth in a production at the Shaw Theatre. He brilliantly describes how he was so awful that the children in the audience would throw sweets at him, and he would actually be booed off in the curtain call. I love him for telling the story and I love how it makes me feel: it's good to remember that there can be disasters in your career from which you think you'll never recover, but in the end it's all just a good anecdote.

Someone else shares an article about a *Game of Thrones* cast member who says she won her role over a 'much, much better' actor because she had more Twitter followers. Is this an actual thing? According to the comments after the article, it most definitely is in Hollywood, where my LA-based British mate has seen numerous casting breakdowns that state, 'Must have over 20,000 Twitter followers'. In the name of God, what is the world coming to? I'm heartened, however, when I think of our most popular and successful TV actors here, amongst them Jodie Whittaker, Olivia Colman, Suranne Jones, Sarah Lancashire, Nikki Amuka-Bird, Siobhan Finneran . . . and note that NONE of them are even on Twitter.

My friends Jason Watkins and Clara Francis are in the *Guardian* Family section talking about the heartbreaking loss of their two-year-old, Maude, to sepsis, six years ago now. I can honestly say that I have never experienced anything as painful or terrible as seeing their suffering as a family during that period and in the months and years that followed. But they are so incredibly inspiring, sharing their story so generously to help give comfort and courage to other bereaved parents and raising awareness for Sepsis UK. A perfect example of using one's profile as a public person (Jason is a BAFTA-winning actor) to put something back into the world.

7 August

Horrible night's sleep and I wake up anxious and tired.

I'm off to Kent again today for *Peterloo* rehearsals at Tilbury Fort so there's some work nerves (we're working with practically the whole cast rather than our little girl-gang) and I have a head full of *The Handmaid's Tale* too, which has been showing on Channel 4, the season finale of which we watched too close to bedtime last night. I think this series has been the greatest piece of telly ever made. Even better than *The Wire* and *Transparent*, I think. Every shot is a work of art, the acting is flawless, the writing is shit-hot, the cast is diverse and the subject matter is as relevant as anything you could ever hope to see. It is set in an ultra-right, ultra-religious future America, where women have zero rights and where our heroine (played by Elisabeth Moss) is required to make babies for wealthy infertile couples. And where everyone is trying to escape to Canada. It doesn't take an enormous leap of imagination to see how close to a terrifying reality this could be. As one character says, 'This stuff doesn't happen instantaneously, but in increments'. But it's bloody harrowing, and properly infiltrated my dreams and nightmares last night.

As part of my ongoing *Artist's Way* 'homework' I write, long hand, a page of A4 stream-of-consciousness every morning. It's a bit like purging: getting rid of all the shit your unconscious throws up as you wake and meet the day. Every once in a while I look back over the half-legible ramblings and try to see patterns or recurring themes. See what constantly eats at me, see what I constantly fail to address, see what resolutions I make over and over, which habits I seem incapable of breaking. Lyss, my youngest, is off to the local drama club, helping behind the scenes as they make an alien invasion film over the week: how brilliant people are, giving up their time to organize stuff like this for kids. Martha, my eldest, is still in London and having a ball at the National Youth Theatre. Kersh is out early to storyline the next series of *Cold Feet* with his writing partner Debbie Oates. So I have a bit of time to sift through some old morning pages. Yep, it's all there: all the old familiar shite. I am half a stone overweight. I am tired. Am I perimenopausal? BORING.

I spend too much time on social media, I feel guilty about my mothering. I make plans to do stuff with the kids, then regret I haven't done what I planned. I want to learn the ukulele. I want to go to a dance class. I still haven't done either. I am jealous of such and such. Such and such has been funny with me. Someone's annoyed me by talking to me about *Corrie*. What shall I do with Mum? I have to learn my lines. Why am I not learning my lines? I have too much to do. I'll never work again. I must be kinder. I must work harder. What a dull fucking puritan I am. And what a CLICHÉ. Jesus. Great, though, to splurge it all on the page on waking and get it out of the way for the day. At least I hope that's what happens. I hope I'm not so dull in my day-to-day dealings with the world. God.

8 August

Early start and we all board the *Peterloo* bus at the hotel and set off to our set at Tilbury Fort, where St Peter's Field has been faithfully reconstructed within the fort. The site of the massacre is a built-up area in the centre of Manchester now. It looks and feels amazing to be here. The huge area is covered in sand and surrounded by period houses, and Henry Hunt's faithfully reconstructed barouche is next to the hustings at the far end of the space. 'Barouche' is a word none of us had ever heard until today and now we all bandy it about as if it's always been part of our vocabulary. 'Back to the barouche!' 'Does that mean the posse in the barouche?' 'Barouche position one or two?' It just means carriage.

It is an eerily still day, the atmosphere is strange. We feel as though we're in a memory. This is the first day we're working with the menfolk which has made us all a bit nervous, breaking out of the comfort-zone of our small female team. Although we're only rehearsing, Mike wants us in costume and the men look fantastic – just like the illustrations from the time. Dorothy (as Mary) is exactly like the drawings depicting the day in her white dress and with her blonde curls peeping out from under her bonnet. We spend a long time working through the logistics of the scene, from the arrival of Hunt's carriage with us all following, to my character keeling over as the men climb down (my big moment!), to the meeting of all the various radicals and reporters on the hustings, to the arrival of the yeomanry and the beginning of the massacre. There is much to cover, and it's tricky to work out exactly how it will be without the yeomanry being on horses (they're just striding toward us in an intimidating manner at the moment, to slightly comic effect) and without the all-important 200+ supporting artists. There has been a bit of Twitter hilarity about a widely shared call-out from casting for 'long-haired, miserable-looking northern men'. We women spend a lot of time sitting in the barouche (BAROUCHE!) and, as usual, there is much pissing ourselves with laughter, especially when they bring the horses in to pull it across the field and into position. The men are seated in it and we women follow behind, as happened on the day. What we don't anticipate is the speed at which the horses will go in order to get through the sand on the ground. We literally have to *sprint* to keep up.

These brilliant women have made this job a complete joy. Rehearsals tomorrow are cancelled and rescheduled for Friday because the weather is going to be horrific. I stay up boozing with the hilarious John-Paul Hurley (who's playing the reformer Saxton in the film) til 4.30am, like a giddy teen.

9 August

Heavy hangs the head, etc. Barely functioning. Thank God I don't have anything to do today. I stagger down the side of the dual carriageway in the pouring rain for half an hour until I stumble upon a roadside Burger King where I cut a tragic figure, eating my bean burger at a dirty table, with a solitary fly buzzing around my head. Someone asks me for my autograph. They don't even ask for my photo I look so bad. The glamour is almost unbearable.

10 August

More of the same at Tilbury Fort, which is such a fascinating place. This Elizabethan waterside structure, spanning acres, surrounded by the most industrial landscape of new Essex, feels like an anomaly. It is ideal for our shoot, though.

11 August

It's fair to say that everyone is getting a bit stir-crazy. It is hot and there is a lot of waiting around in various marquees at unit base and by the field. Because there are so many of us, and more arriving every day (the yeomanry, the hussars, the magistrates, the horse-handlers) there is absolutely no way that we can all have a trailer of our own. It would be like a city of its own. I like it. It feels very egalitarian and, although I always admire people who are able to find their own space and keep themselves to themselves and their energy preserved (and there are those among us who can), I enjoy the chatter and camaraderie of a gigantic canvas green room. Pearce Quigley and Maxine Peake and their fictional family have bought board games, Gerard is teaching Chrissy how to make knots in a long piece of rope, Samantha and I walk around the walls of the fort again and again, talking about feminism, body issues, love, work, family, religion. I have made new and enduring friendships on this job. And although it has had its frustrations, and although I speak not a word in the entire film, I have learnt loads, not just from Mike but from the people I've been spending time with. Sam has the purest heart of anyone I've ever met. I love the way she chats away to Mike without any filter, as she would to anyone, about her new top or the jam she's making or how he's getting on at home. I can tell he thinks she's ace. You'd have to have a heart of stone not to, to be honest.

Dick Pope, the director of photography, and long-time collaborator with Mike, is on set today planning shots, as are the stunt co-ordinators. My character is to be carried off by a couple of stunt constables and when I struggle, get truncheoned. Poor Elizabeth. The women at Peterloo, although out in force, were in a minority, but were disproportionately among the number injured. They were absolutely targeted by the yeomanry, the hussars and the constables, and it's very important to emphasize this in the action. The march to, and meeting at, St Peter's Field in August 1819 was one of the first instances when women organized and were politically active and vocal, and they paid for it dearly.

In the evening most people go home for the weekend. I'm meeting Kersh in London tomorrow to see Martha's National Youth Theatre sharing and to go to the 'evening do' of our friends' wedding so I stick around for another night and have a swim in the hotel pool with Zoe Alker, our third AD. Zoe is a talented writer and filmmaker and is whip-smart. When she graduated from her course at Bristol she sent a handwritten note to Mike Leigh and gave him a link to a short film she made asking him for feedback, inspired by an Arts Emergency badge she'd seen saying:

Sometimes if you want something to exist you have to make it yourself.

He got in touch with her that week and chatted to her about her work and offered her the chance to interview for the post of third AD, even though she had no experience. It was purely so she could watch him work and see a film of this scale being made from the planning stages to wrap. He has been incredibly generous with her and she has been observing his work in this capacity for a year now. What an incredible opportunity for her. She has learned untold amounts. And she has been a fantastic person to have around on set, a real friend to us all.

12 August

I travel to London and hang out on the South Bank with all my baggage until it's time to meet Kersh. I feel completely desperate to be around beautiful buildings and art and culture after a week at the hotel. I go to the National Theatre coffee shop and bump into my old LAMDA classmate Toby Stephens, who I haven't seen in about fifteen years. It's fair to say he's kept himself in better nick than I have. He's rehearsing *Oslo* at the Dorfman (formerly the Cottesloe) and I promise him I'll try to get down to see it. We talk about our year group at LAMDA, and how extraordinary it is that the vast majority of us are still acting or involved in the business in some way twenty-six years on. This is by no means the norm. I think everyone from our year group bar two are still at it. For most people of our age, the reverse is normally the case: normally only about two per year are still performing.

Kersh arrives from Manchester and we travel together to Deptford where we check in to our Premier Inn and stride over to Laban Dance College where we're seeing Martha's group perform a short devised piece. First the whole group of about 300 fourteen- to sixteen-year-olds stand out in the field in front of the school and sing *Lean on Me* and *I'm Only Human* for all the assembled parents. It's completely lovely and very moving. We're then shepherded into various rooms and studios around the building to watch our own children's smaller groups share a ten-minute ensemble piece. Brilliant energy and focus and Martha is just fab. Everyone has a little bit to do, but as an ensemble they work so well together. So much talent.

Later Martha will tell us that it's been a wake-up call to her, seeing how many talented people there are out there, and that it was a bit intimidating to her at times. It is such a relief to see her again. It's been a long two weeks and we've missed her terribly. Seeing all those parents there, watching their kids, waiting to see them afterwards, was a strange experience for us too. I still feel like one of those young people starting out, not like the oldies coming to proudly look on. We realize that we're not the heroes of the story any more, just supporting cast. Just a smiling mum and dad you get introduced to at events like these. Amazing. Life.

16 Aug

I leave my family in our special place in west Wales after a preposterous but worthwhile thirty-six-hour holiday and set off on the epic journey across country by train to Tilbury Fort where I have a stunt rehearsal.

It is the 198th anniversary of the Peterloo Massacre today, and when we arrive on set Georgina, the producer, presents each of us with a little box of beautiful badges with the various relevant slogans printed on them: 'Liberty or Death', 'Unity and Strength', 'Freedom and Peace'. It's a lovely keepsake, but they are deeply affecting too. Only this week there has been a Nazi march in Charlottesville, Virginia, to protest the state's removal of a statue of a Confederate general. Hordes of white men brandishing torches descended on the town and when a counter-demonstration from the left started up, a young woman, Heather Heyer, was killed by a speeding car that ploughed into the crowd. These slogans have never felt more relevant. At lunchtime, Maxine Peake recites a section of Shelley's epic protest poem, 'The Masque of Anarchy', to the assembled cast and crew on our reconstructed St Peter's Field:

> Rise like lions after slumber
> In unvanquishable number–
> Shake your chains to earth like dew
> Which in sleep had fallen on you–
> Ye are many – they are few.

Max performed the poem in its entirety as part of the Manchester International Festival a few years ago at the atmospheric and candlelit Albert Hall. It remains one of my favourite performances of all time.

Later, Sam and I are ushered across the field where there are extras out in force and in costume, adding to the deep sense of history we all feel today. We meet our stunt co-ordinators in an out-of-shot corner and practise being lifted out of the barouche and hammered by the constabulary, ready for when we film this section in a few days' time. Poor Kate O'Flynn, John Branwell and Gerard Kearns have been waiting all day in full costume and make up but are released without filming a shot. It's inevitable, I suppose, that we'll fall behind and lose scenes in a project of this scale. They are all sanguine.

Years ago I remember reading an interview with Meryl Streep in which she said that they pay her for the waiting around; the acting she does for free. And there are worse ways to make a living than knocking about with your mates, reading books and, in lovely Gerard's case, learning his knots.

17 August

6.15am pick-up from the hotel but we don't actually get on set to do anything until about 4pm. I don't mind. This cast is full of interesting souls with endless projects on the go outside of this experience. I spend a lot of time chatting to Dan Poole, one of the hussars, before discovering completely by chance that he is making a documentary about The Space Theatre in Cape Town, and specifically about Brian Astbury. Brian was my inspirational LAMDA teacher who had set up and run The Space, the first multi-racial theatre in apartheid South Africa in the 1970s, and who ran Arts Threshold with us after we graduated. The documentary has been a long time in the making, and poor Dan has been up against it trying to get images and footage from big British arts institutions who own them now, and who have been spectacularly greedy and unhelpful. Luckily, he has been equally helped and supported by talented and award-winning individuals who have offered their time and work on the cheap or for free. Brian has received little or no recognition for his outstanding contribution to world theatre, and for the many and varied careers he has helped launch and nurture over the years. The film will be an apt celebration of this incredible man, who is not getting any younger. It would be a very great thing to show him how appreciated and valued he actually is.

The band is in today playing an array of bonkers-looking nineteenth-century instruments and they herald our arrival on to the field with a stirring rendition of 'See, the Conqu'ring Hero Comes'. It creates a fantastic atmosphere as we film, and the supporting artists are just fantastic as always, really going for it on every take. Later the lads in the band hear that they're finished tomorrow and they are very disappointed in the bar at bedtime. They have done the same intensive character work as we have and feel they haven't been given any opportunity to act or to feel really part of the project. I feel for them. I try to reassure them that for many of us this has been a somewhat frustrating job, that very few of us, in such a massive cast, have had much of an opportunity to be creative or get our teeth into the characters we've created, BUT that we are ALL part of telling this really important story and we should be proud. That many people would have loved to have been in this film, and *we are*. And that is a pretty brilliant thing.

18 August

A much busier day today on the *Peterloo* set. We get into wigs and costumes almost immediately and are soon on set filming wide shots of the arrival of the barouche and the action around it, including my fainting fit as Elizabeth. Last night everyone in the bar put bets on how many times I'd have to faint today, and the guesses ranged from fifteen to forty-two, but in the end it was about eight times, including rehearsals, so that was manageable. A few of the supporting artists thought I'd actually collapsed so I was pretty chuffed about that. Getting recognition where I can.

A massive thunderstorm stops play for a couple of hours in the afternoon and one of the poor actors is knocked off the hustings in the tussle when the meeting gets broken up, but somehow we manage to get all of the wide shots filmed from all angles.

More fantastic chats all day between filming. I am basking in these new friendships. Sometimes it's like we're having one long putting-the-world-to-rights chat and the film is a mere backdrop. We're sometimes in the hotel pool, sometimes in the bar, sometimes in bonnets in a barouche.

19 August

The magistrates have arrived. Scores of familiar and extraordinary faces from stage and screen, but with loads of facial hair. Nice to have some new blood in the 'holding marquee'. Long shots from their point of view in an upstairs window are in the can by lunch and there is much jubilation as we are released back into the world.

I have packed a pair of knickers and a toothbrush and get the fuck out, catching a train to London where luckily my mates Al and Amy can put me up for the night. Zoe has recommended an exhibition on women and surrealism at the White Cube in Bermondsey and I head there and then to the Royal Court to see Lemn Sissay in the thirtieth anniversary production of *Road*, directed by John Tiffany. Culture binge. Filling the flipping well before it dries up completely.

Road was a seminal play in its time, a classic of the 1980s, and written by Jim Cartwright when he was only twenty-four. It's a play that carries huge significance for most northerners who became involved in theatre in any way, sometimes as a direct result of seeing it back then. It marked, for us, a moment in cultural history when, en masse it seems, we all realized that theatre could be about people like us, and places like our towns. The impact it had on so many of us can't be underestimated.

I didn't see the original Royal Court production, but a later one at Bolton Octagon, the first time I ever visited that theatre. A group of us from Accrington travelled over to see it, and I remember being bowled over by the energy of it – the first promenade play I'd ever watched, where we were invited on stage by the cast to dance and had fish and chips in the interval. The last scene, where four of the characters, desperate to escape the poverty and grind of life in Thatcher's Britain, listen to Otis Redding's 'Try a Little Tenderness' in its entirety, remains one of my favourites in any play ever.

And tonight's production delivers again. The cast (including Lemn who is knockout as the narrator, Scullery) are brilliant. I was worried that the play might not have aged well, that its working-class poverty-poetry might seem too on the nose and outdated now, but it is beautiful and, unfortunately, shockingly relevant still. As usual I struggle with the audience. Sloane Square on a Saturday night. There are times when this chippy northerner feels the audience laughter is inappropriate, like they're laughing *at* the characters, not *with* them, and I long for more moments like the one in *Love* at the Dorfman earlier in the year, or indeed in the Bolton production of *Road* way back, where the fourth wall gets broken down and the characters come out among us: where we are made part of what's happening, and *culpable*, rather than being allowed to coolly observe from a safe distance.

But it is a great production and a good night. My old friend and housemate Steven Hoggett, one of the top movement directors in the world, is there too with his husband, Kyle, and we talk for ages about working-class theatre and middle-class audiences and the problems therein. It is fantastic to see him. He divides his time between London and New York now, so I see him all too rarely. In the 1990s for about four years a gang of us lived in a shared house in Kimberley Road in Stockwell. They were some of the most formative years of my life. I think we all feel that. It was a party house, where many fags were smoked and bottles emptied and secrets shared and personalities formed. It spawned a ridiculous amount of highly successful creative artists, including Olivier Award-winning lighting designer Natasha Chivers, top camera operator and photographer Alison Banham (who I'm staying with tonight), actors, radio producers, directors – and Steven whose CV includes *Harry Potter and the Cursed Child* and *The Curious Incident of the Dog in the Night-Time.* Being surrounded by such imaginative, driven and talented people at such a crucial time of my life is probably one of the most significant factors in my having any kind of creative life since. That and Arts Threshold.

Choose your friends well. Be around people who are full of spark and energy and who are supportive and kind and who make things happen, and don't just *talk* about making things happen. Find your gang and hold on to them. I've done it again with my Take Back team, and I'm lucky enough (so, so lucky) to have had my Manchester Female Reform Society gang on this job. It's the secret of life, I'm telling you.

21 August

I think I come near to losing my mojo today. I am 'not in my power', as Sam says. It's difficult to write about a 'hard day' on a film set because that very statement is full of privilege, of course: *How hard can it be, you overblown baby? You're not working a twelve-hour shift in A&E.* But I am struggling a bit and I also don't want to pretend that I'm always capable of Pollyannaing my way through life, just SO GRATEFUL for every second I'm working. After coming back from the weekend in London feeling recharged and restored and ready for the week, it just feels like Groundhog Day to be back in that fucking barouche, doing the same scene at full pelt, with no mics on and in deep background, over and over again. By the end of the day I have reached some weird zen-like state of acceptance. The barouche is my home now. I had a family and a life once. A career. Now I spend my days fainting and being put in a barouche. It is fine.

We're moving on from the barouche and hustings tomorrow. I'm coming to the end of this chapter now and I'm ready. Proud as I am to be part of telling this story, I need life to carry on and to get myself back now. Two days to go.

22 August

Another challenging day, but for different reasons. This time we're called in the morning and do nothing until about 5.30pm. I talk with Sam a lot about what the waiting is doing to us all. If, in the past, anyone had said to me what I'm saying now about the boredom of being held in a hot marquee for hours with nothing to do, I would be scathing to say the least. *Read a book, thicko. Write a letter. Write a play. Use the time.* But inexplicably these things seem impossible to us. I can't explain it, but NONE of us have the energy or concentration to even finish the *Guardian* quick crossword, let alone read a book or even construct a sendable email. The place is teeming with creative and inventive artists and makers, but we are in some sort of stasis. I know that when I'm home again and back to busy normal life, I'll be cursing myself for not utilizing this down-time, but it has just been beyond me somehow. We play some daft games, attempt the aforementioned crossword, try to read the paper, make an escape to the Tilbury Fort souvenir shop for ice lollies.

When it's finally time to walk over to the set, we all stumble upon the scene of the massacre being shot. It is a profound moment for all of us. A lot of us have, I think, lost sight in many ways of the story we're telling. I certainly have. I feel removed from it. But seeing at close quarters the 'yeomanry' letting loose on the supporting artists and particularly the sight of the crowd dispersing in panic, and their screams as the uniformed thugs on huge horses wield their sabres: it is chilling. A line of us stand in silence and some of us get a bit upset. The world is in such a state right now: it's impossible not to hear that kind of screaming without thinking of the recent attacks in Manchester, London Bridge, Barcelona this week, and last week Charlottesville, where Heather Heyer was killed whilst protesting against neo-Nazis. We are suddenly sobered by the relevance of this nearly 200-year-old story and, as we go in to film our reactions to the massacre, I think it's fair to say that we all feel a renewal of our commitment to the telling of it.

23 August

Our last day of filming on *Peterloo*, although late in the morning, our second AD Gayle tells us that they are woefully behind on set and are still completing yesterday's shot list, so we need to prepare ourselves for an extra day. I'm planning on surprising my family back in Wales for the last night of the holiday tomorrow, so this is disappointing news, but it's par for the course on a job of this size and scale, I'm sure. The pace steps up after lunch, though, and we are taken out to the set to practise our massacre stunts with Mike Leigh, Dan the first AD and the stunt team, and we are thrown in at the deep end. Mike doesn't like any of what we practised the other day and we hurriedly change it all. The next few hours are absolutely extraordinary. There are three cameras, and a potentially fiddly and time-consuming blood effect on Dorothy Duffy's character gets ditched for a CGI wound that will be added in post-production. This saves us at least half a day.

The supporting artists and stuntmen are brought in and we *just do it*. We reenact the massacre. It is an incredibly intense few hours after the days and weeks of waiting. The supporting artists are once again exemplary in their energy and commitment. I will write to the agency who has employed and provided them and thank them. Brian and Will, two huge stuntmen, beat and drag myself and Sam out of the barouche and the SA women in their white dresses give them a run for their money, dragging them off us, screaming. It is very moving. We repeat the action over and over and every time there is a level of pandemonium that feels horribly authentic and upsetting. When we finally complete the sequence for the final time, I look across to Dorothy by the hustings. She is hugging a supporting artist tight. They are both crying. The woman in question, Penelope, is a direct descendant of Mary Fildes, Chair of the Manchester Female Reform Society, and Dorothy's character in the film. She was badly injured at Peterloo when a yeoman slashed her across the breast with a sabre. Dorothy, in her white dress and bonnet, looks exactly like the drawings that accompanied the reports of the day. Penelope signed up with an 'extras' agency a few months ago on a whim, and this was the first job she got through them. When she turned up on set she had absolutely no idea what the film or the subject matter was. She only traced her family tree about a year ago and learned about the Peterloo massacre for the first time. Not only seeing this reenactment, but also being in the crowd as part of it, and seeing Dorothy enacting her ancestor's fate so beautifully and with such commitment, was just completely overwhelming. What an incredible coincidence. And a beautiful end to this project.

I hope the film will go some way towards spreading the story of what happened on that day in 1819. It is shocking how few people, even in Manchester, know about it. It was a massive moment in working-class history, and it is not part of the school curriculum. Maybe the release of the film will change that. I hope so. I'm proud to have been a tiny part of the telling of it.

27 August

Right now, Kersh and I are in bed; our kids are still asleep after an epic trip back from Wales taking in multiple breakdowns in our shit old van (sitting in a Pembroke garage, I realized just how inured I am to hanging around now: Mike Leigh's gift to me). Kersh is reading a book he dislikes in preparation for a possible writing project. I am dipping in and out of *I Love Dick,* the cult feminist book by Chris Kraus, on Steven Hoggett's recommendation. I'm not allowed to watch the Jill Soloway show until I've read it. It's making me antsy. A sniff of another kind of life sometimes comes and gets me. I can so easily be transported and feel like we are Lena Dunham and Adam Driver in *Girls,* or the sexy, spied-on East German couple in *The Lives of Others* or even the elderly Parisians in *Amour.* I feel arty and brainy and dark. I am Patti Smith or Glenda Jackson. (True story: I passed my driving test by pretending to be Glenda Jackson when I was seventeen.) But then reality hits and I realize I am just a middle-aged mum, who used to be in *Corrie,* trying to get the holiday washing done and dried before it rains, jogging gracelessly around the block in an attempt to fight off my spreading middle. I read the Review section of the *Guardian* and feel sick with jealousy about all the projects that are going on that I'm not in, and panic about all the books I haven't read and the music I'm failing to keep up with. I uneasily straddle all these self-imposed ideas about myself. It's a sign that I'm doing the work, but not filling the well.

My *Peterloo* women continue to inspire me. Our WhatsApp group is a resource. Fierce and beautiful Chrissy posts an angry diatribe about an RSC production that has cast sixteen blokes and four women, and a recording of her favourite song, Tracy Chapman's 'All That You Have Is Your Soul' about not being tempted by the shiny apple, listening to your own truth, your own soul.

Later, as I'm cooking tea I listen to a recording of an interview between Jude Kelly, Artistic Director of the South Bank and Angela Davis, the legendary African-American civil rights activist and author of *Women, Race and Class*, for the WOW (Women of the World) Festival in London. It is just what the doctor ordered. It's all about everything that fuels and fires me up: feminism of the intersectional, trans-inclusive type, and the importance of keeping on, keeping on even if you might never live long enough to see the fruits of your struggle. Katie West has posted it on our 'Liberty or Death' WhatsApp. Katie is a remarkable person and an enormous talent. She is someone who effortlessly straddles all her worlds. She's working-class Stockport and lives there still. Mention a film, however leftfield and arthouse, she's seen it. She's read Carson McCullers and the beat poets and loves 90s dance music. And she has also seen every episode ever recorded of *RuPaul's Drag Race* and can quote from it extensively. I don't know how she fits in the amount of culture, high and low, that she does *and* work *and* only be thirty-one. She is honestly one of the coolest women I've ever met, but without trying at all, and certainly without signalling it. She is playing Sonya in Andrew Upton's version of Chekhov's *Uncle Vanya* at HOME later in the year and there are these incredible huge posters of her all over Manchester at the moment. I spend a lot of time wishing I was more like her. When we did the read-through for *Blindsided* at the Royal Exchange all those years ago, I remember thinking that that must have been what it was like to have been in a rehearsal room with a young Judi Dench back in the day.

29 August

I have done my back in and am hobbling about like an eighty-year-old. I'm supposed to be running 10K on Sunday. I'll just have to hope it gets better in time. Take Back are at the University of Salford today rehearsing for a huge symposium on theatre and performance for about 300 visiting academics. They've given us a fee and we're erecting the *Under Canvas* tent in the foyer and are performing a mash-up of previous *Ten Takes* for a sharing in the theatre space tomorrow: *Ten Takes on Resistance*. There's a bit of money for everyone involved, which is just great. We've asked our friend Sandra Cole to write and perform a new piece around Black Lives Matter and Peter Keeley has written a new piece on this government's devastating cuts to disability benefits. I've known Peter for many years. He was writing stuff for Contact Theatre back when Kersh started out in a monthly playwriting slam called 'Flip the Script'. Peter has Cerebral palsy, is a wheelchair user and is piss-funny. He just has a brilliant way with language, but his dyslexia and learning difficulties make it difficult for him to put those ideas on paper in an easily readable way, and for him to learn lines. We talk for a long time today about his frustrations as an artistic person. There seems to be nothing in place in a commissioning process that takes into account a person's specific difficulties, and he has had knock back after knock back, despite his story being, I think, unique and important. He has encountered so many setbacks in his life, personally and professionally, I fear that he is in danger of losing his mojo. I would have given up years ago; I don't have an ounce of his resilience.

It makes me think a lot again about the hierarchy of privilege and its intersectionality. That he has a disability is one thing, but he is also poor. Being an actor is expensive, as he says: Spotlight, the casting resource that you have to pay to be part of; Equity subs; travel to auditions, especially when you can't use public transport because of accessibility issues. His piece for *Take Back Our Bodies* was brilliantly received earlier in the year and I know it gave him a boost. We need to build on that now. He's written a full-length play loosely based on his life, all about the loves and losses of a young man with CP, which has just been rejected from the PUSH Festival at HOME unfortunately. I'll read it and see if we can do something with it, even if it's to workshop it and kick it into shape a bit.

Rosa arrives from London. We're including her Theresa May piece again and, this time, having graduated, she's free to perform in it too.

Matt Hassall is directing. He works tirelessly all day, without a break, while we put the tent up and chat about everything we have coming up. The migration project, now called *Borders to Belonging,* is the priority. We can't quite get a structure fixed for the live element, so Becx will write something new to tie all the different themes and ideas together. I don't like the title either. It feels sterile and academic.

Then we have big plans for the NHS project for the seventieth anniversary next year with The Edge Theatre and with Trafford General (the first-ever NHS hospital and around the corner from The Edge), *Take Back Our Girls* for International Women's Day in March and *I Forget Your Name*, for which we have to put in a funding bid as soon as possible. I'd also like us to do something about housing, specifically about the Grenfell Tower tragedy. And we want to make a little online film of Rosa performing 'The Naughtiest Thing I Ever Did'. Before it dates. Although it doesn't look like Theresa May is going anywhere any time soon after all.

30 August

The show at the Salford conference to an audience of academics goes well, I think. It's a bit of a 'Greatest Hits' with a couple of new pieces by Sandra and Peter thrown in and it is lovely to see some of our best pieces from the last couple of years revisited. The wonderful writer Alistair McDowall is on before us doing the keynote speech of the conference and, hilariously, his entire talk is a kind of apology for not being more overtly political in his work and a case for more elliptical forms in expressing big ideas about life and humanity. He is engaging and self-deprecating and his ideas and inspirations are fascinating, but the whole thing is almost a bloody *anti*-introduction to us. I have to make our case to the assembled academics before we launch into the showing, as a company that is about as unapologetically didactic and on-the-nose as they come. Our actors are brilliant as ever and I feel the usual pride as I watch. Matt Hassall has done a fantastic job directing as always. We are so lucky to have him as part of our team. We have achieved a lot in two years, and have made shows about so many topics. There's room for this kind of work and a need for it, too, I'm convinced.

As we all leave at the end of the day, a taxi comes to pick up Peter and the driver makes a horrible fuss about getting the wheelchair into his car and how it won't fit in his boot and how it will rip the upholstery in the back seat. He absolutely does not want Peter and his chair in his cab. Once again, I see the reality of what Peter lives with every day. Everything is ten times as challenging for him. Even getting home after a performance.

At home, my brother, Dave, who is a professor at the University of Leeds (and Rosa and my nephew Joe's dad), has sent me the introduction to his latest edition of *Cultural Industries.* It's a book he has to update at regular intervals as the world, culture and the industries constantly shift and evolve in seismic ways. His words make me cry. It's an academic book, but he is a beautiful and accessible writer and so full of hope and deep respect for the arts and their role in society. I will start this diary with a paragraph from his preface, I think. It perfectly and succinctly sums up what I feel about the role of culture in our lives. He also interestingly quotes the same lines from the song 'Bread and Roses' that I have used in my Arts Emergency talks: 'Hearts starve as well as bodies . . .'. As far as I can remember, we've never actually ever discussed that song or its lyrics. A lovely bit of synchronicity.

31 August

Rosa has an audition for a TV job at Elstree Studios, just outside London, so leaves early for the train. She is doing so well.

The organization Stagetext, which works on in-theatre accessibility for deaf and hearing-impaired audiences, gets in touch asking me to give them a quote championing its work in subtitling live theatre. This is such a fantastic and relatively recent innovation, and has made shows accessible to a whole new audience. Although, as an actor, it's terrifying when you're performing as you have to get the words exactly right.

I've been asked to be part of a Royal Television Society panel discussion about class at King's College, Cambridge in a couple of weeks.

I catch up on a load of emails and letters, and feel virtuous. Back still bad.

1 September

I love this time of year. It feels like another fresh start, a new school year, all new pencil cases and good intentions.

Amy James-Kelly, an actor who used to be in *Coronation Street* with me and who left shortly after I did, has made a film and has invited us to the screening at The Sharp Project in town. Becx and Grant are there (Amy was in one of our showings of *My Version of Events*) and a big team from Reuben's Retreat. Reuben's Retreat is a local charity set up five years ago when Nicola and Mike Graham lost their little boy, Reuben, at nearly two years old to a brain tumour when they were on holiday in the south of England. Nic, determined to honour his memory and make sure that his little life hadn't been in vain, set up Reuben's Retreat in the days and weeks after he passed away. It's an organization that offers breaks to the families of children with life-threatening and shortening illnesses, as well as support and counselling for bereaved families who have lost a child. Kersh and I are proud patrons. I always wear three wristbands: one for Reuben, one for Sophie Lancaster and one for my late, great friend Alex Williams whose mum, Alison, set up the Believe and Achieve Trust, which supports those affected by meningitis, in his memory in Manchester's Tameside. It is astonishing to me how much these three mothers have done to keep their children's memories alive, in the face of such devastating loss. Our little community has done incredible things to make Reuben's Retreat become a reality, and Nic is a force, having raised £1 million in the first two years and bought an old disused hospital next to a park that will become the centre of their work. Amy and her film crew used it as a base while they were filming and were helped enormously by Nic and her family.

The film is lovely, a love story called *Last Summer*, and once again I'm bowled over by the tenacity and creative energy of people who just get on and make things happen rather than waiting for life to happen to them. Amy wrote, produced, directed and starred in the film, which she'll now start taking to festivals. What an achievement.

Becx and Grant have had their debrief at the Royal Exchange about the Co:LAB project, and got excellent feedback. Discussing future projects, they suggested using the theatre's long relationship with

Bruntwood, the massive construction company whose owners sponsor the Playwriting Competition at the Exchange, to try and find an empty building for *I Forget Your Name*. When we put on our one-night-only performance of the immersive piece last year, we had temporary residency in a soon-to-be-demolished old bank and it was a perfect venue. Part of the problem of revisiting it has been finding a building as suitable and user-friendly as that one. Hopefully, Bruntwood may be able to help. I hope so. *I Forget Your Name* was one of our most accomplished and innovative pieces without a doubt, exploring the bureaucracy around the refugee crisis by taking small groups through an interactive experience over the four floors of the huge and abandoned office block. But because of the time constraints (imminent eviction) it was seen by so frustratingly few people. We have always been keen to revisit it.

2 September

I start work in earnest on *The Greatest Play in the History of the World* and stay up til 1am reading and re-reading it and learning lines. It is quite beautiful, I think. Finally, I feel engaged and excited about it. I have space in my head at last.

3 September

I run the Salford 10k for Reuben's Retreat. I haven't run for weeks because of *Peterloo* and then my bad back, so it nearly finishes me off. But I run the whole way and manage it in an hour and eighteen minutes and feel proud of myself. I'm in bed with my lines for most of the rest of the day.

4 September

Peterloo wrap party in London. Great turnout, and it is wonderful to be reunited with my women again, who are out in force and gleefully bonnet-less. A great end to the job.

6 September

There's a big concert this coming Saturday to mark the reopening of the Manchester Arena after the attack in May. The line-up is right up Martha's street, and they are asking people to come on and be interviewed between the acts by the host, Russell Kane, about memories of the Arena and with messages of support. I momentarily think that it might be something that Martha would like to do, as it would mean backstage passes and the chance to meet some of her favourite bands maybe, but when we discuss it as a family we all realize it's a bit soon for us all, still a bit raw. We'll get a takeaway and watch *Modern Family* together instead. It will be a great and defiantly joyful night though, I'm sure, for those who can face it.

7 September

My girls are back to school today and I make sure they're sorted and wave them off before setting off to London for a flying visit.

I'm meeting Toby Clarke from ALT, a fantastic organization in the capital (but coming to Manchester next year) that gives free, high-quality part-time training for people on low incomes. It has been insanely successful already in turning out some brilliant performers, some of whom are now working professionally and some of whom have gone on to places at the top drama schools. The majority are black and their showcases are getting huge audience turnouts from industry professionals and casting directors who are on the lookout for young talent as the business cranks itself into the twenty-first century and attempts to be more representative. In theory. As well as training, the students get headshots and showreels and masterclasses, all free of charge, supported by the Andrew Lloyd Webber Foundation and the Arts Council among others. It's an incredibly exciting venture and Toby is absolutely lovely: completely unassuming and dedicated. And not very good at asking for things. He tentatively approached a few people on Twitter (which is how he found me) who he thought might be supportive, but he is desperate to get word out about what ALT is doing, completely uniquely I think, and to spread the word. I'll do what I can. There's a showcase in December and I suggest that we rebrand it a gala, and try and get some bigwigs in to create a bit of a buzz around it. People's energy and commitment to helping people who are being increasingly marginalized never fails to amaze and move me.

Afterwards I meet Raz Shaw for something to eat and to talk a bit about *Greatest Play*, and to gossip. We haven't got a designer yet. Amanda Stoodley, who I've worked with before, isn't available after all, which is no surprise really – she's very in demand – so we need to find someone else. A woman. Otherwise it's an all-male creative team, which won't do at all.

An article is doing the social media rounds about female playwrights in the top London theatres and how we're getting on in the fight for 50:50 representation in 2017.[4] Pretty badly, according to the blog piece by Victoria Sadler. The Royal Court is smashing it, producing seventeen plays so far, ten of which were written by women, and in second place the National with 30:70 female-to-male ratio. The Old Vic has apparently not produced a single play written by a woman so far this year. There is a big event in January that my mate Connie Hyde is helping to organize for ERA (Equal Representation for Actresses), which campaigns for 50:50 gender equality in casting. But the problems of course spread right through the creative industries, from directors to writers to designers and crews. We have so much further to go across the board.

In the evening we pile over to Burley Fisher Bookshop in Haggerston, where my friend Graham Caveney is launching his memoir, *The Boy with the Perpetual Nervousness*. There's a good turn out and the cellar setting makes it feel really New York and cool. (I am so immersed in Chris Krauss's *I Love Dick* at the moment that being cool and New York is my frame of reference for everything.) I feel my usual gauche and uneducated self among the publishers. I wonder if everyone who hasn't had a university education feels like this to some extent. One of my favourite things about Graham has always been his assumption that everyone is as smart as he is. He never talks down to anyone; you just have to raise your game in conversation with him. Tonight he has chosen an exquisitely written passage that juxtaposes descriptions of his teenaged love for Chrissie Hynde with italicized sections about his priest/headteacher's growing sexual interest in him, so we read it

---

[4] Victoria Sadler, '2017 in Review: The Lot for Female Playwrights Worsens', 4 September 2017.

together. The book is already getting superb reviews in the national press and looks to be a big success. I'm so happy for him, but, as his publisher says in his introduction tonight, one wishes it had never needed to be written. What a cost.

8 September

I see the kids off to school, then get the train into Manchester and head to the Equity office, where I have my picture taken with a giant Equity card to be part of their 'My Union, My Card' campaign, encouraging people to join. Then I stride down to the Royal Exchange to see the lovely green room ladies, Yvonne and Ann, and to make a little film encouraging people to buy £10 tickets on the stage, to be part of the action in the upcoming production of *Our Town* in the main house.

To the People's History Museum next because I have a hankering to see the Peterloo stuff. I stand looking at the huge reproduction of the newspaper illustration of the day and marvel at how much it looks like what we recreated in Tilbury over the summer. A couple of women are trying to work out where the magistrates were as they watched, and from which window the Riot Act was read. I can tell them because of a striking shot in the film of all the men seated in the upstairs window like a painting. There is a lot of preparation already going on for the 200th anniversary commemorations in 2019, including a growing archive of people whose family have links to campaigners, reformers and victims that day. I take some pictures to send to the Female Reformers' WhatsApp group.

On the way back to the station, I get harangued by a gang of pissed blokes outside a pub shouting at me, ''Ey up Harold' (my character Hayley's pre-transition name in *Corrie*). Possibly galvanized by all the pictures of women campaigners in the museum, and PISSED OFF at being shouted at *and* at their blatant transphobia, I give them a gob-full back.

In the evening Martha and I go and see Anna Jordan's extraordinary two-hander, *Freak*, at 53two. It is a brutal, tender, bruisingly honest play about female sexuality, performed to perfection by the two leads. It completely rattles me. Martha seemed to take it in her stride.

Later Kersh and I watch *I Am Not Your Negro*, a documentary about the writer James Baldwin and his friendships with the three murdered civil rights campaigners, Medgar Evers, Malcolm X and Martin Luther King, their legacy and the horrifying history of Black America. It seems fitting to watch it today, just after the Lammy Report in the UK publishes its findings of deep-rooted institutionalized racism in the criminal justice system here. And after a report on Twitter abuse and misogyny reveals over 25,000 offending tweets, nearly *half of which* were directed at one MP, Diane Abbott, Britain's first and longest-serving black female MP. But still the internet is a-buzz with those who continue to deny that there is a problem with racism, either here or in the States. Sometimes it feels like we have so far to go, it's hard to know where to start.

I go to bed a husk, and sleep really badly.

9 September

I Love Dick has become one of my favourite books of the year. It is full of references to female artists I've never heard of (although searching on Google I realize that some of them were part of the surrealist exhibition I saw at the White Cube the other week) as well as stories of lives lived eccentrically and fully in other spaces and time zones. Reading it makes me feel excited and alive, and I can almost hear my brain creaking as it expands and opens. Cross-referencing has taken me (via Google Search) to French sociologists Durkheim and Mauss and Austrian composer Schoenberg, and then to writer Jane Knowles and activist Jennifer Harbury, poet Emmy Hennings and artist Hannah Wilke. It's a proper celebration of women and art, so much more than the infatuated letters that form the framework for the book. And this quote has stayed with me:

Dear Dick . . . what happens between women now is the most interesting thing in the world because it's least described.

10 September

My brother, Dave, arrives from the airport after a week's conference in Stockholm and we have a brilliant day. We talk for hours and hours at the kitchen table and then in the pouring rain as we visit the trig point on a hill in Accrington where our dad's ashes are spread. We talk about the Royal Television Society panel I'm part of later in the week, about class, access and portrayal in TV. His take on this stuff as an expert on the cultural industries and a leading academic in the field is really useful. He believes passionately that the arts should be state-funded and supported in order to ensure full access. He thinks that there are huge problems in representation across the arts; that *because* it has become such a hot topic, creatives are increasingly reticent about telling stories about parts of society that the majority middle-class feel unqualified to tell. And there is little margin for error in such a competitive market.

This is a fascinating take on the access argument, I think. That it's perhaps not necessarily an *unwillingness* in the industries to tell these stories, but that maybe the fear of censure is holding back a more nuanced and fleshed-out portrayal of working-class life now. So the working-class stories we're seeing more of in the current climate are often based on true stories (e.g. *The Moorside*, *Three Girls*), perhaps because accusations of misrepresentation can be then batted away, with the defence of factual accuracy. And people even attacked *The Moorside* for being unrealistic in its portrayal, so unused are we (I think) to seeing 'people like that' on our screens. If people from working-class backgrounds were in decision-making positions and working as directors and writers in the industry, as they once were and as they increasingly *aren't*, then that would make space for more complex portrayals of life in more marginalized parts of society. And if there was more freedom to get it wrong, too, I suppose.

We also talked about our own class. I'm being asked to comment on and discuss the working-class arts issue with increasing regularity. Dave and I grew up in a low-income household (hence the state support we both received at higher education level). However, as we got older our parents started to earn more, as they both worked their way up into clerking and office-management roles. But I don't think this means we changed our *class* as such, in the same way that someone born into a middle-class family wouldn't 'become' working class if they took on a manual job.

Class is so hard to categorize in any kind of definitive way. It's such a complex issue. You can use education (state or private) as a marker, you can use income, but surely a wider degree of cultural capital has to play some role. So for example, a child can grow up with wealthy working-class parents but with no access to the arts. Or could grow up in a home that is middle class in outlook and cultural engagement, but where there is little or no disposable income. We were very fortunate in that our home was unique in that culture – 'high' culture (and I'm emphasizing the inverted commas) – played an important part. Yes, our childhood was about *The Two Ronnies* and football pools and trips to Blackpool, but there were also classical music LPs and Graham Greene first editions and poetry anthologies lining our shelves because of our dad's love of these things. I was, throughout my young life, given opportunities to go to the theatre with school, and grew up valuing words and music because of the home our mum and dad brought us up in. I certainly grew up with privilege, in a *cultural* sense, even if we weren't privileged in a monetary way. But I would not have been able to pursue a career in the arts and to have the life I have now without the support of the state.

I think Arts Emergency have done a good job of dissembling this stuff in choosing who and how to help. Their remit for mentees isn't based on parental income, but on higher education. You are eligible if you are the first in your family to be accessing higher education. Dave went to Oxford and was the first in our family to go to university.

And although I live an outwardly middle-class lifestyle now in many ways, I still *identify* as working class. It's part of who I am. Because of my background. If everyone who becomes a successful artist eschews their class roots, then who can younger working-class people look to for inspiration and encouragement? That's why so many of us continue to proudly self-identify as working class. You can be successful and working class, and I think it's very important to get that message out.

12 September

Meeting at University of Manchester about the Migration Project in October, now called *Be//Longing*. It all seems to be coming along nicely. Loads to do in terms of integrating specific research into the work, and we need to find a couple of actors who can be available for a couple of weeks, but it's definitely coming together.

At home, I have a Take Back afternoon: chasing up pieces for *Ten Takes on Resistance* and making some first attempts at casting. I think

I could have been a casting director in another life. The buzz when your number one choice says yes! We have some great stuff covering issues ranging from women's suffrage to the Grenfell Tower tragedy, from disability cuts to the NHS. Rosa has written a fantastic spoken-word poem about a Tinder date with a Tory. Cathy Crabb has written a lovely piece for a nine-year-old girl and her Polish immigrant grandmother.

I email radio comedy producer Alison Vernon-Smith again about my one-woman piece about Dad, *These I Love*, which I'm more and more eager to record live. She hadn't seen my previous email so I'm glad I followed up.

Kersh has been offered a place on the Writers' Room for a Netflix series, *Medici*. He'll be in London for three weeks in October. I'm so pleased for him. A writers' room environment suits him; writing can be a lonely business. He doesn't miss acting at all, but he does miss the craic, the community.

13 September

Take Back are at the launch of a new organization today called Voices of Survivors. The idea is to bring together the various services for people who have survived, or who are vulnerable to, sexual assault and rape, with the service-users themselves so that those running these services can learn from the people who are actually accessing them, and find out what needs to be improved. We have been asked by Trafford Rape Crisis to come and perform a shortened version of *My Version of Events*, our play about consent, to end the afternoon. We are in and out of the main space at Central Methodist Hall, quickly running through the scenes with our two actors, Shila and Dean, in the stairwell in true Take Back style. We miss some of the speakers but manage to catch a wonderful survivor called Catherine calling for better provision for people with learning difficulties. She says that clearer information and perhaps volunteers who have learning disabilities themselves would create a more empathic and less intimidating process for those coming forward. The aftermath of an assault must be terrifying and confusing enough; it hadn't occurred to me what it must be like for someone with an LD. And people with learning disabilities, as she points out, are a particularly vulnerable group when it comes to sexual crime, and hate crime too.

It is a good and informative afternoon, and Shila and Dean perform really well for the very receptive audience there. We get positive feedback and make some interesting and useful contacts for future work in this area.

15 September

Paula Rabbitt is the very brilliant communications manager at the Royal Exchange and she has kindly agreed to meet me to talk about how together we can best help Toby Clarke and ALT to spread the word about their incredible work. She is full of ideas and, as a board member of Eclipse, one of the country's leading black-led production companies, she has shedloads of contacts who could potentially help raise the profile and support this fledgling organization.

I'm at the theatre to open the new restaurant, The Rivals. It's the first preview of *Our Town*, too, which possibly wins the award for having the nicest cast in the history of theatre. A lovely friendly crowd assemble in the Great Hall for the ribbon cutting and loads of Prosecco and canapés. Naturally, slick as ever, I can't get the scissors to work and have to rip the ribbon with my teeth. It looks beautiful inside the new restaurant and bar, a *long* overdue cosy, intimate space to have a drink before, during and after shows. Good real ale too.

Afterwards a car comes and picks me up to take me to Cambridge where I'm to be part of a fancy-pants panel on class and television at King's College tomorrow morning.

16 September

The Royal Television Society (RTS) has organized this huge three-day conference about the future of the industry, and there are some big players involved. Alan Clements of STV has planned our part of the day and I'm sharing a stage with James Purnell, Director of BBC Radio and Education (and who used to be my MP), Anne Mensah from Sky, Fraser Nelson, editor of the *Spectator*, and Greg Dyke, former Director-General of the BBC, and the only person in that position ever not to have been privately educated. We are here to talk about class and social mobility:

how to quantify it, how to use the data to create better opportunities, to identify the barriers to success in TV for people from low-income backgrounds. It's a good discussion. I bang on about being a product of the state, the usual stuff, and about the scourge of unpaid internships. The BBC have banned them, but now do a two-week unpaid work experience placement for people trying to get into the industry. A young graduate called Suzanne, who was a recipient of the RTS bursary to help her through university, speaks from the audience. She says that this scheme is still not suitable for young people who have no money or support. Most people, she rightly points out, can't take two weeks off work (the work they have to do to live) to stay in London (usually) with no money for travel or food. It feels as though the decision-makers don't actually understand sometimes what it *really* is to be poor. The Chair, Tim Hinckes, is funny and sharp and makes the whole experience lighter than it might be otherwise, and puts everyone at ease. I like him enormously. At the beginning he asks how many of the assembled audience went to private school. It's about 70 per cent, with a significant number of Oxbridge graduates among them. This is part of the problem.

Here are some of the Deloitte figures that are bandied about. I think they're quite shocking.

- 7 per cent of UK pupils attend fee-paying schools.
- 27 per cent of actors in the UK have a working-class background.
- 42 per cent of BAFTA winners were educated independently; 35 per cent of BAFTA winners attended grammar schools.
- 67 per cent of British winners in the best leading actor, actress and director categories having attended fee-paying schools.
- 7 per cent of British Oscar winners were state educated.
- 88 per cent of people working in the cultural industries have worked for free at some point.

20 September

Kersh and I manage a sneaky date in London, seeing the matinee of *The Girl from the North Country* at the Old Vic. It's the smash hit of the moment, the one everyone's talking about, and it doesn't disappoint. It's a new play by Conor McPherson, the music is all Bob Dylan songs and it's set in Minnesota during the Depression. Shirley Henderson plays the mother who has dementia and it's an extraordinary, bold performance, entirely without inhibition: it almost feels punk. I wonder how you get to that, what freedom she was given in rehearsals and how she reached that place. I've never seen anything quite like it. I don't always like her choices but I'm captivated by them. When she sings *Like a Rolling Stone* at the end of the first half, the words, 'HOW DOES IT FEEL?' are full of longing and seem to come from the soles of her feet. She is tiny and bird-like and this huge resonant voice fills the theatre. I think my favourite moment, though, is Sheila Atim singing *Tight Connection to my Heart*: 'Has anybody seen my love?' Her voice is like crystal.

Amy Hodge has sent me Anna Jordan's latest draft of *Mother Courage and Her Children*, which we're hopefully doing as a Headlong/Royal Exchange co-production in early 2019 and that has been given the thumbs-up by the Brecht estate. I devour it in one sitting and my heart starts pounding as I'm reading it, because it's so good, and written in my voice, and I feel completely pumped up and excited about it. Anna has set it in the future, MC's cart is an old ice-cream van, and the world of the war in the play, sometimes so confusing and alienating in other translations, has been simplified to Red and Blue, North, South, East and West. The factions are as irrelevant, as meaningless, as that really. Courage and her children change allegiance constantly in order to survive.

I'm fascinated to know who will be designing it. So much of what I do will be informed by that: whether she's little and wiry or solid like a mule, how well she keeps herself in spite of the grind of survival. Shirley Henderson has made me crave a less self-conscious, less inhibited way of moving and I decide to go and do some dancing and get some singing lessons, start getting prepared. I'm not a great singer, and I don't need to be for this I don't think, but I do want to be able to communicate the songs in a way that makes them completely part of the performance. I want to be able to belt 'em out a bit.

21 September

I find a 5Rhythms dance class in Manchester, at Z-arts in Hulme, and turn up for the session with some trepidation. There's only a couple of people in the upstairs room when I arrive, as well as Chris, the teacher, as he sets up his decks and speakers. I do think about doing a runner before it's too late. 5Rhythms has been around since the 1970s and was created by Gabrielle Roth as a kind of shamanistic, meditative, free expression method. I *know*. What the hell am I doing here? I've deliberately chosen this class because it's not about steps or perfecting a routine, but about losing yourself in an unself-conscious way and dancing for a couple of hours, sober (oh my God) with strangers, to waves of music, going from flow to staccato, chaos, lyrical and stillness. It's all about connecting with your body and freeing your mind. I'm doing it because I love dancing, but am perennially crippled with embarrassment about 'letting go'. And because it frightens the bejesus out of me.

I stand in a corner and warm up a bit as the room fills up, and we get started. There are twenty to thirty of us, and if you were to walk by and peep in you'd think you'd stumbled across a weird cult or some sort of Californian therapy group. I wonder what's brought everyone here. It takes me about half an hour to stop watching myself from the outside and feeling like a knob. After two hours I am red-faced, sweaty and I feel bloody fantastic: the best I've felt in ages. I feel strangely connected to all the strangers in the room and that I can take on the world. I'm so glad I did it. It's sometimes good to leave your cynicism at home. I'll do this again.

22 September

A bit of a daft day running around from appointment to appointment. MediaCity first to do a local radio interview about a poetry event I'm taking part in next week for Hull's City of Culture Festival. It's a good interview but I'm ever so slightly discombobulated by how surprised the otherwise lovely presenter seems that a) I can string a sentence together, and b) that I have any interest in spoken word and poetry. Is it because of *Coronation Street*? Is there still an insidious snobbery about actors from soaps? On then to the Royal Exchange (to the roof garden, which I didn't know existed until today) to make a little online film about theatre and protest that will go out alongside the next production, *Parliament Square*. Is all art political? What part does protest play in art and vice versa? Afterwards I go to the café for a coffee with

Nottingham-based Talent 1st, a group supporting young artists, who are bringing their programme to Manchester next year, and want a bit of help getting people along to take part.

Then I meet my lovely Sam Edwards for tea in The Rivals restaurant and we catch up properly for the first time since the *Peterloo* wrap party. Sam is part of a feminist theatre company called Mighty Heart and they've just secured funding to do a project on eating disorders. She is one of the most naturally creative people I've ever met. She has done 5Rhythms too and loved it also, incidentally, so it's great to share our experiences of that. Just being in her company does my soul good.

In the Great Hall, there is an event taking place, *Come Close – Memories of Partition*. The Exchange has commissioned a series of monologues by South Asian writers for the seventieth anniversary of the partition of India. It's a subject most of us in the UK know little or nothing about, and yet another shameful chapter in the British Empire's history. In every part of the hall, people are performing these specially commissioned monologues, telling these forgotten stories. It's a cacophony of voices in there, quite something to witness. Shila Iqbal performs a heartbreaking piece, *Jai Hind Pakistan Zindabad*, curled up in a dark corner on the floor by the shop, talking about some of the atrocities she witnessed. We then rush over to 53two to see a sharing of our friend Hannah's new play, *Purge*, a really interesting piece about body image and social media. It's packed in the tiny pod theatre, and once again I feel such love for this city and its engaged and committed community of artists and audiences. You could see something every day of the week.

24 September

I return to the Royal Exchange with Martha to see the rest of the Partition monologues, which are being shown in the main theatre space this afternoon. What a brilliant thing to bring these stories here. We learn so much about this brutal and terrible piece of history, so relatively recent too. It's heartening to see such a big and diverse crowd out on a Sunday afternoon to watch.

25 September

This morning I'm filming a short introduction to the play *I Told My Mum I Was Going on an RE Trip*, the verbatim piece about abortion I loved so much earlier in the year. Justine Potter is producing it as a TV piece for a strand of programmes called Performance Live on the BBC, and each play is preceded by a little piece to camera giving some background. I'm being filmed in the auditorium at Contact and there are loads of old *Coronation Street* friends on the crew, which is lovely, but I am strangely nervous and it takes me a few takes to get it right. Why? Is it because I'm performing a script but as myself? Justine says she's never seen me nervous before. I am dry-mouthed and shallow-breathed, and it unnerves me how easily I've been thrown by this simple job. What the hell? Nerves are such a weird thing. And so boring. I get there in the end, everyone is kind, but it has taken me longer than I would have liked, and I leave a bit rattled by the experience.

The Greatest Play in the History of the World has sold out, which is great news. We're putting in an extra matinee on the Friday.

26 September

Back in London for a few days recording a radio adaptation of a Neil Gaiman book, *Anansi Boys*. I am completely thrilled to be working with Nathan Stewart-Jarrett, who I loved so much as Belize in *Angels in America*, and then Sheila Amit from *Girl from the North Country* (she of the crystal voice) walks into studio. I am fan-girling all over the place.

It's a funny script, completely bonkers. I'm playing the ghost of a murdered woman and have to kick Julian Rhind-Tutt (who has turned into a tiger) almost to death in this first scene of the day – even though he's actually in a booth on his own in a separate bit of the studio. I have a great time.

In the evening I catch the train to Brighton, learning lines en route, and meet Becx at the Labour Party Conference dinner. The atmosphere is buzzing down here. Someone describes it as 'conference on steroids'. There's a feeling of great unity and hope. Eddie Izzard is here, as well as Paul McGann, Lindsay Coulson and Tanya Frank. We have a great chat with Tracy Brabin, who used to be an actor and writer and is now MP for Batley and Spen, Jo Cox's old seat. She is relishing the job, despite the tragic circumstances of her getting it. And it's interesting to hear what it's really like in Parliament from someone on the inside. Becx and I have our picture taken with Lord Alf Dubs, a refugee himself as a young boy and a hero of ours. He was responsible for setting out the Dubs Amendment last year to protect unaccompanied child refugees and to ensure that Britain gives them sanctuary. His anger and despair at the government's failure to act on this is very moving.

Liz Dawn and Tony Booth have both died. Liz played the iconic Vera Duckworth in *Coronation Street* for years and was a funny, kind and unbelievably generous woman, and a real character. Tony was probably best known for his role in the comedy series *Till Death Do Us Part* and for being Tony Blair's thorn-in-the-side father-in-law in real life. He used to live in the house we live in now and we spent many entertaining evenings in his rakish company. He was full of scandalous stories and was a true raconteur, a bit of a bounder, with a very colourful life. Both Liz and Tony were big Labour activists and we honour them tonight with a toast. I feel very lucky to have known them both.

27 September

I get back to my London hotel at 2.30am so force myself to have a bit of a lie in as I have a later start at the Soundhouse Studios in Acton. Most of my scenes today are with two radio competition winners. The Carleton Hobbs radio competition has been running in drama schools for years, and each year the winners get a six-month contract to be part of the Radio Drama Company. This year's winners, Tayla Kovacevic-Ebong and Isabella Inchbald, are both in *Anansi Boys*, and are having a ball. And they're both just excellent. Tayla plays about four parts today with a vocal dexterity that I can only dream of. I'm working with Julian Rhind-Tutt again too, who is every bit as piss-funny and charming as I imagined. Even as he hammers me to death (Becky the foley artist smashing an apple in a sock). I LOVE radio.

I cross paths with the actor Tanya Moodie, literally, as she's leaving the studio for the day and she tells me she's in a play this evening at the Print Room at the old Coronet building in Notting Hill, so I decide to go along. I haven't been to the Coronet since it was a cinema back in the 1980s and early 90s (famously the last cinema in London you could smoke in) and it has been transformed into a really exquisite theatre with the most gorgeous, eccentrically decorated and opulent bar I've ever set foot in. The play, *Trouble in Mind,* is by a black actress and writer, Alice Childress, and was written in 1955. It's set in an off-Broadway rehearsal room where a white male director is directing a new 'liberal' play about black people in the Deep South. The heroine, played to oh-my-God perfection by Tanya, becomes increasingly uneasy about the way in which the plot unfolds. If I hadn't read the programme notes, I would have absolutely believed that the play could have been written this year. All the same relevant issues (unfortunately) about black stereotypes in art, about white people explaining black culture and their own hardship to black people, about the underlying scratch-the-surface living, breathing racism in the most liberal of us. I'm shocked/not shocked at all that I have never heard of Alice Childress or her play, and that it's not part of the cannon. It's a great piece of work. During the ovation, the man next to me says 'That's the best play I've ever seen'. And Tanya is something else. I'm so glad for the bit of synchronicity that brought me here tonight.

28 September

I am working with Lenny Henry today, for the first time since we were together in *Broadchurch*. What a lovely man he is and, despite his huge fame, still so open and curious and eager to learn. And I breathlessly get to meet the writer Neil Gaiman too. This has been quite a job. Just a few days in London, but with these incredible artists, including beautiful Adjoa Andoh and Doña Croll and the 100-year-old legend Earl Cameron, who is still working. What a privilege. And I've had incredible conversations, or rather I've been lucky enough to *listen,* as these black actors have talked about their experiences of the industry, the prejudice they absolutely still encounter, the tokenism of many theatre's diversity targets, and their frustration at not being *heard.*

29 September

To Hull for the City of Culture's celebrations and a weekend of poetry and spoken word organized by BBC Radio and called *Contains*

Strong Language. There is a screening of *Black Roses*, the BBC film we made two years ago about the murder of nineteen-year-old Sophie Lancaster, with poetry by Simon Armitage and the words of Sophie's mum, Sylvia, spoken by me. Sylvia is here too with Kate Conboy, her friend and PR for the Sophie Lancaster Foundation, the charity they set up in Sophie's memory. Sue Roberts, the director, who co-directed the theatre production of it at the Royal Exchange with Sarah Frankcom, is the driving force behind the whole amazing festival so she too is here.

But none of us can bear to watch the film again. Simon and I do a short explanatory introduction to the small assembled audience, then we all leave. It's a hard watch and we've all put ourselves through it once too often. Once too often being *once* only for Sylvia. I do an interview with the local news and then when the film ends we go back into the makeshift cinema to do a little Q&A. The atmosphere in the room when we return makes me cry. This harrowing story, so simply told, with poetry and verbatim dialogue, always floors everyone, and it is silent and heavy-hearted with sadness and disbelief in the space: you can feel it as soon as you walk in. It's a story about prejudice and murder and hate, but in its essence it's the story of a mum and daughter, and the magnitude of Sylvia's loss: her tiny, smart, unusual, dreadlocked and pierced teenaged daughter kicked to death for looking different. Everyone always asks about Rob, Sophie's boyfriend who survived the attack, and today is no different. It is lovely that ten years on Sylvia can report that he's finally rebuilding his life, has a new partner and lives in America. He is making art again too. Lots of people donate to the Foundation as they leave.

We then make our way to Hull College where we're treated to a delicious three-course meal courtesy of the catering students, before going to see some poetry. My friend, the poet Mike Garry, is supporting John Cooper Clarke. There is a fantastic punk spoken word artist called Toria Garbutt on first, sharing her beautiful, funny and whimsical poetry about the sometimes *un*beautiful events and happenings that were part of her growing up in Knottingley, a small ex-mining town in Yorkshire. I shoot off after Mike's set because I've scored a ticket to the sold-out Slung Low extravaganza, *The Flood*, down at the docks, starring Take Back regular Nadia Emam. It is a spectacular piece, with boats and fire and junkyard islands out on the water, and films projected on to a fan of fountain spray. We're all given headphones, as the action is taking place quite far out in the harbour, so there's a real mix of the intimate and the epic. Nadia is glorious in it as Gloriana, the elusive goddess of the piece, and there are community groups boosting the numbers and choirs forming a spine tingling soundtrack. I'm so glad I got the chance to see it.

30 September

I've been put up in a lovely and fancy hotel apartment, so I make the most of it and hang out here for the morning learning some lines and doing a bit of Take Back business before making my way to Jubilee Church in the city centre. I'm rehearsing with Jeremy Irons for a live recording of a poetry reading we're doing for BBC Radio 4 tonight called *Hull, A City of Poets In its Own Words.* The writer and presenter is Lindsey Chapman, who is from Hull herself. She's put together a great hour of anecdotes and history about her city, interspersed with poems by, amongst others, Stevie Smith, Andrew Marvell and of course, Hull University's famous librarian Philip Larkin. We have a quick run-through before a public rehearsal in front of a packed audience and it goes down really well. Everyone seems to love it. I think it weirdly works having Jeremy's sonorous tones mixed in with something a little more . . . let's say, *proletarian* from me. Charlotte, the producer, asks me to tone down my accent for 'A Dialogue between the Soul and the Body' by Marvell (I am Body, Jeremy is Soul) and I give it a bit of a go, but to be honest I never feel comfortable speaking in a different voice when I'm not playing a part, per se.

One of the poets featured in the programme is Imtiaz Dharker, whose poetry I included in my *Pick of the Week* earlier in the year. She's been specially commissioned to write about Hull for the City of Culture celebrations, and Jeremy and I are reading a segment of 'This Tide of Humber' together in the live broadcast. In the afternoon, I go to see her read it in its entirety at the university, and watch a dance interpretation of it. I think she may be one of my favourite poets and has such grace as a human being too.

Poet, playwright and performer Lou Wallwein is up for the festival too, and in a whirlwind. *Glue*, her radio play, based on her life in care and on leaving the care system, was broadcast yesterday on BBC Radio 4. She is launching her first anthology of poetry this weekend, as well as performing *Glue* as a one-woman theatre show, and shredding her encyclopaedia-sized social services file in front of a live audience. I catch her briefly between interviews and performances and worry a little for her, that it all might be too much. Like Lemn Sissay, her dear friend and fellow care-leaver, she is most at home making art out of her life, but it seems a lot to be dealing with, even amidst all the excitement. She assures me she's being gentle with herself and has upped the self-care, but it has been a rollercoaster for her for sure.

The live broadcast of *City of Poets* goes well I think. I have a lovely time reading all those beautiful words and feel happy in my skin. Jeremy and I have got on like a house on fire. He is extraordinarily elegant with an edge of the decadent that I find a bit thrilling to be around. Although there is quite an awkward moment when, on picking my case up from a storeroom at the hotel, mid-afternoon, and absentmindedly scrolling through my phone in a random corridor, the door right in front of me opens and Jeremy's little terrier, Smudge, runs out. I am loitering literally *right outside* Jeremy Iron's hotel room. It's not a foyer or anywhere near a lift or a staircase. I am, for no apparent reason, just hanging outside his room, for all the world looking like his number one fan/stalker. There's nothing I can do but style it out: 'Ah, Jeremy, hello! Hmm, I know how this must look . . .'

It's a bit surreal in the canteen having our catering college tea, with Kate Tempest on the next table, Jeremy Irons opposite me, sandwiched between the poets Michael Symmons Roberts (gloriously gossipy) and Simon Armitage. I bloody love my life sometimes. And Lindsey, the presenter, is smart and funny and manages the incredibly stressful job of timing the live broadcast *to the second* with aplomb. I can hear the distant talkback in her earpiece all the way through: 'Slow down! Speed up! We're under . . . add some narration!' and she is like a swan gliding through while her legs go like the clappers under the surface. At one point there is a bit of confusion as Jeremy somehow misinterprets her 'Sloooow down' hand gestures to us as 'speed up!' and rattles through 'To His Coy Mistress' at a rate of knots, much to our surprise and to the panic of the producers in the box.

1 October

The Conservative Party Conference have come to Manchester again. WHY? Martha and I make our way into town to meet up with the Take Back team and also, gloriously, the northern contingent of the *Peterloo* women. The rain holds off, the speakers are full of passion, the streets are full of banners: for the NHS, for the Justice for Grenfell campaign, against fracking, against the cuts. I do a poem I've written called 'The A–Z of Resisters', a celebration of all the assembled activists from every walk of life. I feel very proud to be here with my people.

2 October

The People's Assembly have organized a panel discussion called 'A Media for the Many, Not the Few', at their event tent in Piccadilly Gardens. There's quite a good turnout for a Monday afternoon and it's an interesting discussion on the whole, much more focused on journalism than drama, and very much concerned with mainstream/ establishment media and the alternative/independent press. And the totally unpredicted rise of Jeremy Corbyn that took all the mainstream media by surprise. There's a good discussion about how to make the BBC a truly public service again, representative of the people who own it. The editor of the *Morning Star* says that it would be a mistake to become complacent about protest and mass action because the Labour Party's manifesto has become so representative of many of our aims, and he's right. The continued momentum has to come from the grassroots of the movement. The People's Assembly has done so much to unify the left and to create a vibrant anti-austerity campaign, bringing in all the leftist groups and finding new and creative ways to engage people. They're a brilliant bunch. I trot out the figures about education and talk about access as usual.

Afterwards a journalist from the *Evening Standard* comes up to speak to me and the Chair, Millie. She tries to disarm us with chat about how she's a Labour supporter and how she feels the *Evening Standard*, whose editor is George Osborne, former Tory Chancellor of the Exchequer, is quite balanced in its reporting really. I actually laugh in her face. Millie says afterwards that she was recording us. I will never learn:

chatting away happily like we're old friends. God knows what I said. Fingers crossed nothing worth printing. There are far bigger things going on in the world. The Spanish government have sent in the police to stop the referendum on Catalonian independence and the images of police brutality are shocking. And there has been a mass shooting in Las Vegas at a concert with many dead and injured. It was a white gunman so as usual rather than it being condemned as an act of terrorism, the media are dragging out all the old 'loner' clichés. And still no gun controls and no chance of them with Donald Trump in power.

3 October

Ten Takes on Resistance today, to round off the weekend of protest around the conference and to celebrate Take Back's second birthday. Grant has put together a lovely video compilation of our work so far in photos and statistics, and even we're surprised by the numbers. Twenty shows, sixteen venues, with over 230 creatives writing and performing over 150 new pieces to over 3,000 audience members. Not bad for two years. I am bursting with pride.

Our venue tonight, Central Methodist Hall, is where we first started and we perform to a packed audience. Generation Now from Liverpool perform for us brilliantly again to start the night after a trailer for *Be// Longing* later in the month. Then ten wonderful, varied pieces about resistance. Rosa, my niece, has an audition in London so can't perform her poem herself, so Katie West steps in. Sue McCormick has hurt her back so Vicky Brazier performs her moving monologue about an imprisoned suffragette instead. Lou Wallwein's two-hander is preceded by the best intro video ever, Lou on full throttle ('THE TORIES ARE A BUNCH OF KNOB'EADS!'). The piece is knockout: a group of people pushing down the shit wall that everyone hates in Piccadilly Gardens being an allegory for mass action. And the evening ends with two devastating monologues: Dave MacCreedy as a non-political porter in an NHS hospital in *Death by a Thousand Cuts: Outsourced* watching a young girl die as she waits for an outsourced, private ambulance to arrive; and Sandra Cole bringing her usual magnetic presence to the piece on Grenfell Tower that we asked her to write. It is a major issue of our time, in multiple ways: the culmination of disastrous housing policy;

the unheard voices of social housing tenants; gentrification; cuts to the fire service; benefit sanctions; mismanagement of funds; and out-and-out institutional racism. The Justice for Grenfell campaigners were a huge and deeply moving presence at the demo on Sunday too. Sandra's piece ends with *Power to the People* and the audience jump to their feet as they applaud.

Afterwards we go to celebrate at the pub: Dave, Nisa Cole – our newest director who did such a great job tonight – and I end up in the People's Assembly tent in Piccadilly Gardens with Sam and Ramona, the organizers, drinking red wine until the early hours.

5 October

I am slowly but surely getting back on top of everything after a hectic couple of weeks.

Managed to get over to see Mum, answered emails, learned some more lines (I am still procrastinating like crazy over this, though). The *Radio Times* has asked me to write an opinion piece about the portrayal of rape on TV, as a new ITV series, *Liar*, reaches its conclusion this week. The topic is whether or not we should be telling stories about rape as entertainment. Of course I think absolutely we should. When rape and serious sexual assault are reaching epidemic proportions in our society, drama surely has a responsibility to ask questions about that and to start conversations. This show has been controversial in that the whodunit element (who was lying: the alleged rapist or the victim?) made way for something altogether more important mid-series. It was revealed in Episode 3 that the very nice doctor that the audience were encouraged to believe couldn't possibly do something like that, *had* done it. The issue of the lack of belief of rape survivors coming forward is a huge one.

Alison Vernon-Smith has got back to me about my one-woman show about dad, *These I Love*, and the possibility of doing a live recording of it for radio. She likes it in principle, but bluntly tells me that it's structurally all over the place, that it's unclear what it's about. I feel a bit resistant to this. It's not that I can't be bothered to rework it, it's that I like it as it is. It's about my dad: the way he turned his terrible and tragic childhood around to become a brilliant parent himself; the healing power of music, poetry and nature; the role of daftness in our lives, my childhood, our relationship. We found a box of diaries and notebooks after he died full of beautiful writings about his love of life and his occasional struggles with depression and grief, dating back to the 1940s. These diary entries and poems form the framework for the piece. It's so difficult because it's so personal to me that I'm not sure how much I'm willing to change in it, but I don't know if I'm being a bit precious. Probably. Blimey, writing is so exposing. I'm certain Alison will just think I can't take notes. We agree to meet up and discuss it soon.

In other news, the *Morning Star* newspaper are going to publish my anti-austerity A–Z poem that I read at the demo last Sunday, so I'm chuffed about that.

In the evening I've been invited to the launch of a fund to support young people with mental health problems. The new fund is part of Mosscare St Vincent's Foyer, an organization that provides supported housing for young homeless people, often care-leavers, who have extra needs. It's a brilliant place – one of a couple in existence and with more planned, with creativity at the heart of what they do, and this is reflected at the launch tonight. Wonderful Tony Walsh is hosting and reads some of his inspiring, political and life-affirming poetry. There are songs and performances from some of the young people, including a poem from Hannah, who is a resident at The Foyer, the supported apartment block, here. And the Manchester Dementia Gospel Choir have us on our feet, clapping and singing along, and crying. People are fucking amazing. The world is in such a terrible state, but there are millions of people doing their bit to make it better. I feel like I've met a lot of them this year.

6 October

Jane Montgomery Griffiths is an Associate Professor at Monash University in Melbourne as well as being an actor there, which isn't as unusual for Australia as it perhaps would be here. She played Vivian Bearing, the professor dying of ovarian cancer, in Margaret Edson's play *Wit* there a few years ago and is writing a paper on the effects of playing that character on an actor's physical and mental wellbeing. For example, perhaps psychosomatically, one can take on a character's personality to a degree, or start to become ill as a result, or imagine that you are becoming ill. Also how the role stays with the actor afterwards, what physical transformations were required (weight loss and head-shaving etc) and the psychological effects of those transformations on the performer. She is interviewing women who have played Vivian around the world, and we meet for lunch today in Manchester.

It is such an interesting conversation. It occurs to me that Vivian is the only role I've played in twenty years that has been played by another actor. As well as my character in *Coronation Street*, I've only ever performed new writing on stage, screen and radio. So to hear another person's ideas about the role and interpretations of certain moments in the piece, and to meet someone who knows that character as well as I do, is fascinating. I think playing the role took its toll in more significant ways than it did for me when I did the run at the Royal Exchange in January 2016. An actor who played Vivian in a touring production in Scotland, has said she'd never do it again. Jane herself implies that she needed some decompression time at the end of the performance each night. She also convinced herself that she had the symptoms of ovarian cancer afterwards. For me, strangely, *Wit* was one of the happiest and most satisfying jobs I've ever had. Challenging, of course, on loads of levels: the dense text, the weight loss, shaving off my hair, the accent, being on stage the entire time . . . But, conversely, it was a completely joyful experience. And I would love to do it again.

There are a few reasons for this, I reckon. I felt heard and respected by my director, Raz. The rest of the cast were fantastic and supportive. And, significantly, the end of the play was completely exhilarating, a moment of release for Vivian. A moment of what you might call grace, I suppose. And it was that feeling that I carried into the theatre bar afterwards and into my life, I suppose. All the pain and illness and loneliness Vivian experiences happens during the play; it plays out from beginning to middle to end without interruption. Leaving the stage I was left only with the liberation of the final moment of her being released from it all in death. And this, I hope, freed me up to be present for the audience members who wanted to talk afterwards. Thinking back, as I talk to Jane, I realize that actually I've never been more well than when I was doing that play. And in the preparation for the role, as I've discussed before here, I was informed greatly by my experience of playing Sylvia in *Black Roses*. Understanding that playing the role of someone who has been through something (same with *Broadchurch*) is very different indeed from going through it for real, and you *can*, I think, actually compartmentalize any difficult thoughts and feelings easily in that context. It's a flick of a mental switch really.

The conversation makes me miss *Wit* again, of course, and I email Raz, who says he's been having regular pangs for it too. It will not bloody leave us, that play.

7 October

I spend an overdue and satisfying morning learning lines and working on *The Greatest Play*. God, I love it. Reading the last couple of pages for the first time in ages (as I'm inching through the pages as I learn them) I remember how beautiful it is, full of Kersh's stock-in-trade love of life and utter redemption for his characters.

11 October

Raz, who is directing Kersh's play, is up from London with our lovely designer, Naomi Kuyck-Cohen, to look at the studio space at the Exchange and talk about ideas and concepts. We have a bit of lunch and discuss shoes, a huge part of the show, and whether we can ask the audience to take theirs off as they enter the space. Naomi wants the entire studio to be carpeted in a deep blue, so it might work, but I am aware that it might piss some people off. We settle for a free and easy optional de-shoeing, encouraged by me before the show starts. We all get excited about the possibility of using the audience's shoes to signal the various characters in the play.

I wish Kersh were here. I feel a bit protective of him in his absence, when concepts he's written in threaten to be scrapped to achieve a more minimalist telling of the story. It all feels a bit last-minute too, but I trust Raz, I like Naomi a lot, and I know we'll get there. It's hard to imagine anything really until we start rehearsing. It's a deceptively complicated piece, a love story, but with a load of science in there and moving around in time, too. We all love it, so all will be well. Raz's mum is unwell and he is a bit tired and out of sorts and we have a bit of to-ing and fro-ing by text later making sure we're both okay with everything. I have to be careful not to step on everyone's toes and to let everyone do their jobs. I'm so used to the Take Back way now, where our roles overlap, and where we know each other so well that things just happen very organically and very instantly. I must be careful not to enforce that kind of immediacy on everyone else's process. Butt out, in other words.

12 October

The familiar shaky feeling of exposure this morning. My article on TV and rape is in the *Radio Times* and a few news agencies have picked up on it and quoted from it. I feel pissed off that they call it an *interview with me*, when it's an article *written by me*. Such a tiny detail, but it makes a difference to me: the fact I've been asked to construct an article in my own words, espousing my own views on a subject interesting to me and be paid for it. Not just an actor vox-popping to include in someone else's piece.

And my protest poem is in the *Morning Star*, which makes me very proud, but also completely unnerves me. I fear backlash. I'm scared of criticism and negativity. I fear the thought that I'm pushing myself forward, being bigheaded or showing off, even as I share the piece with my own family. Having strong views, standing up for what I believe in, being heard, doesn't come easily to me, despite appearances. I think this is to do with my gender and my class. I need to start owning it a bit more. I'm heading for fifty, for God's sake. I need to hold on to the positive encounters I have with lovely people every day. And toughen up a bit. An interview with the American actor Frances McDormand, that someone has shared on Facebook, helps. She is sixty, wears no make-up, has had no 'work' done, is working in Paris with the Wooster Group, a New York-based avant-garde theatre company and takes zero-shit from anyone. Yeah. Be More Frances. That's my little mantra today. I'm on my own path.

In the afternoon, I see my first-ever 'relaxed performance' of a play. Relaxed shows are for people who want to come to the theatre, but who perhaps have additional needs. People who, for whatever reason, can't sit still for long periods, or have a young baby they can't leave for the duration; or who don't know, or who can't cope with, the 'normal' constraints and boundaries of being part of a theatre audience. Today, at the matinee of *Our Town* at the Royal Exchange, there is a large group from Moodswings Network, a mental health charity in Manchester, as well as several teenagers and some babies in the auditorium. Youssef, playing the Stage Manager/Narrator of this beautiful play, starts by introducing himself and explaining what a relaxed performance is, before the cast all introduce themselves to us. This production plays with the form anyway, with tables and chairs set out on the stage where cast and audience sit with each other and chat in the pre-show. The actors are in modern dress and speak with their own accents even though the play is firmly set in early twentieth-century America. So the vibe lends itself to this further 'relaxing' perfectly. We are told that the lights will remain up on us throughout and the doors open: people can come and go as they please, can make noise; nobody need feel uncomfortable or constrained. The atmosphere is warm and inclusive.

The difference for me is in my own tolerance of audience restlessness: a flick of a mental switch means I'm completely cool with a toddler shouting out, the rustling of papers from a gaggle of GCSE students, the comings and goings of various spectators. There is something very moving about the added layer of community among us, in this beautiful, timeless play about community. Even as the cast smile and tell us who they are playing in the first moments, I'm getting teary. There is an energy in this space that makes me feel very raw and alert and alive. Sometimes I think this is the most alive I feel – in the theatre, but in *this* theatre in particular. And the diversity on stage is so uplifting, with a deaf actor, Nadia Nadarajah, playing Mrs Soames, and with signing totally incorporated into the scenes. There is a wide and heartening spectrum of ages and ethnicities too. A proper *Our Town* for this town.

The news is full of Harvey Weinstein, the Hollywood producer, who has been making young women's lives hell for years, allegedly inviting actresses to his hotel room, masturbating in front of them, sexually assaulting them and, in some cases, raping them. There are pages and pages of allegations, with pretty much all of Hollywood condemning these alleged actions, but with half saying they apparently never knew and half saying that everyone knew exactly how he operated. It's thrown wide open the abuse of power that goes on right across the industry (here too of course, but particularly in the toxic and deeply misogynistic atmosphere of Hollywood) and has started an important and long overdue conversation. It feels like the collective scales have fallen from the eyes of the world at last and that things might actually start to change now. I really believe that. Actor Emma Thompson appears on *Newsnight* and calls out a crisis in masculinity. And there's the rub. Even the language we use when we talk about these offences reflects an imbalance. These are crimes against women, but we rarely talk of them as crimes committed *by men*. In this same week a report in British schools says that there has been a massive spike in peer abuse among young people – basically, children sexually assaulting other children. And, yes, that means, overwhelmingly, boys sexually abusing girls. Something has shifted this week. It's one of those moments when everyone has to take a look at themselves and ask, 'Could I have done more to uncover this? Expose it? Call it out?' There will be more revelations to come for sure. In UK theatre, there are powerful and feted people notorious for similar abuses: we've all heard the stories, and it feels like their time is running out.

14 October

There is a screening tonight at Salford Arts Theatre of *The Acting Class*, the film I contributed to about working-class access to the arts. It's a really well put-together film, featuring interviews with lots of young people who have been prevented from pursuing a career in acting or going to drama school. These are intercut with bits from those of us who were lucky enough to get there: me, Maxine Peake, Chris Eccleston. I am really impressed with Sam West, who gently and humbly acknowledges his own privilege as he speaks with great articulacy about the need for the arts in every young person's life, even if they don't want to pursue it as a career. The skills you learn in drama, he says, are skills for life: working with others, articulating ideas, thinking critically, speaking publicly, empathizing with others. And those skills should be available to all. There is a great and lively Q&A afterwards. Mike and Dee, who made the film, Tom Stocks, the founder of Actor Awareness, actor Andrew Ellis and I form the panel. Actor Awareness is yet another fantastic organization set up with the aim of creating opportunities for actors, writers, directors and makers who don't have access to more traditional routes into the industry. Tom puts on scratch events and sharings and has created a little community in London.

A lot of the film is about Tom, his difficult childhood, his attempts to raise funds to take up his place at East 15 Acting School, and his determination to carve out a life and a career as an actor, in spite of everything life has thrown at him. He has brilliant energy and is full of righteous anger. There are a lot of young people in the audience asking for advice, wondering how to proceed, talking about the prohibitive costs of just *being* an actor: headshots, Spotlight subscription, showreels, travel to auditions, etc. The conversation naturally leads to the representation of working-class people on TV too. A couple of times I feel a responsibility to bring the conversation back round to a more positive frame. It's so easy for us all to sit together and get chippy about the state of things, and start to get misty-eyed about the golden days of dramas like *Boys from the Blackstuff,* and pretend telly is all *Downton Abbey* these days. It isn't. There are amazing shows being made: in the last eighteen months alone we've had *Happy Valley, Broken, Murdered for Being Different, Three Girls, The Moorside, Damilola, Our Loved Boy,* to name a few.

And the tired old argument that our theatres are exclusive and posh will not wash with me at all. I know from seeing first-hand the incredible community engagement work the Royal Exchange, HOME, Bolton Octagon, Oldham Coliseum and Contact do, particularly with young people, that this isn't always the case. In the 1980s and 90s the Exchange had a bad reputation for not employing any northern-based actors, and some people still believe this to be the case. It isn't. Just look at *Our Town.* And a little row breaks out in the audience at one point when a man slags off the Salford-based Lowry Theatre and says, 'Who in Salford wants to see *La Bohème*? Where are the new plays by Salford writers?' and a woman shouts back, 'I'm Salford born and bred, I love the opera, and I've had two plays on at the Lowry . . . but I didn't see you in the audience!'

If we'd been having these conversations two years ago I would definitely have felt more impotent and hopeless, but the fact is that we are on the cusp of a change in this country. Young people are registering to vote in their droves and the people in power are, for the first time in a long time, having to sit up and take note and start thinking of policies that will win young votes. Labour has recently published a huge piece of research on class and access to the arts, and this will be at the heart of their cultural policy. I feel hopeful that things could be about to shift in wildly exciting ways for young people hoping to pursue a career in the arts.

And young people are constantly filling me with hope. There's a young black director/actor in the film, Elliot Barnes-Worrell, who crowdfunded a short film called *The Works*, with a cast of working-class, mainly black, actors and in which the dialogue is all taken from Shakespeare. He speaks so excitedly about Shakespeare and how he is *our* writer, how we need to claim him back, how we need to be unafraid of the language and ideas in his plays. A young woman in the audience tells another to make her own work. 'Nobody can stop us from making theatre,' she says. 'Get a group of friends and just do it.' How bloody inspiring. Shaban Dar, who is in his third year at ALRA North drama school, is here. Shaban got in touch with Take Back during our *America* rehearsals and came and observed. He has been to every show since and Becx subsequently wrote a piece for him as part of a response evening to the production of *Freak* at 53two. He asks intelligent questions and talks passionately, and without self-pity, about the financial struggles facing drama school-leavers. I am reminded again that, however inaccessible and exclusive and unaffordable things are, there are always people who stand out, who have the extra drive and spark to make things happen for themselves. People like Tom and Shaban, Elliot, the theatre-making girl in the auditorium, who turn up, engage and connect. Who are present. They are the future and it's pretty exciting. We just need as a society to make sure that the world doesn't grind them down to the point that they have to give up.

15 October

Actor Awareness, led by Tom, are running a workshop at Hope Studios this afternoon and he has asked me to pop in to do a Q&A. The fifteen or so participants are deep in conversation in groups when I arrive, all creating a one-minute sci-fi scene, set in a cellar, that incorporates the words 'hate', 'chimney' and 'chocolate'. I can see it's a wrench to break off and listen to me chuntering on for half an hour and they all laugh a bit too readily when I say that to them. There are a range of ages present, all of them trying to break into a career in acting, and eager to know how to do that, without the traditional route of drama school available to them. How fantastic that they can spend a couple of hours on a Sunday getting creative with other like-minded people, for free.

Tom has created something really needed and special. There are lots of suggestions I can make. Manchester is alive with groups and classes and venues. I tell them about the open-for-all writing group at Oldham Coliseum, Scribbles; about the play-reading group at Hope Mill; the free-to-hire space above Gullivers pub. I suggest that they see as much theatre as they can, be seen, make connections, take advantage of the cheap and free tickets available at all the main houses, get to the many fringe venues and make new friends.

I once again recommend Andy Nyman's wonderful *The Golden Rules for Actors,* and then I leave them to their cellars and chocolate chimneys and wish them well.

I've been sent a fantastic book, *Acting in British Television*, by Christopher Hogg and Tom Cantrell. I did an interview with them three years ago when I was at the Royal Court and am chuffed to bits to be featured in the soap opera chapter and that a lovely picture of Hayley, my character in *Corrie*, graces the cover. I read it deep into the night. Not my bit obviously – I'm tired enough of my own bloody opinions on everything – but interviews with Graeme Hawley, my soap colleague, and Jason Watkins, recently a highlight of the BBC comedy *W1A*, as well as the brilliant Nina Sosanya. It's a fascinating read, hearing about different people's techniques and reading Rebecca Front's account of process involved in working on an Armando Iannucci show, which sounds terrifying and exhilarating in equal measure. I think it's a great resource for anyone hoping to have a television career, in front of or behind the camera. Or even anyone who is curious as to how it all works.

17 October

My line-learning is going okay, but it's a slog. I find it much, much easier when I'm on the move, so the dog is getting plenty of windy autumn walks. I do a bit of prep too: dividing the piece into titled units and numbering them, making notes. Normally I do an exercise that involves going through the text and noting down everything that is said about the character, by themselves or by anyone else, and highlighting what we know to be true based on that. This is the framework, the basic structure of the character. Then I fill in the gaps, researching stuff that the character knows about. So, with *Wit*, she was a Professor of Literature specializing in the poetry of John Donne. So I had to know all about that in advance of rehearsals by reading the metaphysical poets and everything I could lay my hands on about Donne. And I usually write a biography of the person I'm playing – in first person, freehand – to flesh out the detail in my head and make them more real to me. There aren't huge amounts of room for this working on *Greatest Play* as I'm really a storyteller inhabiting the world of the Preston Road and the people who live there.

To Hope Mill in the evening to see our friend David Gregan-Jones's new play, *What I Felt Whilst Under You*. It's one continuous hour-long scene between two actors; a study of a marriage, and is really accomplished. I feel the usual complete admiration that people get things written and made and put on. Becx and Grant are here too, and we have the briefest of catch-ups before and after. They are completely on top of *Be//Longing*. I feel terribly guilty for not being more involved, but the combination of Kersh not being around and having to prepare for *Greatest Play* has made it impossible. They are, of course, lovely about it. I miss them.

18 October

It's unusual to have a read-through for a radio drama, especially one you're not actually going to be able to be in, but this afternoon I'm invited to do just that for a Roy Williams adaptation of John Wyndham's novel *The Midwich Cuckoos.* It's an interesting adaptation that looks at difference through a contemporary lens by making the professor black and giving him a deaf mixed-race daughter. There are two directors, Polly Thomas and Jenny Sealey; Jenny is deaf and Artistic Director of Graeae, the world-famous theatre company that puts deaf and disabled people front and centre of their work. Emily Howlett is playing Michaela, the daughter, and is excellent and also brilliant fun. During the break she is full of gossip about the very small deaf theatre community. I love it. I would really like to learn British Sign Language at some point. I've seen a few productions recently where it's been integrated into performance, including in *Our Town,* and I'm sure we'll be seeing more and more of it. I play a posh colonel and have to polish off my rusty RP, sometimes

more successfully than others. My big fat Lancashire Rs ('MaRs BaR in
the CaR PaRk') make the odd appearance and, on one occasion, I
nearly extend the A in 'gas' ('gaaas') and stop myself just in time.

Liz Stevenson was an AD at the Royal Exchange on the Birkbeck
directors' scheme when I did my first job there after *Coronation Street*
(Simon Stephens's *Blindsided* with Katie West). Liz has gone on to do
amazing things. Most recently she's set up a theatre company in her
hometown of Chorley in Lancashire, with her brother and her partner,
called Junction 8. Tonight I take Lyss to see *Under the Market Roof*,
Junction 8's first production, a specially written play set in the actual
town centre market, with a cast of four actors and a community chorus.
We sit with hot chocolate and blankets under canopies and spend
a magical hour as the story unfolds, at the end of which, naturally, I
have tears dripping under my chin. It's another of those experiences:
watching a play about a community, with that community, in that
community. I don't think I love anything more. And the chorus are so
committed and enthusiastic, when they all appear at the end, dressed
in market stall holder costume from across the ages all singing along
to 'Don't Stop Believin'' . . . well, it floors me. Amy Drake, our Take
Back regular and my mate, is the lead. I've never seen her play straight
before (she's a natural comedian) and she knocks it out of the park. Part
of my blubbing is pride. I absolutely love these nights. Everyone is on a
high afterwards. Liz tells me afterwards that it was a slog getting the
play on, making it happen. Nobody understood what she was trying to
do or why, but now she's got this first production under her belt (and the
town has *loved* it) I think Junction 8 will become part of the furniture in
Chorley.

On the long drive home, I listen to a BBC Radio 2 documentary on
Bruce Springsteen, while Lyss dozes in the passenger seat. He talks a
lot about how having children changed his life, how he had to adjust
from a troubadour, transient, nocturnal life and learn how to be present
for his children. I think about my life as a mother, and this diary, and
whether it adequately reflects some of the struggles I have in striking the
right balance. It's a working diary, not a personal one, but the lines often
blur for me, particularly as Martha grows older and her own nascent
passion for, and involvement in, the theatre develops. What's wonderful
is that she will never turn down the opportunity to see a play with me,
so I can easily combine the filling of her well with the filling of mine. We

can spend quality time together doing what we most love in the world. This has deepened and strengthened our relationship. That and protest, as she becomes more and more engaged with the world's injustices and seeks to use her voice to change things. One of the positive things about social media has been the resource it's provided for Martha as she's become interested in feminism in particular, and in other campaigns around global inequality. Lyss is a simpler soul, very much my baby still, right now, and our shared joys are more prosaic: mooching around Tesco, watching kids' telly, going to the park, play-fighting. And sometimes I really, really don't want to break off from work to do those things. It's hard. I can't say in all honesty whether having children has adversely affected my work or whether it's improved me as an artist. I think the time constraints that come from a family's timetable (*I have to learn two pages by 3pm when they get home from school!*) can be useful in terms of focussing the mind. I think I'm aware of trying, and often failing, to be a good role model to them and that might affect my choices. I have certainly turned down work because it's meant being away from them for too long. So is the pram in the hall the enemy of art? It hasn't been for me, I don't think. But it certainly makes things harder, more complicated, and a lot of time is spent seeking balance. Even more time is spent tidying up, shouting, nagging and breaking up fights. Motherhood has been a source of great joy to me, but also my biggest challenge *without a doubt*.

23 October

My friend and neighbor Adam Zane has put together, in a WEEK, a beautiful celebration of the life of the indefatigable Martyn Hett, one of the twenty-two victims of the Manchester Arena attack. Eight actors speak the words of his friends and partners as they remember him: his energy and spirit, his don't-give-a-fuck attitude and his unerring sense of inclusion and fun. The show is one of two evenings at Hope Mill, attended by the friends who feature in the piece, as well as members of Martyn's family. It is quite something to experience it in their company, quite overwhelming. And the title, and the rallying call #BeMoreMartyn, resounds for us all. It makes me miss a younger, dafter, less earnest version of myself. And makes me mourn again the loss of this fantastic force of nature. I am so proud of Adam for getting this on and raising funds for the family's favourite charities at the same time.

24 October

First day of rehearsals for *The Greatest Play in the History of the World.* Kersh and I catch the train into town together, and it feels like a real treat to get the chance to go to work together. Raz, the director, has travelled up from London and we have a meet-and-greet with Pip, our stage manager, and Tara Finney, our producer. Raz suggests that he and Kersh read the play aloud so I can hear it, and I joke that he can't bloody bear to listen to me for an hour even when I'm rehearsing a one-woman show; that I have to listen to him instead. It's helpful, actually – nice to hear the rhythms of it and recognize which bits I know better than others in terms of lines too.

In the afternoon we start to quietly block the beginning, placing the various 'locations' on Preston Road, the world of the play, and discuss how to differentiate between the narration parts of the story and the 'lecture' about The Golden Record on NASA's Voyager One, which forms the framework of the play. Again I'm reminded of how lovely it is as a piece, and it is really wonderful to be part of something so full of heart and optimism and Martyn Hett-like lust for life. It's a love story set against the backdrop of the two Golden Records which were sent out into interstellar space in the 1970s, full of sounds and images portraying life on earth, in case intelligent life elsewhere ever comes across it. The earth feels like a pretty bonkers place right now, so this little piece of unapologetic romantic storytelling, about living fully and well, feels just the ticket. There are so many resonances with *Our Town*, which Kersh had neither read nor seen before writing this, that it feels like a perfect bit of programming, entirely by accident.

We see James Fritz's *Parliament Square*, the Bruntwood Prize-winning play in the main house at the Exchange in the evening. I like it considerably more than Raz and Kersh do. It's flawed and loses its way a bit halfway through, but the first act is highly theatrical and utterly compelling, and the performances are spot on. It's a play about a person being pushed to the edge of what she can tolerate in watching the world suffer, and the consequences of her decision to take drastic action in a moment of extreme protest.

25 October

I have an annoying and untimely cold, which, alongside some classic actor anxiety dreams, is disrupting my sleep, so I feel pretty knackered in rehearsals this morning. In spite of this we have a really productive day, and manage to block and roughly run through a third of the play. I'm keen to get on my feet and start moving as soon as possible, so that it will be in my muscle memory as well as my head.

We play with shoeboxes and slippers, which denote the various people in the story, and try out using borrowed footwear from audience members for some incidental characters, which I think will work really well. We're staging it in traverse in the studio, with rows on either side of the length of the space, which works perfectly for the world of the road. But I'm finding the use of two placed microphones at either end, for use in the Golden Record sections, a bit clunky. Well, the getting to them and back into the world of the here-and-now story again. We're going to have a look tomorrow at the possibility of pre-recording those sections and overlaying them, so that the action itself doesn't get so broken up by me getting to the mics. What is great (and I'm sure Raz would say otherwise!) is that it feels like a real collaboration in the room. I don't feel I can't suggest things or say what doesn't feel comfortable for me. My big challenge is going to be properly engaging the audience, eyeball to eyeball, and varying the musicality of my long narrative sections; not falling into a rhythm or a pattern of speaking that becomes one-note or one-tone. I think we're on track, though. I feel a bit less panicked about the amount of time we have left after today.

I've been sent a great play to consider for next year, *The Almighty Sometimes* by Kendall Feaver, about the mother of a spirited teenage daughter who is wrestling with mental health and medication and creativity, another Bruntwood Prize-winner from two years ago. It's really special.

27 October

Production meeting today so all the creative team are in town: Naomi, the designer; Jack Knowles, the lighting designer; Tara, our producer; and Mark Melville, our composer/sound designer. Raz and I meet early to carry on blocking the end of the play so I can attempt a full run for everyone in the afternoon. God, it feels long. It runs at an hour and twenty minutes which is about fifteen minutes too long and by the end I'm completely sick of the sound of my own voice. But as a first stagger through after only four days it's not bad. I need to be much more on top of the lines in the last section, but we have another week so I'm not too worried.

Kersh and I go for a pint in the evening and make some cuts. There is so much lovely detail in the first half of the play, but in the second half we need to crack on with the plot. My head feels fried from remembering all the words and the moves. There is a lot of action concerning shoes and slippers and moving them and myself around the space, and I'm knackered from trying to keep it all in my brain. Next week hopefully everything will go in a bit deeper and it will be easier. I've decided to accept the play at the Exchange, *The Almighty Sometimes*. It's beautifully written, and it feels like a proper old-fashioned play, where people talk to each other in scenes, and I'm looking forward to that. Norah Lopez Holden, who was so fantastic in *Our Town* the other week, will play my daughter and Katy Rudd will direct. It's funny to think what a big part of my life these names will be in a couple of months' time, because the people you rehearse a play with become really important to you really quickly, I find. There's something about this job that accelerates friendship.

29 October

Get-in day at Hope Mill for *Be//Longing* and finally an opportunity for me to pull my weight and do something for this project. I've had to leave so much of it to Becx and Grant because of rehearsals for *Greatest Play*, and it feels good to be with them, embracing the chaos, again. Most of the set is at Becx's flat which need loading into a van and taking to Hope Mill, where we spend several hours assembling and taping cardboard boxes. These will form the basis of the set, like the warehouse in the refugee camp at Calais. We've taken out all the usual theatre seating and replaced it with ad-hoc camping chairs and folding plastic seats to create a thrown-together space.

There is so much to do. Grant has done an incredible job, aided by his brilliant dad Tony, making ten freestanding telephone posts to dot around the theatre. When you lift the handset you hear a monologue, written by Becx and based on the research she's done about experiences of migration. There are several beautiful installations all around the space, made from maps, suitcases, sand, children's clothes, life jackets, as well as our tent from the B!RTH Festival. I think it's going to look amazing. It has been very freeing to have a budget for once. This is Grant's absolute forte and although he's worked far too hard as always and looks about to drop, I know he's excited about this one. And it is so good to be with my gang, catching up as we work.

30 October

Early start at the Swan Street rehearsal room to do an interview with BBC Radio 4 about regional theatre, with the poet Michael Symmons Roberts chairing a discussion between me, the lovely playwright Simon Stephens and the theatre critic Kevin Bourke. It's an interesting and lively discussion covering funding and sponsorship and the role of theatre in a region: whether it has a duty to reflect its audience or whether we should be producing work with more universal appeal. A bit of both, we agree. Theatre should definitely hold a mirror up to its audience, but we all come to the conclusion that we should also challenge them. We shouldn't always give the people what they want: we should sometimes give them something new, something they've never seen before. There is much talk about the relevance of the Manchester International Festival, of which I'm a big fan, precisely because it offers something that might be outside our normal experience as a regional audience, something unapologetically esoteric and experimental. And it's clear that none of us really know what Manchester's newest space, The Factory, will add to the theatrical landscape. It is such a huge space, none of us feel sure as to what it could house, really, but time will tell.

All of us big up Sarah Frankcom, Artistic Director of the Exchange, for really changing the landscape of theatre here, pushing boundaries in terms of risk-taking but also doing incredible work in trying to make the place more accessible, affordable and diverse. We agree that HOME has found its place in the city by offering something entirely unique, something more director-led and European in approach. We all leave pretty pumped-up about the current state of theatre in Manchester, actually. Simon is about to become Professor of Playwriting at Manchester Metropolitan University, which is wonderful news for the city too. He is utterly charming and generous.

I do a phone interview for a piece in the *Guardian* about auditions. So much changed during the sixteen years I was in *Coronation Street*. Actors used to be given travel expenses to attend – there were no self-tapes. You weren't required to learn the scene and turn up with a ready-for-an-audience performance. But the biggest change that I've noticed (more from talking to younger actors, really) is that you're not told if you don't get the job. This courtesy seems to have become an anachronism and that feels very wrong to me: waiting for weeks to hear until you finally have to assume you haven't got the role is utterly detrimental to the mental wellbeing of auditionees. I am going to talk to Equity about this. It feels like such a small inconvenience for a casting department, particularly in the age of cut-and-paste emails, but would make such a difference to actors, who have so little control over their lives and careers anyway.

Rehearsals are fun. We start at the beginning of the play again and do more specific work on blocking. I'm feeling a bit more confident that we'll be ready: we have a few more days yet. We're rehearsing later all this week, just afternoon sessions, so I can spend some time with the kids at half-term and go straight to Hope Mill in the evenings for the performances of *Be//Longing*.

31 October

After rehearsals I walk over to Ancoats for the first night of *Be//Longing*. Everyone is stressed. Artists are trying to finish off their installations in the main space as Matt rehearses the actors and last-minute lighting tweaks go on. The space looks incredible, totally transformed, and the various pieces of art are interactive and affecting.

A van is parked outside with the door slightly ajar, from which Kersh's piece about people-smuggling plays on a speaker. As you walk through the foyer past hanging lifejackets, Louise Wallwein's epic poem about volunteering in Kos and Lesbos plays. Matilda Glen's corner installation in the dust-sheet-covered bar makes the link between colonialism and migration, and brings the human aspect of the crisis into sharp relief: embroidered facts on tatty pieces of clothing and furniture, old photographs – relics of a life. In the main space there is a pile of suitcases spilling out sand and the detritus of a life on the road: baby bottles, mobile phones, socks. When you touch the handles of the cases, refugee stories read by actors play. The same artist, Sophie Mahon, has loaned us her beautiful copper world map, too. When you place your hand on a country it plays a chord, each region a different deep and resonant sound. It is impossible to make discordant music in this world.

Our old favourite, the *Under Canvas* tent, sits at the back of the space amidst an Amnesty exhibition of photographs, and a TV plays a film about an astronaut's experience of seeing the earth from space, and the difficulty in accepting boundaries on returning to land. We manage to get the place ready in the nick of time, and everyone breathes again as the theatrical aspect of the experience begins. There is an old piece of canvas hanging to make a makeshift screen and we start with a film of the dance piece that Grant has made: Yandass dancing among chalked boundaries in a black box over a soundtrack of negative social media comments about asylum seekers and a banging piece of music by Keeley Forsyth. As the piece progresses, she dances away the chalked lines until she is covered in chalk dust in a boundaryless space. Then Becx's play begins and it is perfect.

In the forty minutes of the piece, performed by our actors Nadia Emam and Darren Kuppan, we are taken on a tram journey to the 'most important meeting' in a young asylum seeker's life; we sit with a newly arrived young mother in a cockroach-ridden bedsit; and empathize with the refugee who no longer wants to speak of anything that led him to this point. But we are also reminded that migration isn't exclusively the preserve of those fleeing terror and war: a couple set up an English restaurant when they emigrate to Spain; someone starts a new life in Australia.

It is a rallying cry for connection, for reaching out beyond boundaries. The line 'In a café in Colwyn Bay, someone has a cup of tea with a stranger from another country' resonates, and inspires us to see beyond the headlines and the numbers and the faceless masses, as well our own notions of what migration is, and see each other as human beings without borders.

I couldn't be prouder.

1 November

Wonderful news for Kersh, who has been accepted onto the *Coronation Street* writing team. This will give him some stability and, more importantly, a gang. Writing is such a solitary business, and the *Corrie* team are a famously gregarious bunch. It will be a big change for us and he'll be required to be away at conference several times a year, but it is great news. We feel as though we have come full circle. It's almost four years to the day since I filmed my last scenes there and now Kersh is starting on his own *Corrie* adventure, as we do our play together, too. It feels as though there's a lovely synergy to it all, to this period of our life together.

After a good afternoon's rehearsal, in which we accidentally run the play (I start the first half and kind of keep going . . .), it's the official gala opening of *Be//Longing* for the researchers at the University of Manchester. It seems to go well and everyone appears impressed by the scope of the work we've done; the scale of the piece has exceeded what they expected. And once again everyone comments on how theatre can, in a matter of minutes, bring to life and humanize the necessary facts and figures of important academic work. The post-show discussion is lively. Becx is on the panel and we are challenged about our work 'preaching to the choir', as usual. It is frustrating, this assumption that we somehow make this work for our own gratification; that the work in itself, the bringing of audiences together and the emboldening of thought and implicit call to action isn't enough. There are many companies who are funded to take work into schools and communities. It's just not what we do.

2 November

A week to go before we open *The Greatest Play in the History of the World*. Another run today and it's still too long, despite more cuts. It's getting sharper and more specific every time, but the saggy sections are standing out more as a result. I am going to have to do some serious work this weekend, on line specificity in particular. I'm doing a bit of paraphrasing and every single run I manage to skip a section. This has been the hardest play I've ever had to learn. The pace of it is crucial, it is incredibly wordy, and the action necessarily jumps around in time in a non-linear way that makes it easy to get lost. I can feel myself getting a bit knackered, mentally, with these long days rehearsing then Take Back in the evenings. I need to step up the self-care a bit and make sure I'm sleeping and eating well. All will be well.

A piece I've written for the *Guardian* about art and politics, inspired by the *Be//Longing* experience, has gone online, and apparently the trolls are out in force. I don't read the comments. I know better. Kersh says that someone in Tasmania (!) has been inspired by the article to make a similar piece there, that there are many positive remarks, but others apparently label me a middle-class luvvie and question who has funded this. *Them*, no doubt! It's all good. As I watch the play again in the evening and hear the stories that have come from the research of the Migration Lab – real stories of real people struggling and surviving, living through things I can't begin to imagine – I feel, I *know,* we're on the right side of history. That the work we're doing here is meaningful: that it is ultimately about empathy and connection and kindness. About seeing each other as human beings, striving to understand, working to change things, staying hopeful. The last lines of the play say it all:

And in Brazil
And in China
And in Syria
And in Iran
And in Afghanistan
And in a house in Moss Side
And on a bench in Hulme
And on a train platform in Euston
And in Belgium
And in Miami
And in Kabul
And here
And here
And here
The sun rises
And the sun sets
And we wait for a new day.

ACKNOWLEDGEMENTS

First, thank you so much to Anna Brewer, Lucy Brown and Camilla Erskine at Bloomsbury for trusting me with this and for all the help and support. Sorry about the long sentences. Welcome to the world, Emily! Thank you to Lisa Carden for your kind patience with my Oxford commas and misplaced zeds.

I've been lucky enough in my life to have had more than my share of ace teachers; special thanks to Olga Mulderrig, Mr and Mrs Walmsley, Martin Cosgrif, Colin Cook and my friend, the incomparable old git, Brian Astbury.

I've always loved being part of a gang; I'm a pack animal. Thank you to the many and various gangs I've been proud to be part of over the years: Accy College, LAMDA, Threshold, the Kimberley Roaders, the *Corrie* cast and crew, my Maundy Grange family, the People's Assembly, Team Take Back. And of course the Women of the Manchester Female Reform Society, whose friendship sustained me through much of 2017. Liberty or death! No onions!

All on *Peterloo*: Mike Leigh, Georgina Lowe, Helen Grearson, all at Thin Man, the cast and crew and especially Zoe Alker.

Jon McGrath, Sarah Sansom and Lemn Sissay and the Royal Court Theatre.

Thank you Becx Harrison and Grant Archer, my comrades and friends. I am 95 per cent more knackered than before I met you, but it's totally worth it: my life is 95 per cent richer for having you in it. I'm proud of us. Even though we still don't know what we're doing.

Mothy – I am your Miss Spider always.

Sarah Frankcom, Ric, Amy and all at the Exchange. Yvonne and Ann.

The Greatest Team in the History of the World (Tara, Pip, Naomi, Jack, Mark) and especially Razzle, my friend and collaborator. I don't understand why I love you as much as I do, but somehow I do. It's just weird.

All at Lou Coulson Associates: you are amazing, as is the gang at CLD.

My family: Grandma Joan, Wayne, Jen, Sophie, Lottie; Helen and my wonderful nephew, Joe. Thank you, Dave, my brother. Our long putting-the-world-to-rights chats are soul food to me. I forgive you for squeezing toothpaste in my eye when we were kids. I still like The Housemartins.

Martha and Lyss, I'm prouder of you both than you'll ever know. I'd be even more of a wanker if I didn't have you two to keep me grounded. Tidy your rooms, be kind, set the world on fire with all that smartness and talent and beauty and fierceness. Your dad is the best man in the world. Be nice to him.

Kersh, I am the ruler. I am the wind beneath your wings and don't forget it.

Thanks to my brilliant mum, still coming to see everything and even sometimes missing 'Come Dancing' because of it. I love you. You always let us live our own lives even when our choices must have seemed bonkers to you. Dave and I owe everything to you and Dad.

Finally, I dedicate this book to my beautiful and courageous niece Rosa who, shortly after I'd finished writing it, was shockingly diagnosed with germ cell ovarian cancer and undertook treatment with unbelievable grace, spirit and bravery. Rosa, I'm prouder of you than you'll ever know. We all are. I love you. Now go set the world on fire, sis.

INDEX